Cyberpolitics in International Relations

28-

Cyberpolitics in International Relations

Nazli Choucri

The MIT Press
Cambridge, Massachusetts
London, England

MIT Press books may be purchased at special quantity discounts for business or sales promotional use. For information, please email special_sales@mitpress.mit.edu or write to Special Sales Department, The MIT Press, 55 Hayward Street, Cambridge, MA 02142.

This book was set in Sabon by Toppan Best-set Premedia Limited, Hong Kong. Printed and bound in the United States of America.

Library of Congress Cataloging-in-Publication Data

Choucri, Nazli.
Cyberpolitics in international relations / Nazli Choucri.
    p. cm.
Includes bibliographical references and index.
ISBN 978-0-262-01763-3 (hardcover : alk. paper) — ISBN 978-0-262-51769-0 (pbk. : alk. paper)
1. Internet and international relations. 2. Technology and international relations. 3. Internet—Political aspects. 4. Information technology—Political aspects. I. Title.
JZ1254.C47 2012
327.10285'4678—dc23
2011048194

10 9 8 7 6 5 4 3 2 1

Contents

Acknowledgments

I am grateful to many colleagues, collaborators, graduate and under-graduate students as well as postdoctoral associates at MIT and Harvard University for their assistance throughout various phases of research for this book. The brief observations that follow do little justice to their contributions or to the depth of my appreciation.

First I would like to thank the MIT and Wellesley College students who, through their participation in the MIT Undergraduate Opportunity Research Program (UROP), contributed to the background research, data gathering, and exploratory work so central to the framing of this book: Jessica Choi, Russell Kooistra, Jessica Malekos-Smith, and Charles Patterson. I am grateful to the graduate students in the MIT course on *Cyberpolitics in International Relations* offered for the first time in the fall term, 2011, who elected to examine different conceptual, operational, and empirical facets of linkages between cyberspace and international relations.

The basic research and manuscript preparation was undertaken under the auspices and with the support of the Project on Explorations in Cyber International Relations (ECIR), part of the Minerva Program funded by the Office of Naval Research under award number N00014-09-1-0597. Any opinions, findings, and conclusions or recommendations expressed in this book are mine and do not necessarily reflect the views of the Office of Naval Research.

I would like to thank the members of the ECIR Project, a joint MIT–Harvard University research team, for their insights into the conduct of multidisciplinary research, including review of disciplinary assumptions as well as the cross-disciplinary critiques of field-specific fundamentals—and differences in the meaning assigned to seemingly simple words or phrases.(For example, when computer scientists refer to "hot spots," they do not mean those parts of the world with a high probability of war and violence. By the same token, the seemingly simple concept of "control" means different things in different fields.) For these reasons, and many others, I am most appreciative of the help in clarifying prevailing understanding of "cyber" inherent in "cyberpolitics."

I am grateful to several colleagues who helped me to understand some of the complexities of cyberspace on the one hand and of international politics on the other. I thank Joseph S. Nye Jr. at the Harvard Kennedy School of Government, for discussions of the theoretical legacies in international relations, which provide important linkages between cyberspace (a new arena of human interaction) and cyberpolitics (a new mode of politics with new types of conflicts as well as new opportunities for cooperation). I am especially grateful to David D. Clark of the Computer Science and Artificial Intelligence Laboratory (CSAIL) at MIT who devoted considerable time to introduce a political scientist to the intricacies of Internet architecture and the various debates surrounding the choices made early on as well as the evolving implications for cyberspace broadly defined. Stuart S. Madnick at the MIT Sloan School of Management helped clarify many conceptual and definitional challenges connected to the concept and the term "cyberspace," and in this process developed the foundations for an ontology of cyberspace.

Thanks are due to the ECIR postdoctoral associates—notably Shirley Hung, Robert Reardon, Aadya Shukla, and Chinton Vaishnav—for their own contributions to this multidisciplinary initiative. The ECIR graduate research assistants also helped articulate some of the thornier issues; the assistance of Jeremy Ferwerda and Dara Fisher, are especially appreciated, as are the contributions of Jesse Sowell and Josephine Wolff

I would like to thank Gaurav Agarwal for research assistance and for analysis and reanalysis of empirical data—especially the data that appear inconsistent or fraught with ambiguities in definition, provenance, and rules for enabling internal consistency in measurement and reporting. Thanks are due to Patricia McGarry for managing the format requirements of the MIT Press. Elizabeth Nigro carried the burden of checking many drafts of this book and provided invaluable assistance in the preparation of the final version for the MIT Press. She has been remarkable in her attention to details.

Finally, I am grateful to Clay Morgan at the MIT Press for his support of this project and, especially, for steering the manuscript through various phases of a complex review process, and always with patience and perseverance.

I
New Challenges to International Relations Theory and Policy

1

Introduction

Cyberspace is a fact of daily life. Because of its ubiquitous nature and vast scale and scope, cyberspace—including the Internet and the hundreds of millions of computers the Internet connects, the institutions that enable it, and the experiences it enables—has become a fundamental feature of the world we live in and has created a new reality for almost everyone in the developed world and for rapidly growing numbers of people in the developing world.[1]

Until recently, cyberspace was considered largely a matter of *low politics*—a term used to denote background conditions and routine decisions and processes. By contrast, the matters of interest in *high politics* have to do with national security, core institutions, and decision systems critical to the state, its interests, and its underlying values.[2] Nationalism, political participation, political contentions, conflict, violence, and war are among the common concerns of high politics.[3] But low politics do not always remain below the surface. If the cumulative effects of normal activities shift the established dynamics of interaction, then the seemingly routine can move to the forefront of political attention. When this happens, it can propel the submerged features into the political limelight.

In recent years, issues connected to cyberspace and its uses have vaulted into the highest realm of high politics. We now appreciate that cyberspace capabilities are also a source of vulnerability, posing a potential threat to national security and a disturbance of the familiar international order.[4] The global, often nontransparent interconnections afforded by cyberspace have challenged the traditional understanding of leverage and influence, international relations and power politics, national security, borders, and boundaries—as well as a host of other concepts and their corresponding realities.

Many features of cyberspace are reshaping contemporary international relations theory, policy, and practice. Those related to time, space,

Table 1.1
Characteristics of cyberspace

- *Temporality*—replaces conventional temporality with near instantaneity
- *Physicality*—transcends constraints of geography and physical location
- *Permeation*—penetrates boundaries and jurisdictions
- *Fluidity*—manifests sustained shifts and reconfigurations
- *Participation*—reduces barriers to activism and political expression
- *Attribution*—obscures identities of actors and links to action
- *Accountability*—bypasses mechanisms of responsibility

---

permeation, fluidity, participation, attribution, accountability, and ubiquity are the most serious (table 1.1). Individually, each feature is at variance with our common understanding of social reality and with contemporary understandings of international relations. Jointly, they signal a powerful disconnect.

Cyberpolitics, a recently coined term, refers to the conjunction of two processes or realities—those pertaining to human interactions (*politics*) surrounding the determination of *who gets what, when,* and *how*,[5] and those enabled by the uses of a virtual space (*cyber*) as a new arena of contention with its own modalities and realities. Despite differences in perspectives worldwide, there is a general scholarly understanding of the meaning of "politics." It is the complexity attending the prefix *cyber* that distinguishes this newly constructed semantic.[6]

This book asks several questions. How can we take explicit account of cyberspace in the analysis of international relations and world politics? What are the notable patterns of cyber access and participation worldwide? What new types of international conflicts and contentions arise from activities in cyberspace? What are the new modes of international collaboration? What are alternative cyber futures? In sum, how do we address the new imperatives for international relations theory that emerge from the construction of cyberspace?

Historically, the social sciences were formed into disciplines by first separating humans from nature and then separating various aspects of human activities for knowledge development. This strategy allowed detailed and focused inquiry into one sphere of human activity while ignoring others, a practice that contributed to the rapid advance of knowledge. Empirical evidence subsequently compelled us to expand beyond discrete areas to appreciate society-nature connections. In recent years, we have also become increasingly cognizant of the importance of multidisciplinary and interdisciplinary perspectives.

The same general observations pertain to the study of international relations. Traditional approaches to theory and research in international relations, derived from experiences in the nineteenth and twentieth centuries, are largely state-centric. They focus on major powers and power politics. The terms of engagement are human-centered, defined largely by social parameters.[7] The traditional view is beginning to be supplemented by the recognition that human action is sensitive to the feedback dynamics and interconnections between the social system of humans and the environmental system of nature.

That same adjustment or transition has not yet occurred with respect to the cyber domain, however. International relations theory has yet to recognize the implications of cyberspace for the conduct of international relations, notably in relation to the pursuit of "power and wealth" (Gilpin 1987). The remainder of this introduction defines the contours of this investigation with respect to space and cyberspace, politics and cyberpolitics, and introduces the theoretical framework for the chapters that follow.

1.1 Cyberspace and Cyberpolitics

Traditional international relations theory is anchored in and refers to interactions in physical venues.[8] All forms of space in international relations provide opportunities for expanding power and influence in world politics. In this book, the term "space" refers to domains of interactions that (1) create potential sources of power, (2) provide for an expansion of influence and leverage, (3) enable new services, resources, knowledge, or markets, and (4) realize further potentials when reinforced and sustained by technological advances.[9] When the activities of one actor threaten the sovereignty, stability, or security of other actors, then space becomes a critical variable in international relations. Traditionally, the notion of space was closely coupled with territoriality. Clearly, this connection is loosening rapidly.

The fundamentals of space revolve around the characteristics of the playing field—that is, *who* can play, *how,* and *why.* Some significant spaces manipulated by humans in modern times—enabled by major advances in science and technology—are well known. Among the most familiar are those wrought by traditional forms of *colonialism* and imperialism, modes of expansion and control of foreign territories that are driven by economic, strategic, and political motivations for control and domination. Colonization involves the physical movement of people, the extension of power outside political jurisdiction, the political and military control of other territories, and the imposition of national jurisdiction over foreign lands. In recent times, new spaces were shaped by deploying sheer physical force combined with the power of competition, innovation, and the spirit of adventure. Historically, only major powers, the most affluent and militarily powerful, could effectively compete in the colonization of territory and the exploration of *outer space*. These spaces were clearly understood to be where the quest for power lay. National prestige, positioning in the international landscape, wealth enhancement, and strategic advantage in military competition were all pursued through physical expansion into territories or into the atmosphere. In their different ways, both colonialism and the race to space controlled rather than leveled the playing field. The field itself was defined by the few states that could afford to play.

More recently, advances in technology, buttressed by scientific innovation, have allowed access to new forms of space. Notable among these is *nanospace,* where micro-miniaturization affords activity in a previously inaccessible domain. Nanospace holds considerable promise for medical and military applications. Technological innovation has also enhanced our ability to delineate knowledge about genetic properties and has generated a realm of activity in another previously inaccessible territory. The power of *genetic* space, greatly expanded with the charting of the human genome, is also at a relatively early stage of entry into the field of international relations. These technologies can potentially be abused to produce destabilizing weapons of mass destruction, especially as they become more economical and the ability to manipulate them becomes more widespread.

Cyberspace is yet another arena.[10] Created through technological innovation, it is a venue that allows users to engage in activities conducted over electronic fields whose spatial domains transcend traditional territorial, governmental, social, and economic constraints. Historically, access to and participation in the cyber playing field was limited to the most powerful; the nature of the venture and its organizational complexity restricted the number of players. By contrast, access to cyberspace is available to more and more people around the world. By 2010 the number of people with Internet access had reached nearly two billion. This space offers new opportunities for competition, contention, and conflict—all fundamental elements of politics and the pursuit of power and influence.

Cyberspace

The historical and philosophical roots of the term *cyber* are often considered to lie in Plato's allegory of the cave in the *Republic*. Its semantic identity (for the modern age) is derived from the term *cybernetics*, the study of communication and control rendered famous by Norbert Weiner in *Cybernetics: Or Control and Communication in the Animal and the Machine* (1948). Weiner's exposition influenced Karl W. Deutsch's *The Nerves of Government* (1963), which remains the single most important entry point into political science and political inquiry. By connecting the notions of cybernetics and space, William Gibson (1984) is generally regarded as providing the first formal designation for the new arena of interaction we now know as cyberspace.[11]

While the designation of cyberspace marked a shift in understanding, more important are the features of cyberspace that allow interactions among humans in ways not previously possible. Especially important are the ways in which cyber venues are used to shape ideas, exchange information, and increase access to knowledge and alternative modes of reasoning.

As access to and participation in virtual arenas increased, the concept of cyber took on rich new connotations. A range of metaphorical meanings is now attached to the term, and "cyber" is associated with a panoply of immersive environments, the possibility of interacting with synthetic entities, and a variety of gaming experiences, many if not all reflecting modes of expanding the frontiers of virtual space and human imagination. Over time, the term cyberspace has taken on many different meanings derived from its fundamental features, those pertaining to networked, computer-sustained, computer-accessed, and computer-generated multidimensional artificial, or "virtual," reality (Benedikt 1994b, 122). The term is commonly anchored to Internet applications. But the two are not identical: electronic connectivity needs to be distinguished from its enabling circuitry, on the one hand, and from arenas of interaction characterized by actors, actions, and outcomes on the other.

Overall, the global information infrastructure consists of communication networks, information hardware and software, applications, and the people who create content or use content or enable the generation of added value and new communications-based activities (Spinello 2002, 2–3). This general description points to a complex arrangement that invokes a wide range of roles and functions. David D. Clark (2010) extends this characterization, organizes the cyber domain systematically, and proposes a layered model of cyberspace. This is the view of cyberspace adopted in this book. Consistent with Clark's layered model, we view cyberspace as a hierarchical contingent system composed of (1) the *physical* foundations and infrastructures that enable the cyber playing field, (2) the *logical* building blocks that support the physical platform and enable services, (3) the *information content* stored, transmitted, or transformed, and (4) the *actors*, entities and users with various interest who participate in this arena in various roles. All of these layers, functions, and entities are relevant to cyberpolitics in international relations, but to different degrees and in different modalities.

As an amalgam of interoperable networks, the Internet has become a critical part of the emerging global communication infrastructure. When the World Wide Web came along it was described as "a killer application . . . that took the Internet from a relative handful of enthusiasts into the domain of serious, commercial, and governmental users."[12] The information content layer is expanding at exponential rates. New information is being generated and transmitted, and more mechanisms are being created to facilitate content use and reuse. Such trends involve innovative organization and business practices, new state-based initiatives, new rules and regulations, and new institutional mechanism of management and regulation. David D. Clark (2010), again, captures the decision systems of cyberspace by detailing the tremendous range of actors and entities involved in the operation of cyber venues. At the most general level, these include the Internet and computer industry players, those involved in applications and software development, content providers, governments, international organizations, managers of cyber venues, nongovernmental organizations, and, most important, the global user constituency of individuals and groups.

Over a relatively short period of time, what was initially constituted as a neutral domain of interaction created by technological innovations flowing mainly from the United States came to be influenced if not dominated by political contentions, both in the United States and elsewhere. The cybersphere is now a venue for competition among interests and interest groups, as well as an arena for conflicts and contentions surrounding the increasingly visible hand of government. We can no longer ignore the political salience of cyberspace: As one astute observer has noted, cyberspace is becoming "heavily contested, colonized, and reshaped by governments, militaries, and private corporate and civic networks."[13]

Cyberpolitics

All international relations involve politics in one way or another, implicitly or explicitly. The laws of politics, though subject to debate among some political scientists, generally refer to regularities of human behavior across time and space. Often, variation is explained in terms of issue area, empirical referent, specific modalities, or exceptionalism, to note some of the most common terms. Insofar as there is as yet no decisive account or description of cyberpolitics, the language and concepts we use are the familiar ones of politics in kinetic domains.

Combining Lasswell's (1958) definition of politics as the authoritative allocation of values in society with David Easton's (1953) stark statement about *who gets what, when,* and *how* leads us to the most generic and appropriate view of politics, relevant in all contexts, times, and places. With the creation of cyberspace, a new arena for the conduct of politics is taking shape, and we may well be witnessing a new form of politics as well.

These dual insights into the nature of politics, while initially articulated for the individual polity or the nation-state, carry powerful meaning that is readily transferable to the international arena. They also skillfully draw our attention to issue areas dominated by the politics of ambiguity, areas where the domain is unclear and the stakes are not well defined. We must also keep in mind that politics consists of "the more or less incomplete control of human behavior through voluntary habits of *compliance* in combination with threats of probable *enforcement*" (Deutsch 1968, 17; italics in original). Moreover, politics is "the interplay of enforcement threats, which can be changed relatively quickly, with the existing loyalties and compliance habits of the population, which are more powerful but which most often can only be changed more slowly" (ibid., 19).

All politics, in cyber or real arenas, involves conflict, negotiation, and bargaining over the mechanisms, institutional or otherwise, to resolve in *authoritative* ways the contentions over the nature of particular sets of core *values*.[14] As Harold Lasswell noted, the "study of politics is the study of influence and the influential." The influential people "are those who get the most of what there is to get" (Lasswell 1958, 3).[15] When politics is evoked, power is a necessary corollary.[16] Since politics, by definition, involves some struggle, even in the most collaborative of situations, the capabilities available to the participants become important determinants of potential outcomes; and the final outcomes must be viewed as authoritative in nature—subject to the next round of contention.[17]

Since politics in any domain is about influencing, shaping, or controlling the authoritative allocation of value surrounding who gets what, when, and how,[18] the political stakes are usually recognized as such by the participants, and their interactions are designed to gain advantage, if not to "win" entirely.[19]

The conjunction of politics and cyberspace has reinforced some of the fundamental precepts of politics as expressed by Easton, Lasswell, and others; it has expanded its manifestations, enhanced the potential for political participation, and created new possibilities for expressing views, voicing political positions, and joining political activity. It is difficult to identify an area of politics that is devoid of cyber-related manifestations. While it is not possible to delineate the full implications of cyberspace for politics and political behavior, observers and analysts alike are gradually converging on some broad considerations.

For example, politics in cyberspace is reflected in the title of Richard N. Rosecrance's *The Rise of the Virtual State* (1999). The essence of the virtual state lies in its ability to garner the power of finance and ideas and transform them into sources of global influence. Seemingly simple in its conception, this presumption has pervasive implications. It calls into question the fundamentals of traditional politics among nations based on competition for territory, trade, and military prowess, replacing these with new parameters, such as education, skills, knowledge management, and various manifestations of "brain power."

Rosecrance argues that while all nations are gradually moving toward the virtual state, some will do so faster and more decisively than others. These will be the global "brains," and the rest will remain as global "bodies." Through this striking image, Rosecrance suggests that investment in knowledge is the fundamental source of national power and social effectiveness. Even if one questions the substitution of brains and bodies, it remains the case that in almost all societies, access to knowledge ranks high in national priorities, although this ranking is not necessarily accompanied by effective action.

Other examples are illustrated in the July 2000 special issue of the *International Political Science Review* titled "CyberPolitics in International Relations." The articles highlight the virtual domain as an important area of research in the field of international politics and interstate relations.[20] The conduct of cyberpolitics across a wide set of issue areas, along with commensurate changes in political discourse and interactions, has generated worldwide effects and has led to the articulation and aggregation of new interests, as well as new patterns of international relations and new modes of institutional responses and global accord. It also prompted debates over alternative world views and policy positions. Of special relevance here are the debates over what policies will shape the global agenda.

Toward the end of the twentieth century the sanctity of economic growth came under scrutiny, and its intellectual foundations and philosophical supports became the target of inquiry and serious recasting. The contending perspective, that sustainability is equally important, has gradually risen to global prominence. But the contours of sustainability and its knowledge base remain to be clearly defined. The political contentions now revolve around articulating and controlling the authoritative definition of sustainability. The French scholar and former government official Christian Brodhag suggested a connection between cyberspace and the quest for sustainable development (Brodhag 2000).

Such arguments point us to the potential synergy between cyberspace (a new arena of interaction) and sustainability (a new imperative for theory and policy). Shaped by some shared tendencies, such as dematerialization, decentralization, denationalization, and deterritorialization, this convergence creates new opportunities for countervailing pressures and new sources of satisfaction and dissatisfaction. At this point, the proverbial Pandora's box of competing interests and powerful contentions threatens to spring open and seriously undermine twentieth-century understandings of structures and processes in international relations.

These issues are embedded in a new politics that is becoming sufficiently pervasive as to constitute a fundamental feature of the changing international landscape of power and influence. Figure 1.1 depicts in a highly formalized way two different processes. One is the use of cyberspace or e-venues for shaping politics in the kinetic or traditional domain. The other pertains to uses of traditional instruments for shaping the configuration of cyberspace itself. The relationships in this figure cover a broad set of behaviors, real as well as virtual. Even without reference to specific actors, agents, interests, explicit or implicit rules, or relative gains and losses, we can already delineate different trajectories or manifestations of cyberpolitics.

The figure highlights the pervasiveness of politics (real and virtual) and the pervasiveness of cyber venues (for the pursuit of goals in real and virtual domains) by depicting (1) the overarching interactions between the real and virtual domains of politics and (2) the connections through cyberspace, the shared venue of interaction. This duality is especially relevant since, as Bernardo A. Huberman has written, "the Web

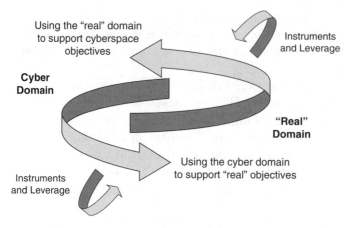

Using the "real" domain
to support cyberspace
objectives

Instruments
and Leverage

**Cyber
Domain**

**"Real"
Domain**

Using the cyber domain
to support "real" objectives

Instruments
and Leverage

Figure 1.1
Trajectories of cyberpolitics.

has become a veritable laboratory, where one can study human behavior with a precision and on a scale never possible before" (Huberman 2001, 16). It is not yet clear whether political discourse via cyber venues consists of a parallel mode of discourse or, alternatively, whether political discourse is assembled first in real venues and then exported or steered toward the cyber domain. Another hypothesis holds that the discourse is interactive across real and virtual domains and that the cumulative effects, if any, will be observed if they shape the outcomes of political behavior in real institutional contexts. In any case, the articulation and aggregation of interests are fundamental to all forms of politics. To the extent that cyber venues are used for such purposes, they must be seen not only as enablers but also as important multipliers.

1.2   Anchors for International Relations Theory

In international relations, the sovereign state is the key organizing principle in world politics. However, global realities early in the twenty-first century are severely constraining the implementation of sovereignty precepts, and, legal posture aside, sovereignty has become a definitional factor rather than an empirical reality. Territorial boundaries, a corollary of sovereignty, define the jurisdictions and the limits of state authority. Joel R. Reidenberg aptly notes that for centuries, "regulatory authority derived from the physical proximity of political, social, and economic communities" (Reidenberg 1997, 85). The delineation of state borders is often subject to conflict, contention, and great uncertainty. Man-made, borders delimit the jurisdictions of states and signal where one jurisdiction begins and others end, thereby delineating the legitimate exercise of political authority.

Tradition in International Relations

Standard textbooks on international relations still tend to focus on interactions among nation-states and assume the state to be the central actor in the international system. The number of states, their relative power distributions, and the strategic and security relations that link them together shape the contours of the subject matter. States in principle are autonomous in the conduct of authority within their jurisdictions, even though the impacts may be felt elsewhere.[21] The gradual recognition of other actors on the world scene is usually accompanied by stressing their subservience to the state, despite the growing influence of multinational corporations, the emergence of robust international organizations, and increasing evidence of a growing worldwide civil society.

Cyberspace has created new conditions for which there are no clear precedents. There is as yet no consensus on the "next steps" to take to incorporate cyber venues into contemporary discourse on sovereignty, stability, and security, but some contending positions are already discernible. One view holds that cyber realities undermine state sovereignty in notable ways (see, e.g., Kahin and Nesson 1997). In this view, cyberspace "is destroying the link between geographic location and: (1) the *power* of local governments to assert control over online behavior; (2) the *effects* of online behavior on individuals or things; (3) the *legitimacy* of the efforts of a local sovereign to enforce the rules applicable to global phenomena; and (4) the *ability* of physical location to give *notice* of which sets of rules apply" (Johnson and Post 1997, 6).

Another line of thinking holds that despite the emerging power of virtual reality, the fundamentals of state sovereignty remain robust, as revealed in various successful efforts in democratic as well as authoritarian states to regulate the transmission of content. At most, the new arena is neutral with respect to impacts on sovereignty. Jack Goldsmith and Tim Wu (2006, 58) remind us that the "Internet is not 'unbound with respect to geography'" and that specific technical norms operate to reinforce the foundations of what we consider sovereign boundaries. These include the usual directives of "choose a country" or "choose a server," for example. Such location-sensitive elements suggest that cyberspace does not entirely undermine the relevance of territoriality.

Yet another view proposes that cyberspace is fundamentally generative in both technological and social terms, and as such contributes to reframing conceptions of sovereignty and the role of the state, most notably in the provision of public goods. This view is consistent with that of Jonathan Zittrain (2008), who argues that the Internet empowers citizens, facilitates innovation, and enables a host of yet unexplored possibilities.

Cyberspace empowers and enables individuals in ways that were previously not possible. This empowerment is manifested through communication, expressed perceptions, organization, and preparations for action.[22] All these activities may challenge traditional concepts of sovereignty. At the same time, cyberspace provides new venues for the exercise of state power in all the usual ways and allows a focus on sovereignty and territoriality as the ultimate principles on which to justify moves of choice in cyberspace. It has also given states new points of control. But the state is no longer the only actor wielding this power—perhaps not even the dominant one in cyber venues. The cyber international "landscape" of actors, actions, technology, and power relations is rapidly changing.

The major trajectories of international relations theory throughout most of the twentieth century—superceded by novel ideas and critical reframing during the latter decades of the century—cannot be readily imported into the cyberworld of the twenty-first century. To illustrate characteristic features of these trajectories, we note briefly three distinct perspectives, each with a specialized focus on a particular *problemwatique* in international relations. One is *realism* (and its variants), which focuses on national security, power politics, conflict, and traditional warfare, so dominant in the immediate post–World War II period. In the context of state-to-state interactions, where the pursuit of power and of wealth dominates, this theoretical perspective is not entirely consistent with the conditions that shape cyber security and the potentials for cyber war. Such theorists generally converge on the view that might is right, thereby adding an element to an already complex inference, that might *ought to* make right—in this way transforming an apparently empirical statement ("is") into a normative one ("ought").[23] Further, realism is anchored in major power politics. Access to cyber venues is potentially available to everyone and everywhere. In terms of today's international relations, it is not yet fully clear what cybersecurity actually entails or what "might" may signify in the cyber domain. Clarifications, adjustments, and theoretical innovations are needed to retain the uses of realist theory in any of its forms.[24]

A second perspective we note here is that of *institutionalism,* a tradition with a long historical record rooted in early liberalism. Institutionalism is concerned with cooperation, coordination, and formal and informal mechanisms of collaboration, as well as mechanisms to routinize the international behavior of states.[25] Whereas everyone appreciates that the sustained coordination in the real world requires some form of institutionalization based on the convergence of norms, the requisites for managing interactions in the cybersphere are not clearly understood (see table 1.1). The insights of institutional theory may indeed have some direct implications for the management of cyber venues. But there is one important caveat: institutionalism in international relations is a state-based logic for regulating interstate interactions.[26] Cyberspace has been constructed by the private sector and its operations have been managed by the private sector. The state is a latecomer to this domain.[27] Adjustments to theory must take place since the state itself is increasingly vulnerable to cyber threats.

Third is *constructivism,* an amalgam of earlier initiatives focusing on perceptions, cognition, beliefs, values, symbols, and similar variables that has evolved into a theoretical approach emphasizing the subjective.[28] A more recent addition to international relations theory, constructivism is still under some degree of construction, so to speak.

Each of these three theoretical modes considers a particular slice of international relations to the exclusion of others, and has little room for linking across perspectives.[29] Traditional theory focuses on socioeconomic, political, and strategic issues for the state system, with considerably less attention to non-state actors. With few exceptions, theory concentrates on static analysis rather than on the dynamics of transformation and change, and thus tends to obscure, if not ignore, the feedback effects and lagged or longer-term effects of short-term changes. Moreover, the globalization process, so significant at this time, has engendered only limited consensus for a dominant theory of international relations politics and practice.[30]

Challenges for Theory

If international relations theory is to take account of twenty-first-century realities, it must address at least three major challenges that may distort our vision of the present and our understanding of the future. The first challenge is to recognize and represent critical interconnections among *systems of interaction,* not only the social and the environmental systems but also the cyber system, a distinctive system of interactions whose features differ from those of the social system or the environmental system. Theory must take into account, even anchored at the intersection of the kinetic and the constructed cyber.

The second challenge is to address the dynamics of *transformation and change.* When change is the focus of inquiry, as in power transition analysis, it is derivative and situational rather than fundamental or definitional.[31] Understanding change requires in-depth analysis of the underlying drivers that shape the nature of the transformation.[32] Thus, the challenge here is to examine the roots of change and their interconnections, and bring these to the foreground in an exploration of twenty-first-century international relations.

The third challenge is to render an accounting of *actors and entities* in world politics consistent with empirical conditions. For most of the twentieth century, theory focused on the major powers, and the rest of the world was viewed as residual, expected to conform to major power rules and principles. A power-based hierarchy was considered the "normal" organizational construct of the international system, even after the end of the Cold War and the dissolution of the Soviet Union, and with it the polarity that had dominated the post–World War II period. We now recognize the diversity of state and non-state actors in the international system, as well as the importance of diversity in attributes and capabilities. The old anchor must be replaced by a more up-to-date view of today's international system, in which the power of the weak can be devastating in its own right.

The construction of cyberspace is clearly a globalizing phenomenon, irrespective of how one views the globalization process itself. Its organization and management are under the control of a wide range of non-state actors, and its properties differ significantly from those of the social system and the environmental system. Cyber-based interactions are already recognized to influence human activities at all levels of analysis. Consequently, the sovereign state, the anchor of traditional theory, finds itself in an increasingly complex international system, far different from the structure of the nineteenth century and most of the twentieth century.

1.3 What Lies Ahead

This book is in two parts. Part I defines the contours of the inquiry over three chapters. It presents the theoretical framework and the empirical context, defines the research strategy, and outlines the key conceptual and political challenges. We draw on the theory of lateral pressure—an empirically grounded approach to change in international relations—to explore the emergent parameters of real and cyber international relations in the twenty-first century.

Chapter 2 lays out the theoretical framework that guides our investigations. We address the three challenges identified above and connect the cyber and the kinetic features of international relations. More specifically, this chapter seeks to (1) provide conceptual order, (2) identify connections between cyber and kinetic international relations, and (3) highlight core anchors for the rest of the book.

The logic for drawing on and extending the theory of lateral pressure, grounded in the three challenges noted above, is: First, the theory was originally designed to describe systems of interaction, human society, and the natural environment, and thus provides some directives for addressing and incorporating the constructed cyber system. Second, invoking concepts of transformation and change, lateral pressure theory is anchored in the assumption that international interactions are shaped by uneven rates of change in growth and development among various actors, large and small. Third, the theory allows diverse actors and entities to influence international interactions in different ways.[33]

Chapter 2 addresses cyberspace as we consider the implications of these basic features of the theory. The logic of lateral pressure theory extends the traditional Images or level of analysis presented by Kenneth Boulding (1956), who introduces the concept of Image and Kenneth N. Waltz (1959), who develops the concept as a device to describe and analyze international relations in terms of the individual, the state, and the international system. Lateral pressure theory extends the notion of Image or levels of international relations by (a) differentiating among the social system, the natural environment, and the cyber system at each level; (b) introducing the global level as a fourth image; (c) concentrating on linkages among levels of analysis, beginning with the individual and moving on to the state system, the international system, and the global system, and (d) also exploring the reversal of influences, namely from global system, for example, to the other levels with various combinations of interaction and influences in between.

Chapter 3 focuses on cyberspace and is entirely empirical. Its purposes are (1) to highlight some characteristic features of cyberspace as a domain of interactions, (2) to examine the new geography of cyber access and participation, (3) to map the richness of the cyber access ecosystem, and

(4) to present some new patterns—for example, the cyber bipolarity between China and the United States, and the emergent cyber races among other countries. In light of the changing and ever expanding global connectivity, some important questions include the following: What are some of the major patterns of cyber access? How extensive is cyber participation worldwide? To what extent is the cyber view of the international system consistent with the usual kinetic-based perception?

From the perspective of lateral pressure theory, cyber access is both a determinant and a consequence of transformation and change. The empirical observations in chapter 3 provide useful information about the evolution of the cyber domain and the participants therein. It allows us to consider various propositions, including the view that, in the short run, uneven access to cyberspace reflects the distribution of power and capability of states in the international system. Gradually, the diffusion of capabilities is expected to lead to the expansion of cyber access, and participation in cyber venues will increase at rapid rates. In the long run, these changes will lead to new opportunities for the flow of information and influence, new ways of exerting power and leverage, and new demands for norms and structures to reduce threats and vulnerabilities.[34]

Cyber access per se provides little insight into the content or the substance of cyber interactions, and even less information about leveraging cyber venues to enhance power, capability, and performance. Accordingly, chapter 4 focuses on matters of content—the substance of interactions—and the use of cyber venues in the pursuit of such objectives. This chapter concentrates on knowledge as a particular form of content and networking as an increasingly powerful knowledge-diffusing and knowledge-enhancing mechanism.

With the increased politicization of cyber-based interactions, there are growing efforts to control access as well as content, and these efforts threaten the system neutrality of cyberspace supported by the United States and other Western countries. The conceptual issues in this chapter are critical to all levels of analysis and may well shape future directions of cyber venues and participation.[35] We ask, what is the value of knowledge in international relations? What are the models of knowledge value? We then turn to networking and introduce the notion of knowledge-networking multipliers—the elements that reinforce networking systems —and ask, how do they work? Knowledge is an advantage in power relations, and knowledge about contentious political issues in particular provides contenders with an edge. But when the contours of an issue and its knowledge base are not clearly defined, the politics revolve around gaining control over the authoritative definitions of the domain itself. The last section of chapter 4 examines the emergence of the demand for knowledge about the challenges of sustainability (rather than the conditions for growth) to enhance the resilience of social and environmental systems (rather than the expansion of physical output), insofar as established knowledge systems reinforce the growth paradigm that, by definition, restricts the supply of sustainability-centered knowledge. We return to this issue in the last chapters of Part II, where we explore emerging priorities on the global agenda as the international community grapples with threats to security, survival, and sustainability and develops an awareness of the enabling power and potentials of cyber venues—all in the pursuit of an emerging global agenda.

Part II examines the dynamics of cyberpolitics at different levels of analysis. We explore contentions over the authoritative allocation of cyber value surrounding who gets what, when, and how. The arguments increasingly involve all entities in international relations, both state and non-state actors (the individual, the state and non-state entities, the international system, the global system), as well as linkages among them.

Cyberspace, as noted, empowers the individual in new and powerful ways, though there is variation in the degree of power wielded by individuals in different states. Different parameters of action are possible in cyber venues, and these cannot always be ignored by the state. Access to cyber venues facilitates access to information and, more important, to knowledge. To date, the technology of cyberspace privileges the individual relative to the state in one important way: it is seldom easy to assign responsibility to a specific individual for the transmission of a cyber message.

If this situation persists, then the individual level of analysis in international relations theory may well assume a new importance, greater than anticipated in traditional vision. The aggregative powers of cyber access, which allow individuals to combine to form various types of entities that transcend territorial boundaries, provide a strong reinforcing mechanism. Some of the newly aggregated entities can be seen as "normal" non-state actors, others may lack a label or description, and still others may operate behind a veil of secrecy. But they all affect the state in one way or another.

States are far from equal in attributes and capabilities, or in power and influence. Chapter 5 presents an empirical analysis of the state, the second image in traditional international relations theory. Drawing on the constitutive power of the master variables—population, resources, technology—introduced in chapter 2, we organize the sovereign states into six empirically defined groups, which we call profiles, in order to examine the characteristic features of each profile, the membership of individual countries in each profile, and the distribution of different profile groups over time. This method results in an internationally consistent view of the international system over time, along with a comparison of attributes and capabilities across profile groups. If there is one overarching finding in this chapter it is that almost all states, rich and poor, are already engaged in various forms of e-governance and continue to reinforce the conditions required for effective performance. Closely connected to e-governance is e-participation. While the evidence points to more rather than less e-participation by states over time, more important is the impact. How effective is e-governance? What is the impact of e-participation? Again, there are some unexpected findings.

The international system, the third image, consists of sovereign states as key entities, as well as non-state actors and intergovernmental institutions. They all operate in a world that is increasingly connected via cyberspace—often in tightly coupled ways. There is much in this new world that challenges the state, but in the cyber domain, boundaries are permeable and information, ideas, interests, and the like can circulate with little regard for territory or jurisdiction. This means that the usual instruments of the state are not always transferable for use in the cyber arena. But the state is adapting. States are developing and deploying new instruments of control, and in many cases they clearly aspire to become the major player in the cyber arena.

In the cyber domain as in the kinetic arena, politics is fundamentally about control over the authoritative allocation of value in terms of who gets what, when, and how.[36] Chapter 6 concentrates on patterns of cyber conflicts just becoming evident in international relations, and chapter 7 explores observed patterns of cooperation and collaboration. In each case we must ask: what is new and distinctive to cyberspace versus what is old, that is, what reflects usual international mechanisms of collaboration.[37]

Chapter 6 examines a wide range of international cyber conflicts and newly apparent threats to the security of the state. Despite the variety of conflicts and the incompleteness of information, we are nonetheless able to identify three general types or clusters of conflicts, with different characteristics, varying degrees of intensity, and different manifestations. Some are about claiming the future, others about managing the present.

First are contentions over the management of cyberspace and the operational features of the Internet. Examples include the end-to-end argument, the view that "code is law," and network neutrality. These contentions are generally considered to be low politics. They appear to be largely technical in nature, but their effects are highly political, as they bear on who gets what, when, and how. A second type of cyber conflict involves the use of cyber venues for strategic advantage and leveraging political control to regulate cyber access or deny access to content deemed undesirable. The third type of cyber conflict involves threats to national security and generally revolves around issues of the militarization of cyberspace, the conduct of cyber warfare, cyber threats to critical infrastructures, various types of cyber crimes and espionage, and the use of cyber venues for conducting competitive politics in the traditional sense.

Chapter 7 explores the other side of the international interaction ledger, modes of cooperation and collaboration in a cyber-intensive world. The creation of cyberspace has already required new mechanisms of coordination and collaboration to develop norms and standards, support the technological foundations of cyberspace, and ensure its sustainability. As noted earlier, cyberspace is managed with reliance on private sector entities, a situation that is not always viewed with favor in an international arena dominated by sovereign states. The traditional international institutions also seek to influence the management of the new arena and use it for a wide range of mission-oriented purposes. Concurrently, all the players, state and non-state, involved in shaping the evolving global agenda are increasingly drawing on cyber venues to reinforce the central trajectories of that agenda.

A number of collaborative interstate activities have focused on the governance of cyberspace.[38] International initiatives have been created to track and measure cyber threats around the world, such as Computer Emergency Response Teams (CERTs). A second type of collaborative cyberpolitics revolves around the quest for norms and agreements on the provision of cyber-related public goods. Examples include knowledge provided through cyber venues, the legitimization of cyber rights (analogous to human rights), and the creation of new norms for cyber behavior. The third and most comprehensive form of cooperative cyberpolitics has to do with the formation of the twenty-first-century global agenda, broadly defined. Specific examples of cooperative activities in this arena include supporting and reinforcing the expansion of cyber access and use worldwide, legitimating new forms of cyber-based activities to buttress the developmental agenda, and using cyberspace to strengthen transitions toward sustainability and thus reduce threats to the viability of social and environmental systems. An important question is whether the observed patterns of cooperation and collaboration are "new," that is, distinctive to cyberspace, or alternatively are manifestations of the usual modes of international collaboration.

Chapter 8 concentrates on the global system, the fourth image in international relations. The global system is the overarching domain that encompasses the individual, the state, and the international system and all combinations of actors and entities, actions, and behaviors within and across these levels, as well as all of their environmental life-supporting properties. This chapter focuses on the real, kinetic features of the global system that shape and are shaped by actors, entities, and capabilities at different levels of analysis. Its purpose is to provide a "tour d'horizon" of dominant forms of human behavior and impacts on their social and environmental systems. Guided by the theoretical framework outlined in chapter 2, and consistent with its application to the state system as described in chapter 5, the discussion in chapter 8 highlights global features of the master variables—population, resources, and technology—and identifies some critical dynamics of transformation and change.

Especially important at the global level is growth in the size and diversity of decision-making entities, state and non-state, whose activities often have far-reaching, even global consequences. We seek to delineate the fundamental attributes and features of the system as a whole that transcend state boundaries. Are there real properties of the global system—other than those understood to exist at the state or international levels—relevant to cyberpolitics worldwide?

This chapter demonstrates that the global playing field enables the conduct of and participation in many different games with different rules and regulations by different players with different levels and types of capabilities. The large number of decision entities complicates the usual calculus of the pursuit of power and wealth at all levels. The global system as a whole is increasingly vulnerable to a broad range of hazards created by human activities. In this chapter we detail the foundations for the gradual convergence of cyberspace and sustainability—in substantive as well as policy terms—and the nature of the cyberpolitics surrounding this convergence.

Earlier, in chapter 4, we pointed to the need for new knowledge focusing on the domain of sustainable development. The initiative to develop this body of knowledge has led to the gradual formation of "sustainability science," defined in *Science Magazine's State of the Planet 2006–2007* as "a new field of sustainability science is emerging that seeks to understand the fundamental character of interactions between nature and society . . . [and] encompass[es] the interaction of global processes with the ecological and social characteristics of particular places and sectors" (Kennedy and the Editors of *Science* 2006, 165). This global agenda, committed to transitions to sustainability, is intersecting more and more with a dynamic and increasingly complex cyber ecosystem.

Chapter 9 focuses on the synergy created by the mutually reinforcing dynamics of cyberspace as a new arena for human interaction, on the one hand, and the international community's efforts to explore transitions to sustainable development on the other. We argue that these two independent processes are converging, with potentially powerful international impacts. As a vision for a better future, sustainability shares some critical properties with cyberspace as a new arena in international relations, such as dematerialization and decentralization. Chapter 9 reviews the central place of knowledge management in the cyberpolitics surrounding sustainability.[39] Many countries, especially the developing states, experience difficulty in accessing knowledge, even when mechanisms for cyber access are in place. We examine potential measures to reduce barriers to knowledge provision and access and consider which knowledge provision principles can help expand knowledge relevant to sustainability, with brief reference to the design and operation of emerging knowledge-based cyber systems for sustainability.

In chapter 10 we revisit key theoretical issues raised in chapter 2 in order to take stock of the major findings and suggest how they may help improve our understanding of twenty-first-century international politics. With the benefit of hindsight, we recognize that increased access to cyberspace (1) enables new voices in communication and e-networking, (2) facilitates the development of new content, notably knowledge, (3) helps consolidate political discourse and the formation of cyberpolitics in the pursuit of norms, goals, and modes of behavior at all levels of social organization and over time, (4) provides new venues to organize and articulate demands for collective responses to shared problems, and (5) eventually helps institutions construct strategies for managing responses.

In this discussion we point to shifts taking place in the international system in terms of its traditional physical properties. We refer to these shifts as lateral realignment, to indicate an important extension of lateral pressure theory. Such a realignment will be increasingly dominated by cyber-based interactions. We then construct four visions of alternative cyber futures, any one of which could conceivably be rooted in this emerging realignment. Finally, we examine the critical contingencies and contentions surrounding the future of cyberpolitics in international relations.

2

Theory Matters in International Relations

This chapter presents the theoretical frame used in this book to explore cyberpolitics—the conjunction of human interactions (*politics*) surrounding the determination of who gets what, when, and how[1] and actions enabled by the uses of virtual spaces (*cyber*)—in international relations. The purpose is to develop an approach to integrating kinetic and cyber domains by focusing on levels of analysis in international relations—the individual, the state system, the international system, and the global system—and their linkages and interactions. Extending the lateral pressure theory, we examine the dynamics of transformation and change that shape and reflect the complex interconnections and interdependencies within and across levels of analysis— for the kinetic international system (and the natural environment) as well as interactions in the constructed cyber system.

We begin with a brief introduction to lateral pressure theory and then focus more closely on each level and its interconnections with other levels. Accordingly, this chapter can be viewed as both a theoretical road map and a reference guide for the rest of the book.

2.1 Lateral Pressure Theory: The Basics

Lateral pressure refers to the propensity of states to expand behavior outside territorial boundaries. The theory seeks to explain the relationship between the internal growth and international activities. It addresses a simple question: why do certain types of international behaviors or activities appear to be more prevalent for some countries than for others? Alternatively, why do some states engage in some types of international behaviors and not others?

The historical record demonstrates that national or territorial expansion is a common feature of the human experience.[2] The development of lateral pressure theory to date can be viewed in three phases. The first phase consisted of two large-scale studies, a cross-national analysis of the forty-five years leading up to World War I (Choucri and North 1975) along with follow-up inquiries, and a detailed quantitative inquiry into the political economy aspects of war and peace in Sino-Soviet-U.S. relations during the decades following World War II (Ashley 1980). These studies used statistical analysis and econometrics model assumptions and estimation procedures.

The second phase in the evolution of lateral pressure theory is illustrated by the detailed analysis of Japan over the span of more than one hundred years (Choucri, North, and Yamakage 1992). Focusing on growth, development, competition, warfare, and reconstruction in Japan, the study brought to light the ways in which a state sought to manage its resource constraints and adopt internal and external policies to meet its core demands, and found itself engaged in competition and conflict it considered essential for its survival. The study, which looked at one country in three different time periods, demonstrated the invariant structural features and the alternative pathways for system adjustments in response to internal and external constraints.

The third phase of lateral pressure theory began with the construction of an exploratory system dynamics model of twenty countries, both industrial and developing, by Annababette Wils, Matilde Kamiya, and Choucri (1998), who extended the analysis of internal sources of international conflict and examined the nature of feedback effects, that is, how international conflict influences and even alters the master variables of the state, and changes the internal sources of conflict as well as propensities for particular modes of external behavior. Subsequently, Corey Lofdahl (2002) modeled the relationship between the internal dynamics of growth and development rooted in the master variables, on the one hand, and propensities toward particular patterns of international trade and their environmental impacts on the other. A few years later, Anne-Katrin Wickboldt and Choucri (2006) used fuzzy logic to systematically and precisely locate and track relative changes in the distribution of states within and across profile spaces, across geographic regions, and over time.

All these initiatives were valuable in their own right. Each provided important insights into and evidence about the overall antagonizing process that leads to overt conflict, violence, and war. By definition, these processes are evidence of nonsustainability and the power of system-threatening dynamics. But the creation of cyberspace and the expansion of human activities in this space have no precedent, and may have unanticipated impacts on the state and the international system as a whole.

The driving logic in lateral pressure theory is rooted in the volume and nature of human demands—needs, wants, desires, claims, and counterclaims—and the ways in which societies seek to meet these demands. The theory addresses the sources or roots of such a tendency, the transitions to overt action, and the consequences thereof.

Aggregated to the social level, the causal drivers can be traced to interactions among population dynamics, resource endowments, and levels of technology and skills—the master variables. These shape the articulation of demands and the consolidation of capabilities. Through a set of intervening processes, states seek to close the gap between the actual and the desired, by expanding their behavior beyond territorial boundaries. Expansion leads to intersections in spheres of influence and potentially to competition and conflict, including military confrontation. Alternatively, propensities for expansion may be blocked in various ways—by internal capabilities or by external conditions—leading to frustration, tension, conflict, escalation, and possibly warfare.

But none of this is inevitable. Intersections in spheres of influence can enable the recognition of common constraints or common aversions and thus lead to cooperation rather than conflict. Policy options, choices, and decisions can shape a variety of behavioral trajectories—subject to the characteristics of the state profile that define the parameters of potential behavior. The core inferences, however, address the consequences of lateral pressure, whether the pressure is motivated by economic, political, military, scientific, religious or other factors.[3] The entire process and the behavioral outcomes can influence the international system in various ways and, depending on the nature of the activities, can shape the global system as well (Choucri and North 1989). The remainder of this chapter expands on this general logic. It extends the levels of analysis in new directions, starting with the individual level, the first image in international relations.

2.2   Cyberpolitics at the Individual Level

Lateral pressure theory is anchored in the view that all social systems are shaped by individuals in their efforts to meet their needs and demands. Social outcomes are often less the result of conscious value-maximizing choices than of inertia, habit, and a mixture of personal and organizational purposes and adaptations. In any case, social habit patterns are usually the outcome of some earlier discrete (conscious or unconscious) individual choices made by the members of the population at large or by an individual or individuals in a bureaucratic or government context.

At its origins, the theory of lateral pressure characterized the individual explicitly as an energy-using and information-processing entity (North 1990, 11) operating in social and environmental contexts. Human actions that affect the natural system feed back into the social system and may have repercussions that are not susceptible to power-based instruments of control.[4] This is in sharp contrast to traditional international relations theories that define the individual in strictly social terms.

Aggregated at the level of the society, the state, and the economy, the most fundamental individual demands (needs and wants) are driven by the quest for security and survival, and the most basic capabilities are leveraged for this purpose. Demands combine with capabilities to produce actions; the outcome is contingent on capacities, knowledge, skills, and access to resources.

In general, the larger the number of people in a community, organization, or society, the greater the volume of needs, wants, and demands. Demands are sets of determinations that derive from a perceived (or felt) need, want, or desire for the purpose of narrowing or closing the gap between a perception of fact (what is) and a preference or value (what ought to be). To meet demands, and to close the gap between "what is" and "what ought to be," we need capabilities. Capabilities are attributes that enable performance and allow individuals, groups, political systems, and entire societies to engage in activity to manage their demands.

Central to the capability of the individual and the social order is knowledge—the foundation of technology at all levels of analysis and in all forms of social aggregation. With the construction of cyberspace, the development of and access to knowledge are greatly facilitated. Francis Bacon gave expression to a timeless truth: "Knowledge is power." Many aspects of ongoing globalization are knowledge-driven, and knowledge intensity is one of the most significant features of the world economy in the twenty-first century. While enhanced economic dependence on knowledge is well recognized and has fueled competitiveness worldwide, the role and impacts of new knowledge are considerably less apparent in development contexts. Chapter 4 explores knowledge, as distinct from information, as a key factor in international relations, along with the role of cyber-enabled networking in the expansion and diffusion of knowledge and the demand for new knowledge.

First Image Cyberpolitics

In the context of *Man, the State, and War* (1959), Kenneth N. Waltz, a leading scholar of international relations, provided a specific place for the individual in a "three-image" construct, noted earlier, to describe behavior in international relations. Strictly construed, the individual, the first image, is the sole thinking, feeling, and acting system in politics. Enabled by infrastructure developments, buttressed by institutional supports, and steered by policy directives, the individual today is endowed with access to cyber venues and enabled in ways that were not possible earlier. Access to cyberspace and participation in cyberpolitics facilitate the formation and articulation of demands and enhance the development and deployment of capability.

Also indicated earlier is that lateral pressure theory places the individual in a social and environmental context. This view differs from the conventional standard of *Homo economicus,* the isolated individual entering an impersonal market at a particular point in time. It is also at variance with *Homo politicus*, a not too distant cousin of economic man. In behavioral terms, the individual is both an economic and a political person as a function of a particular role at any point in time or in different contexts. Both the market and the polity are well understood with respect to properties and modes of behaviors.[5] In reality, however, the *homo* is far from simply *politicus* or *economicus*. Both are social beings traditionally seen in a physical context and yet an integral part of the all-encompassing natural environment.[6] Notably underemphasized are the implications of information processing and access to knowledge.

In the twenty-first century, the individual is able to express both view and voice through cyber venues, despite various state efforts to control cyber uses, different levels of access to cyberspace, and differences in knowledge and skills.[7] Cyberspace enhances individuals' ability to articulate concerns about their insecurity and to voice demands for security. In international relations, security is generally seen largely in the context of the state (the second image). If we consider that freedom of speech, in real or virtual domains, is a key element of human security, then we can track cyber-related linkages, conceptual and political, connecting the first and second images, or levels of analysis.

Individuals and groups have found many ways to use cyberspace to bypass the power of the state and pursue their own goals, thus drawing attention to units of decision other than the state itself and to the gradual emergence of new organizational principles in world politics. In some parts of the world, notably democratic countries and aspiring democracies, political blogs have become mechanisms for the articulation of interests and for the aggregation of individuals or groups into a critical mass. This kind of activity is possible when the political rights of individuals are articulated, understood, and protected by the social contract and the principles of the political system. (It should also be noted that online speech and organizing appear to be effective in some politically repressive countries.)

Because potentially anyone can engage in cyber interactions, it is often difficult to differentiate the personal from the social, the private from the public, the political expression from the statement of threat, and so on. By participating in cyber venues, individuals transcend the bounds of sovereign territoriality and even formal identity. To be effective on the ground, so to speak, individual voicing requires the articulation of interests and their aggregation for behavior. We cannot assume that cyberspace provides a full alternative to the traditional requirements of interest articulation and aggregation.[8] Nonetheless, we must now recognize *Homo cybericus,* whose creation is a function of cyberspace and whose persona may be either *economicus* or *politicus,* as the case may be. Both constructs are relatively well understood with respect to primary properties and modes of behaviors, though neither internalizes the natural environment or, as yet, the cyber environment.

The enabling power of cyberspace provides new and different parameters for potential behavior. While each person individually or in the aggregate is embedded in and bounded by the realities of the natural system and the parameters of the social system, strong demands (high motivation) may compensate for low capabilities, just as high capabilities can compensate for low demands (or low motivations).[9] Access to cyber venues facilitates the articulation of distinctive claims and demands and greatly augments the potential audience. Such developments underscore the increased importance of the cyber-connected individual in twenty-first-century world politics. Cyber access leads to aggregation of interests, group formation, and the creation of new technologies to further enhance communication and accelerate information transfer. These effects, however, have a counterpart in the increasing assaults on privacy, human rights, and political rights as a result of individuals' presence in the cyber context—a threat that receives its own treatment later in this book.[10]

In sum, lateral pressure theory presents an integrated view of the twenty-first-century *Homo individualis*—the first level of analysis in international relations—as that of the human being embedded in interconnected systems, (the social and the natural), and now interacting in the cyber system as well. Each system is characterized by different properties, time frames, and attributes, both physical and virtual. Jointly, they constitute the overall context of human activity. In this connection, each statistic is both an indicator and a consequence of a discrete decision by an individual human being governed by his or her preferences. Statistics involve descriptions of and generalizations about aggregates, but it is difficult to trace the direct relationship between and among the individual, the social, and the state.

2.3   Cyberpolitics of the State System

The state encompasses a wide range of organizational entities through which individuals interact with each other and with their social, natural, and now cyber arenas and make claims on one another. The only legal entity enfranchised to speak on behalf of its citizens in international forums, the state is defined as sovereign in international law. Its primary goal is to ensure the security and survival of itself within a formal boundary that is impermeable, at least in principle. Its borders are recognized internationally.

In practice, however, the state cannot always control its borders and guarantee its sovereignty, meet its objectives, or retain control over its instruments of force. It is not always able to serve as an effective institution in the eyes of its citizens. While it remains the only voter in international forums, it is no longer the only voice heard at the international level. A wide range of non-state actors have increasingly populated the international ecosystem.

Master Variables

Lateral pressure theory argues (and demonstrates empirically) that all states can be characterized by different combinations of levels of population, resources, and technology—the master variables—and that the different combinations yield different state profiles. Each of these variables is obviously not a singular factor but a cluster of constructs (and attendant indicators or subvariables).[11] They are also highly interactive.

The elements of *population* include changes in the size, distribution, and composition of populations. *Technology* refers to all applications of knowledge and skills in mechanical (equipment, machinery) as well as organizational (institutional) terms.[12] The underlying driver is knowledge. *Resources* are conventionally defined as "that which has value." Extending this basic definition to include all elements critical to human existence (e.g., water, air, food) provides a perspective on the concept of resources intimately connected to requisites for basic survival. Technology may require new resources, which often calls for the deployment of specialized capabilities. Herbert Simon has described technology as "stored knowledge" and has highlighted key impacts on society (Simon 1983, 391).[13] Indeed, the increased knowledge intensity of economic activity points to the enhanced salience and politicization of knowledge. Chapter 4 examines the cyber-enabled politicization of knowledge supported by networking functionalities.

Indicators of population, resources, and technology, the master variables, are the observed outcomes of a number of widely dispersed decisions made by individuals (e.g., investors and voters), all coordinated through institutional mechanisms, private and public, the fundamental channels through which the social order is managed. The efficacy of institutions is contingent on the characteristic features of the master variables on which they are based.

State Profiles

Derived from the master variables—population, resources, and technology—the concept of the *state profile* provides an internally consistent and simple way of representing differences among states and a method for calculating the differences (Choucri and North 1989).[14] As table 2.1 shows, the formal definitions of state profiles are based on different ratios of the three master variables. Introduced originally in the context of the real-world international system, the state profile is a good predictor of both power indicators and attendant behavior patterns (Choucri and North 1993a).

Table 2.1
State/Profiles

Formal state profile definitions			
Profile 6:	Technology >	Population >	Resources
Profile 5:	Technology >	Resources >	Population
Profile 4:	Resources >	Technology >	Population
Profile 3:	Population >	Technology >	Resources
Profile 2:	Population >	Resources >	Technology
Profile 1:	Resources >	Population >	Technology

Note: See Choucri and North (1993a) for the initial specification, and Wickboldt and Choucri (2006) for an extension of the logic to differentiate empirically among countries within each profile group.

For convenience, state profiles are displayed in terms of a knowledge-intensive, technology-driven perspective, indicated by the italicized technology variable along the diagonal of table 2.1 (though this is not a necessary feature of the theory or of the concept of profiles).[15] The table can be reorganized to show a population-first array or a resources-first array. Any change in the master variables—any change in levels or rates of change—generates changes within the state, which in turn create changes in the distribution of profiles across states. The nature of the changes depends on the particular master variable that drives the overall profile. For example, if growth in the technology variable (and its underlying knowledge assets) is greater than growth in the population or resources variable, then the state will be moving along a technology-led trajectory. It also depends on the roots of change, that is, the sources of influence that drive the changes in question. Moreover, changes at the state level will have an impact on the overall structure of the international system.

The state profile provides the first-order or baseline features of behavior propensities, namely, the readily available options for behavior (which we have termed in another context "potential behavior"). These options consist of the range and types of activities that can be normally be undertaken, given the available capabilities. Box 2.1 describes the critical features of each profile and hypotheses about expected behaviors.[16] Choucri and North (1993a) determined empirically that the state profile is also a good predictor of the attendant environmental degradation. We have also validated, to some extent, the environmental inferences associated with each profile.[17] In chapter 5 we explore whether the state profile is an equally good predictor of state behavior in cyberspace.

We would generally expect a high degree of congruence between level of economic activity and wealth, on the one hand, and participation in cyber venues on the other. If this association is borne out, we may infer that the indicators of power and influence so important to our understanding of world politics to this point are robust. However, cyber access is rapidly increasing worldwide, especially in China. If the expectation of congruence between economic activity level and participation in cyber venues is not borne out, then we must infer the development of new configurations and alternative patterns of influence as new segments of society participate in cyberspace.

Governance and Security

While the master variables are the core building blocks of theory, lateral pressure stipulates that moving up the causal logic chain toward

Box 2.1
State profiles and expected behaviors

Descriptive Hypotheses

Profile 1: Resources > Population > Technology

Defined largely as resource-intensive and technologically constrained entities, the countries in this group are driven (and shaped) by the dominating strength of their potential resource availabilities relative to population, in second place, and technology, in third place. These countries have high resource intensity and relatively less technology intensity. Typical basic resources include agriculture, grazing, lumbering, mining, and other natural resources. We would not expect these countries to be engaged in cyberspace activities. Exemplary countries are Angola, Bolivia, Liberia, and Zimbabwe.

Profile 2: Population > Resources > Technology

In contrast to profile 1 states, profile 2 states are driven by the dominant strength of their respective populations and secondarily by access to resources, with technology in third place. Technologically constrained, these countries tend to be among the poorest and the least developed, although a few, such as India, have made spectacular advances in recent years. Some countries are likely to have a modest degree of access to cyberspace. Profile 2 states include Bulgaria, Egypt, Indonesia, Morocco, and Vietnam.

Profile 3: Population > Technology > Resources

Similar to profile 2 states, profile 3 states are driven by population dynamics but differ in that their technologies surpass their resources, which are third relative to population and technology. Thus, with populations that are dominant and technologies that are advanced relative to their resources, profile 3 countries exert strong pressures on their limited resource base, at the risk of becoming seriously dependent on external sources for meeting needs and demands. Profile 3 states include China, Cuba, Malaysia, Jamaica, Turkey, and Thailand.

Profile 4: Resources > Technology > Population

Profile 4 states are noteworthy for having large territories, reasonably advanced technologies, and relatively small populations. Their resource intensity calls for better methods of exploitation, access, and use. Because of the high relative salience of technology, cyberspace access and use are highly likely. Examples of profile 4 countries are Argentina, Australia, Canada, Chile, Oman, and Uruguay.

Box 2.1
(continued)

Profile 5: Technology > Resources > Population

Profile 5 countries are technology dominant, with resources in advance of their populations. These countries, which include the United States, have technology and resource bases that are adequate relative to their populations. To the extent that their populations increase, these countries will become candidates for profile 6. But if their technology base declines substantially relative to their extensive resources and limited populations, they risk falling back into profile 3. Leadership and higher participation in cyber venues are characteristic of this profile. Other examples of profile 5 countries are Finland, Norway, Sweden and the United States.

Profile 6: Technology > Population > Resources

Profiles 6 states are characterized by technology intensity, but their populations are large relative to their resource access. These countries tend to exert maximum (yet ever increasing) pressures on their (relatively) limited resource base. Because of their technology dominance, these countries are leaders in the cyber domain. A large number of countries fall into profile 6, including Austria, Bahrain, Denmark, France, Mexico, and Poland.

Note: The examples of countries in each profile group are for the year 2009.

organized collective behaviors (which include institutionalized governance) is necessary if we are to account for and differentiate among types of actual behavior. As new expectations are generated, larger amounts of raw materials and other resources are likely to be demanded, and the role of institutional mechanisms is reinforced further. In addition, a society's access to resources depends considerably on its capabilities, power, and ability to muster and exert influence. In principle, governance and institutions are the mechanisms that protect the social order in the sovereign state. The theory recognizes that the underlying logic leading to collective behavior and state action is mediated by institutions and instruments of governance.

In terms of lateral pressure theory, all forms of governance emerge as a response to two basic challenges to security and stability. The first challenge is to achieve a balance between the demands or loads on the system and the deployment of available institutional or other capabilities.[18] The second challenge is derivative, namely, to constrain system threats and enhance system supports. Conflict and warfare represent system threats that have the potential to overwhelm system supports. Depending on the scale and scope of the gap between emerging threats and supporting mechanisms, we could observe the breakdown of processes that protect the deployment of internal authority. By extension, the logic of conflict itself is a manifestation of system breakdown. Conflict and war—the latter considered the conduct of politics by "other means," as Carl von Clausewitz famously put it—are testimony to the ineffectiveness of the usual political processes.

Gabriel Almond and H. Bingham Powell (1966) identified the fundamental capabilities central to the performance of the political system, namely, extraction, distribution, regulation, responsiveness, and symbolic identity.[19] These are generic and critical institutional capacities for all states, across space and over time. Empirical evidence suggests there is a close positive correlation between institutional quality and level of national income.[20] Simply put, the higher the gross domestic product, the greater the rule of law.

In recent years economists have begun to reconsider the role of governance in the process of growth, according it greater attention than was traditionally the case in this literature. Central to the foregoing is the definition of *rights* in society—namely, what rights govern who gets what, when, and how, and how such rights are allocated.[21] However general this inquiry might be, states are far from uniform in the ways they construct their internal modes of governance and define political rights and responsibilities; there are no elements common to all states that serve as guarantees for various forms of freedoms.[22]

e-Governance

The state today is confronted with new challenges and opportunities. Cyberspace has opened up a new context of interaction, one that allows action and reaction within and across levels of analysis and enables the transmission of content through mechanisms that were not available earlier. The constitutive pressures of cyber access are potentially powerful enough to alter the nature of interactions, if not the stakes themselves.

All of this is reinforced by a varied population of stakeholders voicing new interests and aggregating and mobilizing for political action. In general, we would expect to find differences in patterns of cyber access across state profiles. Indeed, states characterized by technology intensity are, unsurprisingly, those highest in cyber participation. At the same time, however, given rates of cyber penetration, we would expect all states to show increasing e-participation and governments to show increased uses of e-venues in meeting their responsibilities. Such a finding would support the entire state system becoming more and more cyber-centric. We show these patterns in chapter 5.

Many states have begun to routinize service delivery via cyber venues, with different levels of success. The degree of effectiveness depends on the reliability of cyber access, clarity of purpose, and specificity of instructions. While we would expect industrial states to excel in the use of cyber venues, "leapfrogging" initiatives—states moving from lower to higher levels of development via innovative technology development— are already observable. Since the international community is committed to enhancing e-readiness and e-participation in all countries, we would expect the capabilities of political systems to strengthen and the delivery of services to improve. We would also expect political participation and interest articulation to increase.

The politicization of demands and the attendant bargaining processes eventually result in the determination of who gets what, when, and how. None of these factors is neutral with respect to cyber access and its impacts. Then, too, the use of cyberspace to consolidate political influence could well create a market for loyalties. We would expect such a market to be enabled significantly by cyber access as buyers and sellers compete to influence the authoritative allocation of value in the domains of interest. A related and growing feature of second image cyberpolitics is as a venue for the struggle over the management of constraints. When rendered legitimate, constraints become embedded (and embodied) in law, the ultimate authoritative manifestation of values and their preservation.

States have not been slow to control access to cyber venues or to prosecute presumed offenders. Some states go to great lengths to limit the exposure of their citizens to messages deemed undesirable. Many governments have become major players in cyberspace to exert their power and influence and extend their reach as well as their instruments of sanction and leverage. Some examples are provided in chapter 6.

One of the major challenges for the state system is to reach agreement on cyberspace norms and operational goals, given the considerable degree of discord among them. If the foregoing logic holds, we would expect to see a growth in national and international institutions designed specifically for cyberspace management. Indeed, there is evidence for this, as shown in chapter 7 and further elaborated in chapter 9.

Cybersecurity

The conventional way of thinking about national security is in military terms: the security of the country's borders and the country's ability to defend itself against military incursions.[23] The imperatives of the twenty-first century necessitate a reconsideration of the traditional conceptions of security. In today's world, the security and survival of societies, at various levels of development and industrialization, are threatened in ways that transcend the traditional security calculus. Environmental variables as well as internal sources of instability might threaten national security. Most relevant for our purposes, the conventional security view is only beginning to incorporate the potential of cyber threats.

With these considerations in mind, we argue that national security must be seen as a function of four distinct but interconnected dimensions, each with its characteristic features, variables, and complexities: external security, internal security, environmental security, and cyber security. The overarching proposition is this: *a state is secure only to the extent to which all dimensions of security are strong.* While we are concerned primarily with cyber security in this book, it would be a mistake to ignore the other dimensions.

External security refers to the ability to defend territorial boundaries against military threats and is foregrounded in the traditional view of state security. Central to realist theory in international relations, external security refers to the security of the homeland.[24]

Internal security is achieved through the stability and legitimacy of the institutions of governance and their strength relative to sources of threat emanating from within the boundaries of the state. The term underscores the importance of the overall capabilities of political systems, not just military ones, as first formalized by Almond and Powell (1966). The nature of the threat is not as relevant to the definition of this component as are the sources and severity of the threat.

In democratic societies in which the political process is regarded as legitimate and its mechanisms are routinized, the state is not threatened by internal contestation of its process. Where the political system itself is not seen as fully legitimate, or if it is dependent on the use of force, either the police or the military, internal security is not ensured, and national security may be threatened more by internal conditions than by external factors. In such cases, access to cyber venues can readily become part of the "arsenal" threatening the state's internal security and stability.

Environmental security is achieved through the resilience of the life-supporting properties of nature in the face of pressures generated by the master variables—population, access to resources, and technology. We define environmental security as the ability to meet the demands of the population, given its access to resources and the level of technology in the context of a given natural environment.[25] Implied in this definition is a relationship (or ratio) between the loads or pressures on the environment and environmental resilience in the face of these pressures.[26]

Cyber security, the fourth dimension of state security, has fast become a fundamental feature of overall national security. It refers to a state's ability to protect itself and its institutions against threats, espionage, sabotage, crime and fraud, identify theft, and other destructive e-interactions and e-transactions. In the absence of precedents, the best that can be done at this point is to delineate the numerator (pressures) and to observe the denominator (capacities), with a view to analyzing their relative behaviors over time. In most nations with cyber access, any individual or group can broadcast a message with a reasonable expectation that it will not be effectively—or at least not completely—regulated, controlled, or otherwise policed. The numerator is likely to be considerably greater than the denominator in most cases, most of the time.

Cyber security shares with environmental security the important attribute of transcending—or perhaps encompassing—the social order. In principle, a nation could extract itself from the cyber domain if it were able to control all points of access by its citizens or all ways in which users could mediate their communication via intermediary destinations.

Framed in abstract and stylistic terms, this view of national security obscures the fact that different components do not necessarily tend in the same direction and may interact with one another. Such caveats aside, this four-dimensional view is likely to be more robust in the twenty-first-century context than the traditional military-centered definition of national security.[27] On balance, the more robust the individual security variables are, the stronger is the state's overall national security.[27] We thus anticipate a greater complexity of national security policy processes as we begin to explore the full ramifications of each of the constituent dimensions. All of this becomes increasingly important for the international system, the third image, since cyberspace is an arena of interaction that has no historical precedents in theory or practice.

2.4   Cyberpolitics of the International System

The international system consists of the individual sovereign states and all other actors and entities that operate across sovereign boundaries. If there is one powerful outcome of the forging of cyberspace, it is the expansion, enablement, and proliferation of actors and networks, creating a remarkable density in networks of interests. With one exception, the United States, the sovereign actors are relatively recent contenders for influencing how cyber venues are shaped. More to the point are the cyberspace-enabled capabilities of such networks. The private sector has been the central venue for the construction and operation of cyberspace. Nongovernmental organizations (NGOs) have been involved in the management of cyberspace since its early development.

Actors and Actions

Richard A. Ashley (1980) extended the lateral pressure theory and demonstrated that the nature and mode of state expansion in international relations are important determinants of subsequent actions and reactions among states. Choucri and North (1975, 1993) showed in qualitative and quantitative terms that, in general, the strength of a country's lateral pressure correlates positively with its power, a concept that is almost universally used but rarely well defined, and usually related to, even derived from, economic performance. Efforts at the conceptual integration of the natural and the social systems include North (1990), Choucri and North (1993), and Lofdahl (2002).[28]

Lateral pressure theory provides a more detailed and nuanced view of the sources of power, the types of leverages, and the behaviors that can be inferred as a result. Pollins and Schweller (1999) and Wickboldt and Choucri (2006) show that when states extend their behavior outside territorial boundaries, they will encounter other states similarly engaged. North (1990) reminds us that, in this process, modes of bargaining and leverage are shaped by each side's real or perceived capabilities

Empirical evidence shows that intersections of spheres of influences, in which one state seeks to expand control over the influence domain of another state, inevitably fuel prevailing hostilities and reinforce an emerging dynamics of military competition leading to arms races. The essential challenge for states is how to navigate through the critical disconnects between their own demands and those of others, and their ability to meet their demands. The concepts of "soft" power and "smart" power—important additions to contemporary discourse—significantly broaden the theory and practice of leverage and influence (Nye 2011). These two ideas point to the varied assortment of leverages available to all actors to navigate rough political waters in ways other than through conflict and violence.

But the state is not the only expansionist actor. Non-state actors in great variety are also extending their activities beyond their home borders. Multinational corporations are among the most prominent.[29] Corporations conduct most of the world's economic activity, serving as producers, managers, and distributors of goods and services, and their operations include a variety of hazardous and pollution-intensive activities. Paradoxically or predictably, corporations are also central to solutions, whether the problem is environmental contamination or cyber insecurity.

While the expansionist activities of corporations and those of the state represent two different trajectories of collective action—and their conceptual underpinnings and extensions have effectively developed independently—the behaviors of these entities are often interconnected. As a jurisdictional actor, the state undertakes investments and thus engages in state-firm interactions and often intervenes in economic sectors and issue areas.

Elsewhere, we have observed that the relationship between corporate entities and the sovereign state is framed by the characteristic features of the state's profile, on the one hand, and the dynamics of corporate expansion on the other. For example, in early phases of development, a country generates neither outward nor inward corporate investment activity, largely because of the country's limited infrastructure and institutional and organizational capability. Over time, as a country increases its capabilities through its private organizations, it generates a range of cross-border activities and may even become a net outward investor. Eventually, the capabilities of corporate entities, rather than the power and the profile of the home country, become more significant. In this process the firm's strategies become increasingly decoupled from the home state and its profile. Corporate policy becomes set largely within the firm's "organizational field" (Fligstein 1990, 5–11),[30] a concept that carries much of the expansionist core of lateral pressure.

The influence of other non-state actors has grown gradually and systematically, and different types of NGOs have different propensities toward particular types of external behaviors. For example, some religious institutions have established formally recognized organizations within and across state boundaries that are understood as such by state authorities. Private voluntary organizations that seek to improve the human condition also cross borders and, in principle, span all parts of the world. Often they work with and have the blessing and the support of the home state. But if the mission of the subnational and cross-national non-state actors is to alter the prevailing structure of power and wealth, then the increased density of decision units in the international system may harbor new sources of instability. If there is an increasing divergence of interests, there will be the propensity to further support this divergence.

More and more aggregations of groups and networks are transcending the borders of the state and state-bound norms to conduct purposeful action in the international arena. Over time, the respective positioning of governmental institutions and NGOs in international forums has changed.[31] Many different types of nongovernmental arrangements have also arisen, endowed with different degrees of formal designation or legal status, and the complexities of these arrangements and the expansion in scale and scope make it extremely difficult to generate a total census of non-state actors at any point in time.[32] However, while non-state groups have been accorded observer status or otherwise allowed to participate in international forums, only states are formal voters and decision makers. Chapter 8 shows the increasing density of decision-making entities worldwide.

International Interactions

While the creation of cyberspace is the result of the activities of a large number of individuals (the first image) operating within the rules of the state (the second image), the omnipresence and utilization of cyberspace are cross-national in scale and scope (the third image), and cyber activity has become a major feature of interaction at all levels of analysis in international relations. At the same time, all of the usual features of international relations remain salient; so far, none seem to have been displaced by a cyberspace alternative. Cyber access is likely to generate a greater propensity for diversity in both conflict and cooperation and increasing demands for institutional innovations. Chapter 7 explores these and related features.

Conflict and Violence

In the realm of real international politics, several key concepts contribute to our understanding of conflict and violence in major ways. These include the *conflict spiral* (e.g., Holsti 1972), the *arms race dynamics* (pioneered by Richardson [1960]), and the *security dilemma* (notably Herz 1950; Jervis 1997). Less understood but equally important is the *peace paradox*: the possibility that any initiative by one of the adversaries to reduce hostilities and de-escalate violence—to give peace signals—will be considered by the others a sign of weakness and thus an opportunity for taking the offensive and making a move to gain advantage.

The dynamics of conflict and warfare, traditionally framed in the context of state interactions, must now be reassessed to take into account non-state groups and attendant networks. This reassessment will become increasingly critical if the frustration of the population is channeled into support for non-state groups that are sources of terrorist recruitment.

As yet, there is little systematic accounting of the sources and consequences of cyber threats from state or non-state entities. Nonetheless, many instances of system-threatening cyber behaviors on issues ranging from conflicts over the control of rules and regulations for managing cyber systems and interactions to a wide range of antagonizing activities are already apparent. Do the conventional dynamics of conflict and warfare operate in cyberspace? Do cyber venues enable new and different forms of conflict and warfare? Chapter 6 defines the terms of the debate and addresses these and related issues.

Cooperation and Coordination

International institutions and their multilateral foundations are considered to be the formal mechanism of cooperation for the third image.[33] They are the core venues for decision making among the member states—the ultimate actors, agents, voters, participants, and constituencies. The origins of intergovernmental institutions are usually traced back to the founding of the International Telecommunication Union toward the end of the nineteenth century.[34] At the turn of the twentieth century there were fewer than forty such institutions; by the onset of the twenty-first century the number had increased to roughly four hundred (Zacher 2001, 418).

Changes in international institutional arrangements often reflect changes in the distribution of influence throughout the international system. As Friedrich Kratochwil and John Gerard Ruggie stated many years ago, international organizations as a subfield of international relations had "its ups and downs throughout the post–World War II era and throughout this past century for that matter" (Kratochwil and Ruggie 1986, 753).[35] Increasingly, however, evidence is appearing of institutional learning and development. While the evidence may be subject to contention, a notable shift toward knowledge-based institutional policy appears to be emerging. Differences in institutional performance are to be expected, but a considerable degree of innovation is clearly taking place on matters of process, over and above matters of content.

These issues and the underlying conditions point to a "global governance deficit," a concept coined by Peter M. Haas (2003). However, newly formulated strategies of international institutions are expected to take account of, and be responsive to, the intergovernmental arrangements already in place.[36] Changes in the parameters of permissible behavior at any level of analysis are seldom shaped on short order.

In the arena of international cooperation and coordination,[37] are any of the system-supporting tendencies in traditional international relations portable to the cyber domain? Are there new or different cooperative modes in the new arena? If experience in the physical international system is relevant to the cyberworld, then methods of effective representation, routinized mechanisms for participation, established venues for accountability, and operational mechanisms will eventually have to be worked out. These issues are addressed in chapter 7.

2.5   Cyberpolitics of the Global System

Transcending the international system, the global system is the overarching context for human life as we know it. A system of systems, it encompasses the social system and all its activities, the natural system and its life-supporting properties, and cyberspace and all its functionalities and generative properties and potentials.

As articulated by North (1990), the fourth level takes in humanity and the Earth, its geological and geographic features, its flora and fauna, and even the Sun, all of which provides a unique and indispensable environment. Whatever humans do that drastically interferes with the natural system at any level can have global repercussions. Repercussions at the global level could have local implications; this is a case of linkage effects that poses specific challenges for theorists of international relations.[38] With the construction of cyberspace, this global concept assumes new proportions.

Levels and Linkages

Embedded in the foregoing is a simple reality: the fourth image is the "final aggregator" of human tensions and threats that have the potential for eroding life-supporting properties. We define twenty-first-century globalization as a process that is (1) generated by uneven growth and development within states, which (2) leads to the movement of goods, services, ideas, and effluents across national borders, such that (3) globalization contributes to transformations of socioeconomic and political structures within and across states, and also (4) creates pressure on prevailing modes of governance, thus (5) generating demands for changes or expansion of the modes of governance. We stipulate, however, that cross-border movements of people, goods, services, influences, and so forth lead to globalization if, and only if, they alter the fundamental characteristics of state and society and result in the loss of discretion over decision making.

Over time, significant changes in the drivers as well as the dynamics of growth and development shape new spaces or arenas of interaction, create new loads on national and international systems, and generate added pressures for existing institutions. As a result, institutional arrangements are unable to meet growing expectations. The outcome is a gap between actual and desired governance. This gap forges new demands for governance or, alternatively, demands for new governance. It is this process that leads to the creation of new governance capabilities. We have seen and will continue to see a wide range of institutional innovations.

Put differently, the globalization process begins with first image dynamics—the demands and capabilities of individuals. Aggregated to the social level, such dynamics shape the movements or flows of goods, services, people, and ideas across territorial boundaries; they stipulate a set of changes in structures and processes according to a causal logic and draw attention to the feedback dynamics across the second and third images. The implications of the fourth image for the properties of the second image can be derived from Litfin (1998); the impacts of second image decisions on the global system are also taken into account.

This logic provides a clear means for connecting the fourth level to all others.[39] In many ways, it is consistent with the view expressed in *The Oxford Companion to Politics of the World* by David Held and Anthony McGrew in their article "Globalization." They define globalization as the "process (or set of processes) which embodies a transformation in the spatial organization of social relations and transactions, expressed in transcontinental or interregional networks of activity, interaction, and power" (Held and McGrew 2001, 324).

The globalization literature is especially relevant for our understanding of cyberspace, given its focus on flows of goods, services, people, and other factors across state boundaries. Especially relevant to the systematic and quantitative study of international relations is the set of analyses in Pollins and Schweller (1999), which focuses on "linking the levels," as well as deriving implications from international relations to shifts in U.S. foreign policy over long spans of time. The logic itself provides useful guidelines for understanding cyber influences.

Some countervailing trends are noteworthy. On the one hand, cyber access and use can legitimately be characterized as chaotic, reinforcing global anarchy (as understood in international relations). No one is in control. On the other hand, the expansion of cyberspace and cyber participation may push for governance patterns—structures and processes—that transcend territorial sovereignty and rein in the chaos of interaction. We cannot anticipate how the contentions surrounding who governs (or will govern) the future of cyberspace will be resolved, nor can we predict the extent of future disruptive uses of cyberspace for gains on the ground. Further, cyberspace could well alter the traditional distributions of voices in international relations. It has already shaped new domains for interactions relevant to the first, second, and third image levels, created and communicated new demands, and forged new capabilities.

An empowering mode of cyberpolitics that spans both the second and the third images, at times implicitly and at other times explicitly, relates to vertical linkages in information generation and communication to and from the grassroots. Top-to-bottom patterns are amply demonstrated in many areas of activity within the state. When the linkages cross state boundaries or are supported by international institutions, the enabling potentials are notable. In general, bottom-to-top communication appears to be a less traveled path. However, if stakeholders are mobilized and organized, then access to cyberspace becomes a major asset. Some of these developments are converging around the notions of a civil international society and civic global responsibility. In both cases, the qualifier "civic" reflects a new recognition of non-state agencies and the potential legitimization of the international civil (in contrast to state-centered) society. We return to these issues in chapter 9.

Decision and Policy
Cyberspace allows both the constraints and the opportunities rooted at the local level to extend within and across levels of analysis nearly unimpeded and to circulate through the global system. Overall, participation

in cyber venues facilitates both the demand for political participation and the supply of potential possibilities, at all levels of analysis.

On the demand side, a growing number of Internet sites are being used as a conduit to express positions, make demands, and call for action. By the same token, cyber venues enable the supply of policy responses to be manifest.[40] There is growing evidence of the provision of government services through cyber arenas, the use of cyber facilities by candidates during electoral competitions, and the resort to cyberspace to pursue a wide range of political objectives—again at all levels of analysis. In Part II of this book we explore how different trajectories of demand and supply influence propensities for conflict, cooperation, and the global agenda, all in different ways.

Dilemmas and policy deficits aside, there is a mounting international consensus driving toward some form of sustainability for the peoples of this world and in all political entities. This conception of sustainable development commonly appears in the context of social systems, countries, economies, or states. Yet its fundamentals are relevant and applicable to other units and other levels of abstraction and with other forms of aggregation around various organizing principles.

Although states are the only voters in international governance, non-state actors are increasingly using cyber venues for interest articulation and aggregation, as well as for the pursuit of their mission, and thus can influence the priorities and performance of international organizations. Almost all international institutions have used cyberspace to extend their reach and performance in their primary domains of responsibility, as well as in the education and knowledge development initiatives.

While contentions surrounding global accord may not be as dramatic as those pertaining to peace and war, they can change prevailing modes of interaction and the postures and priorities of different actors. When international institutions serve as the consolidators of the new norms as well as the drivers for implementation, the impacts on international relations may be pervasive. When cyber venues are used to pursue institutional objectives, the impacts may be even more pervasive.[41]

All of the foregoing is part of the world in which cyberspace was created. The virtual cyber domain is now a normal aspect of the human experience. If twenty-first-century international relations theory is to address cyberpolitics as an important aspect of the field, then it must recognize the critical fundamentals of time, space, permeation, fluidity, participation, attribution, and accountability noted in chapter 1. These features define the essence of cyberspace, distinguish between the real domains and the cyber arenas, and create new possibilities—as well as new constraints—in contentions over who gets what, when, and how.

Anticipating the growing salience of cyber venues throughout the remainder of the twenty-first century, as well as the constitutive impacts of cyberspace, we are confronted with two challenges for research across all images. The first is to account for the clear evidence of the expanded scale and scope of human activities and attendant policy spaces. Decisions and policies pertaining to the fourth image are made at the other levels of analysis—if and when the various constituencies recognize the need to make decisions. The second challenge is to understand the full manifestations of cyberpolitics in existing and new policy spaces.

These challenges are especially relevant at a time characterized by struggles over the management of cyberspace, on the one hand, and, on the other, the near universal recognition of the need to develop and implement a worldwide strategy in response to scientific evidence of climate change resulting from human actions. Although the fourth image is not a decision system in the usual sense of the word, it is nonetheless affected by human decisions at all levels of analysis.

In sum, the creation of cyberspace with opportunities for cyberpolitics opens up a new set of global opportunities and challenges. The formal recognition of a fourth image, the global system, itself raises new issues. Which aspects of this system are real and which are virtual? More important, does this difference matter? If so, how? If not, why not? Also relevant is the question of linkage: How do the real systems interact with the cyber systems at various levels of analysis? What geographies help address these questions?

In chapter 3 we present trends in cyber access and explore changes in levels of rates of participation in cyberspace. Our purpose is to provide a mapping of the cyberspace domain based on the most recent empirical data.

3

Cyberspace: New Domain of International Relations

Cyberspace is such a recent phenomenon that its enabling capabilities are only now becoming apparent. In human history the expansion of frontiers created new spaces for human activity. Earlier initiatives, such as the discovery or exploration of outer space, were impressive in their own right; at the time they were considered near miracles. But the construction of cyberspace as a virtual reality has no precedent, nor does its configuration in terms of global scale and scope. This chapter examines patterns of cyberspace participation and differentials in cyber access and introduces some features of cyberpolitics explored in later chapters.

Access to cyberspace access per se provides little insight into the nature or the impacts of the interactions that take place. In the absence of an established research tradition on cyberpolitics or of common understandings of cyberspace in international relations, it is useful to highlight some basic features. By way of introduction, figure 3.1 presents a timeline of the evolution of cyberspace focusing on key institutions, major outcomes, and operational networks. This figure also points to a remarkable trajectory, a limited user base at UCLA in 1969 to more than one billion users globally in 2007.

3.1 The Mapping Challenge

The *HarperCollins Atlas of World History* (1999), edited by Geoffrey Barraclough, with its combination of visualization techniques and textual annotations, represents a stylized synthesis of the major historical, political, geographic, and developmental trajectories in human history. As such, it is very effective (and representative of works that follow similar practices). It describes a changing new "reality" in clear and understandable ways. By contrast, mapping the unknowns of cyberspace, the subject of a 1999 *New York Times* article by Pamela Licalzi O'Connell, seeks to

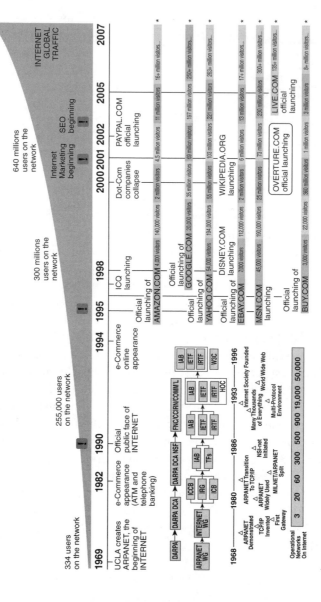

Figure 3.1
Evolution of the cyberspace: Key milestones.
Source: Leiner et al. 2009.

delineate cyberspace according to its virtual features and enabling potentials. These two mapping initiatives do not share common conventions.

Mapping cyberspace is often based on a variety of idioms and models, including spatial models, neural networks, spiderlike systems, and multilayered structures, among others. Using a language reminiscent of the early colonial exploration by European powers, the pioneers of cyberspace remind us that maps are needed not only to navigate toward and through the unknown but also to chart the new terrain and delineate its topography.

To state the obvious: the construction of cyberspace has already demonstrated powerful political implications. It is not only the permeability of territorial borders that characterizes the cyber age but also the prevailing ambiguities about the possibilities of effective control over *who* transmits, *what* is transmitted, *when, how,* and with *what effects.* The comparison between the exploration of outer space and the construction of cyberspace shows a few sharp differences. Venturing into outer space is reserved for a few technologically advanced nations, and space travel is controlled by those directly involved. It was and is a game for the few and the powerful. By contrast, access to cyberspace as a virtual domain of interaction is available in principle to anyone. Despite specific constraints, barriers to entry remain trivial compared to those for outer space. Even when barriers to cyber access are acknowledged to be serious, if not overwhelming, there are powerful forces pushing for their reduction.

Until the mid-1990s, cyberspace was largely "free space," associated with somewhat muted debates surrounding matters of price, cost, quantity, demand, and supply. The explosion of use had not yet led to the commensurate explosion of electronically based profit seeking. It was also "open space" in terms of limited efforts by states to control access or content.

A system that had originally been initiated by the U.S. Department of Defense as a means of ensuring the operation of its computer networks in case of nuclear attack gradually evolved into a network for governments and universities to use. It was not until the end of the century—1999—that the full implications of a worldwide commercial explosion became realized. By then, the large-scale connectivity enabled by the Internet had taken off.[1] This development created cyber interactions for the pursuit of power and the pursuit of wealth.

Describing the development of cyber venues is inadequate as a means to display the full features of the new playing field. Any effort to map cyberspace confronts a dilemma of massive proportions. Attempts to determine the scale, scope, configurations, and reconfigurations—elements distinguished by their elusiveness, despite their material and electronic foundations—yield only the roughest approximations at best. Even the notion of a moving target escapes the challenges at hand. Indeed, any reference to statistics or to mapping e-domains becomes out of date almost as soon as it is completed.[2] By the end of the twentieth century, it was estimated that there were more than 150 million users of the Internet worldwide, a figure that was expected to reach 700 million (see the United Nations Human Development Report, United Nations 1999, 58). It was commonly argued that the "Internet's strengths and weaknesses lie in the large number of users, anonymity, and free access" (Livnat and Feldman 2001, 19).[3] More than 80 percent of users today are outside the United States. Compared to earlier innovations—the radio, the television, the personal computer—the Internet is the fastest-growing information mechanism in human history. The pattern of Internet usage at the end of the first decade of the twentieth century is shown in figure 3.2.

To date, trends of cyber practice worldwide exhibit no shared economic or business model and no common valuation framework. There

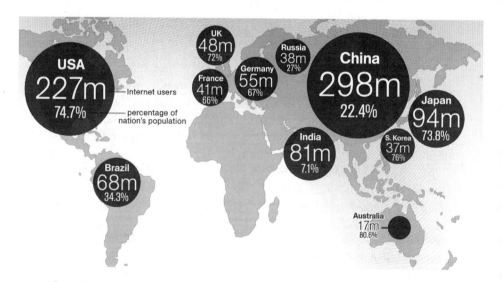

Figure 3.2
Worldwide Internet user statistics, 2009.
Source: July 29, 2009: Sydney, NSW. A News.com.au graphic of Internet users by country as of 2009. Pic. Simon Wright. © Newspix.

are significant obstacles constraining assessments of cyber traffic and cyber content, as well as compelling and still unresolved dilemmas related to the assignment of content ownership, the protection of privacy, the impacts of size and market share, and the assessment of future infrastructure requirements. In 1999, the United Nations Development Programme (UNDP) argued that the Internet "runs along the fault lines of national societies, dividing educated from illiterate, men from women, rich from poor, young from old, urban from rural" (United Nations 1999, 62).

To address prevailing inequalities in cyber access at the end of the twentieth century, the UNDP and other international institutions and private organizations initiated programs to build cyber access capabilities in developing countries. In its work in Egypt, India, and Estonia, the UNDP focused on the underlying idiosyncrasies in the socioeconomic conditions of these three very different types of countries and produced communications and cyber strategies for each country that enabled even the most peripheral communities to become connected and linked to the mainstream. In Egypt, the pilot program for a national strategy of Technology Access Centers provided services associated with connectivity and capacity building. In India, the M. S. Swaminathan Research Foundation targeted the most remote villages with supporting services to enable group-based access. In Estonia the strategy was to push Internet access for all citizens, and to a large extent, and this objective was realized. We return to these and other cases in later chapters.

Disparities aside, widespread access to electronic communications enabling cyberspace entry, along with reliance on advanced technology for generating, storing, and diffusing information, has become a reality of life in industrial countries and is shaping new frontiers in developing societies.[4] All evidence points to a continued extension of this capability to all parts of the world. A compelling argument can be made that the Internet reduces marginalization and increases empowerment in social, political, and commercial terms. When governments move toward an "Internet-push" strategy, they may find it necessary to exercise new controls. Figure 3.3 shows requests for content removal in 2011.

3.2 Differentials in Access to Cyberspace

Turning to a worldwide comparative analysis, we focus on a range of differentials across a set of indicators, notably regional differences, differential cyber access relative to population, and differences in patterns of language use.

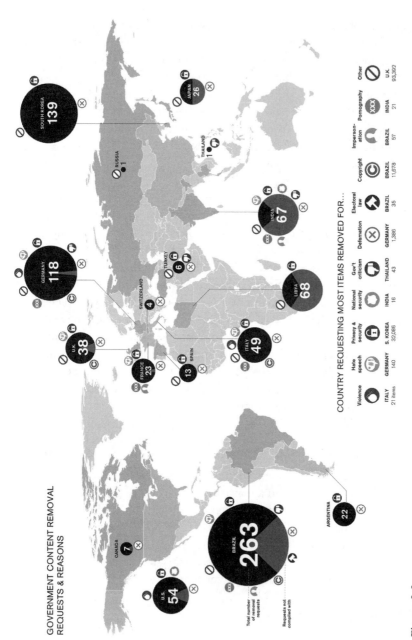

Figure 3.3
State content removal: requests and reasons.
Source: Graphic design by Tommy McCall/Infographics.com, from Bergstein, Brian, "Going Offline: Google reveals how often governments ask it to banish things from its services and how often it complies," *Technology Review* 114 (6): 30–31. © 2012 Technology Review, Inc. 85459:112JM.

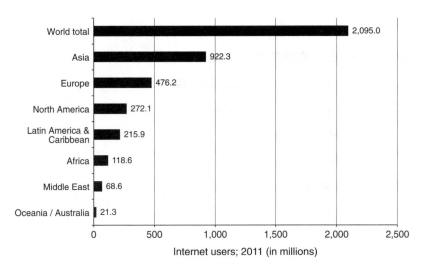

Figure 3.4
Internet users by geographic region, March 2011.
Source: Internet World Stats. © 2001–2012, Miniwatts Marketing Group. www
.internetworldstats.com/.

Differential Regional Access

Figure 3.4 shows the distribution of Internet users by geographic region
as of March 2011, and figure 3.5 shows the Internet penetration rates
by region for the same period. The differences are largely indicative of
future potentials, and suggest two different trajectories for the least-
developed states. The first is the possibility of "technology leapfrogging,"
in that these states could benefit directly from the innovations and the
applications of information technology in industrial states. The second
is that with access to cyber domains and their attendant applications, the
benefits accrued in industrial countries could eventually result in analogous, if not similar, benefits for developing countries.

In 2003 the Organisation for Economic Co-operation and Development (OECD) issued its first major report on information and communications technology and economic growth. Defining each of these terms
carefully, the OECD focused on economic performance and various indicators thereof.[5] The basic conclusion was that "information and communications technologies (ICT) are important, with the potential to
contribute to more rapid growth and productivity gains in the years to
come" (OECD 2003, 3). More important than this general observation
are the details in the data, especially those relating to differences across

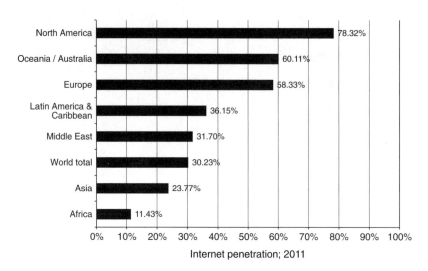

Figure 3.5
World Internet penetration by geographical region, March 2011.
Note: Internet penetration is percent population on the Internet.
Source: Internet World Stats. © 2001–2012, Miniwatts Marketing Group. www
.internetworldstats.com/.

countries. According to the report, ICT is currently "an important driver
of the acceleration in productivity growth in a limited number of OECD
countries, notably Finland, Ireland, Japan, Korea, Sweden, and the United
States" (ibid., 40).Clearly, the spread of e-networks is accelerating in
industrial countries, giving rise to a diverse range of modalities and applications. Several modes of transition have been identified as facilitating
the impacts of this segment of a country's infrastructure on its economy.[6]

These inferences and others in the report are subject to data limitations (as the OECD is careful to point out),[7] and they obscure some
important differences among OECD countries. Based on surveys of businesses with ten or more employees, the analysts concluded that the most
important impediments to cyberspace usage were, in descending order
of importance, lack of security, slow speed of communication, absence
of competency, and cost of Internet access (ibid., 29). We return to this
barrier set later in the discussion when we consider impediments to cyber
access in developing countries.

Human skills and organizational factors appear to be more important
in generating cyber usage than technical factors, equipment, cost, access,
and other variables. Reduced cost of access is a necessary but not suf-

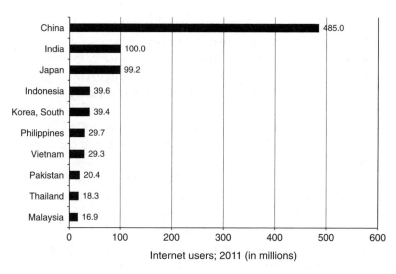

Figure 3.6
Asia—Top ten Internet users, March 2011. *Excludes Hong Kong and Macau.
Source: Internet World Stats. © 2001–2012, Miniwatts Marketing Group. www
.internetworldstats.com/.

ficient condition to enhance cyberspace usage. For example, in the OECD
report, countries with stricter product market regulations were also
those with lesser ICT-related investments, as were countries with stricter
employment protection legislation. The message that legislation matters
is loud and clear. Less clear, however, is what type of legislation and how
it would matter.[8]

In Asia, the growth of the infrastructure for cyber access is easier to
discern than elsewhere because of the clarity of the evidence. Figure 3.6
shows the top ten Internet users in the region in 2011. In terms of
numbers alone, China's population exhibits a very high cyberspace presence. Such numbers suggest that China will become the largest Internet
user, far outstripping the United States, with India possibly becoming the
second largest user.

It may be an accident of history, or perhaps one of proximity, that
these countries tended to follow the well-known "Japan model" of technology advance in the development of their information-related products. Along with the growth of the information technology export
industry, there was also growth in the products targeted for domestic use
only. An expanding domestic market is most notable for India and China,
a factor that contributes to enhanced cyberspace use. On a worldwide
basis, the region as a whole is more of a producer than a consumer of

ICT products and services.[9] Far more remarkable is that in 2000, Internet users in four countries exceeded that in the United States.

The user rate is highly polarized, however, in that countries other than those noted above fall very far behind. The most salient barriers to cyber access in Asia are the absence of viable business models, the unevenness of network and security conditions, and the cumbersomeness of online e-transactions. These countries also have in common with OECD countries the basic reality that Internet access is both driven and constrained by cost factors—that is, affordability.

A few years ago it was argued that in Latin America and the Caribbean, as in some other regions, income was a good predictor of access to cyberspace, all other things equal; but other things are seldom equal. Interestingly, in Latin America, small and medium-sized enterprises have cyber access rates that do not differ too greatly from those of large enterprises. Also interestingly, the South American countries and Mexico rank among the highest states in the world engaging in e-governance activities (Economic Commission for Latin America and the Caribbean 2003, 65). Figure 3.7 shows the ten Latin American countries with the highest Internet use per population.

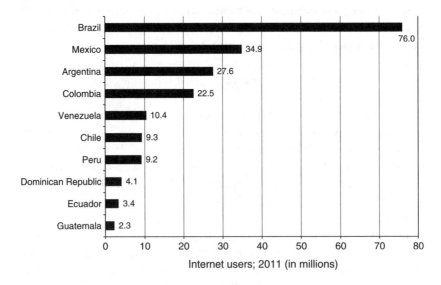

Figure 3.7
Latin America—Top ten Internet users, March 2011.
Source: Internet World Stats. © 2001–2012, Miniwatts Marketing Group. www .internetworldstats.com/.

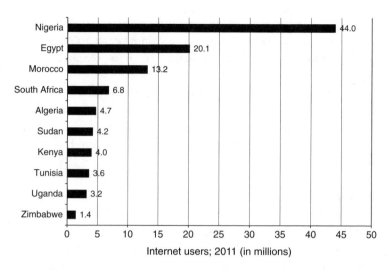

Figure 3.8
Africa—Top ten Internet users, March 2011.
Source: *Internet World Stats*. © 2001–2012, Miniwatts Marketing Group. www
.internetworldstats.com/.

Figure 3.8 shows the participation of Africa's population in cyber venues. The pattern is consistent with the continent's general level of industrialization and overall development.

More surprising in light of the revolutionary events of 2011 is the situation in the Middle East and in the Arab countries (see figure 3.4). In 2003, the UN's *Arab Human Development Report* sent shock waves across the region with its powerful criticism of development and, most notably, of applications of information technologies in Arab countries. The report focused on three specific problems: (1) the region's growing knowledge gap, (2) barriers to knowledge, including cultural, economic, societal, and political factors, and (3) the imperatives for social reform as a requisite for a knowledge-based society in the Arab countries (United Nations 2003a). Indeed, the term "backward" may not be too stark a descriptor of cyber-related conditions in the region.

The low level of cyberspace access in Arab countries can be traced to a variety of factors, most in the domain of high politics. (Later in this chapter we show that these low access rates are now accompanied by high rates of growth.) The most important aspect of the report by far is its emphasis on the importance of freedoms of opinion, speech, and assembly through good governance, coupled with the need to foster a broadminded knowledge mode for the Arab countries. Interestingly, however, while the report stresses the importance of transcending language barriers for access to knowledge, it does not speak to the importance of developing local Arabic content, which is the nucleus of developing local knowledge.

In sum, regional disparities notwithstanding, the evidence shows a sustained push around the world for more and more Internet users. Specific predictions are difficult, however, since empirical observations about conditions facilitating or impeding cyber access are often outdated almost as soon as they are made.

Differentials in Language Use
While most people in the world do not speak English, English is still the dominant presence in cyberspace. But it is rapidly declining in terms of total global users. Figure 3.9 shows the major languages used on the Internet for 2011 in millions of users.

Figure 3.10 shows the distribution of languages on the Internet by percent usage and the inset shows the growth rate. The inset conveys an important sense of scale and scope, as well as showing dramatic changes from 2000 to 2011. This figure highlights an important new element in cyberspace, the growth of the Arabic language. In light of the significant

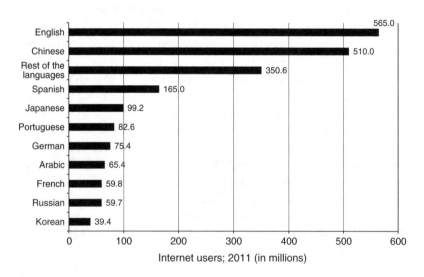

Figure 3.9
Top ten languages on the Internet, May 2011.
Source: *Internet World Stats.* © 2001–2012, Miniwatts Marketing Group. www .internetworldstats.com/.

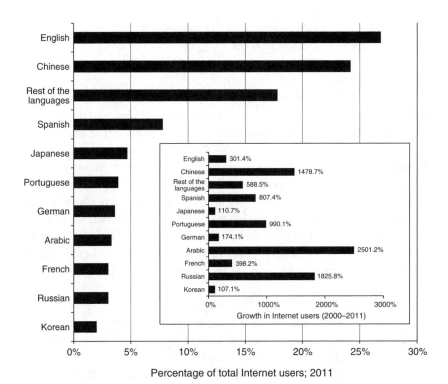

Figure 3.10
Languages of Internet users, May 2011.
Source: *Internet World Stats*. © 2001–2012, Miniwatts Marketing Group. www
.internetworldstats.com/.

lag in Arabic language use compared to other non-English languages, the
dramatic expansion (although from a low base) is noteworthy.

While international institutions as well as other agencies, both private
and public, allow the selection of alternative languages on their websites,
the choice is usually among different Western (often Latin-based) languages. Even with appropriate allowances for diversity, the world's population that speaks "something else" is not likely to be speaking a Western
language.

3.3　Sources of Variation

Against this background, we now turn to some significant features
of participation in cyber venues that provide more insights into the
contemporary cyberspace ecosystem. These include ratcheting effects,

bandwidth, and mobile technologies, as well as some inferences that can be drawn from the evidence so far.

Ratcheting Factor

Differentials in access to cyberspace notwithstanding, everyone is potentially being ratcheted upward into a participatory cyber-based culture—but from different access conditions and with considerable unevenness in levels and rates. Ratcheting per se does not provide an explanation for the patterns observed or any clues that would generate theory of cyber access. But ratcheting appears to be a systemic element of the new arena and a fundamental feature of an ongoing globalization process. While an exponential expansion of virtual materials can be expected, we can say very little about the nature of the content, the quality of the information, or the value of the knowledge that might be extracted from cyber-based repositories. Matters of knowledge are addressed in chapter 4.

Cost and Bandwidth

Despite vast improvements in the infrastructure for cyber access, differentials in the cost of access create serious impediments to virtual participation worldwide. Figure 3.11 presents statistics (for select countries) on users, broadband penetration, and GDP per capita for 2010. Even with the rapid growth in bandwidth in recent years, many parts of the world are left behind. Delays in communication cannot be attributed simply to bandwidth but more properly to user proximity to an exchange point. Generous bandwidth facilitates communication, clearly, but it also creates enabling conditions for innovation. In 2008 the *OECD Observer* openly declared that the "potential for further growth is enormous" (OECD 2008c, 15). Yet it is difficult to ignore signals of the digital divide.[10]

In sum, significant barriers to entry involve limited bandwidth, limited reliability, uneven cost structure (including hardware and infrastructure prices), and limited institutional performance. The gains due to cyberspace access can also be offset by barriers more related to content than to infrastructure. Among these barriers are the explosion of information of indifferent quality, difficulties in tracking data sources and questionable methods used to interpret data, a rapid expansion of both the Internet infrastructure and the user base, and, most important, the language barriers noted above. It is tempting to draw the simplistic conclusion that the non-Internet world is being marginalized—outside the pale of communication highways—yet we observe countervailing indicators all the time.

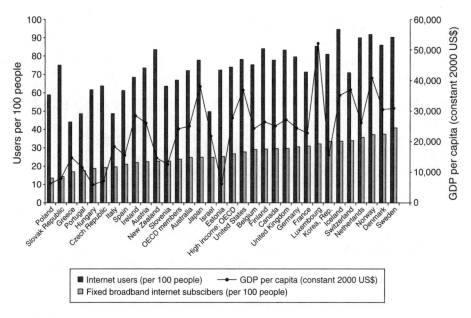

Figure 3.11
GDP per capita, and Internet and broadband Internet subscribers in OECD member states, 2010.
Source: Data from the World Bank: World Development Indicators.

Mobile Technology Effect

All of the trends in this chapter can best be appreciated in the context of the growing diffusion and uses of various forms of information technologies worldwide. We now consider one more significant development, the increased competition in mobile technologies, shown in figure 3.12. The growth of mobile uses and users is already a powerful enabler of cyber access in both the developed and the developing world. In a later chapter we consider the role of mobile communication technologies and social media for coordinating political protest and eventually revolution in Egypt and Tunisia.

Almost all of the analyses, estimates, and forecasts about cyberspace activity focus on advanced industrial countries. It is assumed, implicitly if not explicitly, that this new venue of social interaction will remain concentrated if not monopolized by the global North. The global South is obviously a latecomer, collectively and in terms of its individual components. At the same time, it is important to recognize the speed with which connectivity is taking place in the global South and the rate at

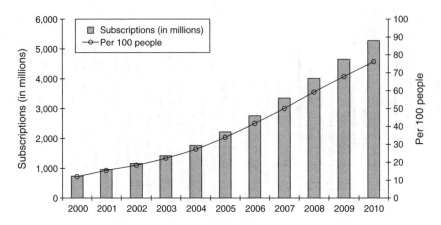

Figure 3.12
Global mobile cellular subscriptions, 2000–2010.
Source: Data from ITU World Telecommunication/ICT Indicators database.

which users are coming on board, a trend likely to result in greater diversity in cyberspace. It is possible that this diversity is both enabled by and enabling a companion process, namely, an increasing distribution of participation in cyber activities.

For industrialized countries, there is very little empirical or systematic analysis of the specific drivers of cyber access. In general, we assume that investments in access mechanisms are simply part of the normal trajectory of technological advancement. An early study of the OECD countries exploring various regression (ordinary least squares method) models found that economic wealth and open telecommunications policy are the best predictors of Internet connectivity (Hargittai 1999). Interestingly, these were wealthy countries (compared to global averages), and, by extension, they were pioneers in establishing electronic connectivity. While empirically derived results may not be surprising, the fact remains that wealth and policy matter.[11] This study also highlighted the importance of participatory politics—such as in Western democracies—for pushing toward greater cyber access, with an implied positive feedback.

For developing countries the patterns are more varied and the knowledge generated about recent trends is more descriptive and qualitative than empirical and quantitative. Methodologically, most assessments are based on statistical observations or questionnaires, country case studies, informal interviews, and summary evaluations of e-readiness for economic growth and business opportunities—all defined in the most general of terms. An analysis of "first-generation" e-readiness assessments shows that roughly 137 countries have been assessed by at least one set of tools, fifty-five countries have been assessed at least five times by different organizations, ten countries have been assessed more than eight times, and many of the poorest are assessed almost as soon as the tools appear, raising questions about the robustness of central tendencies (Choucri et al. 2003)

Social Media and Cyber Access

So far this chapter has focused on various aspects of Internet access in quantitative terms, with little emphasis on content, uses, or the motivations of users. On the basis of metrics alone, however, it is difficult to overlook the growth of the world's largest social networking platform, Facebook. A Facebook index—its penetration rate as a proportion of the Internet penetration rate—as of August 2010 is shown in figure 3.13. Of relevance here is the worldwide distribution of users, the site's uses for purposes other than strictly social, and its mobilization potentials. The popular press has been much faster to appreciate the significance of this phenomenon than has the international relations community as a whole.[12] Facebook was launched in February 2004 and one year later had one

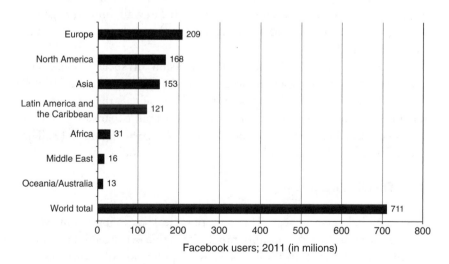

Figure 3.13
Facebook users worldwide by geographic regions, June 2011.
Source: Internet World Stats. © 2001–2012 Miniwatts Marketing Group. www .internetworldstats.com/.

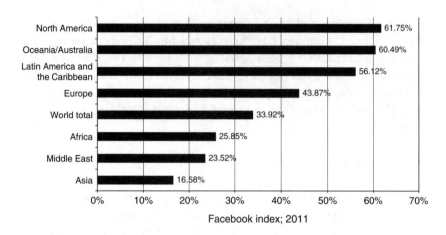

Figure 3.14
Facebook index by geographic regions, June 2011.
Source: *Internet World Stats*. © 2001–2012 Miniwatts Marketing Group. www
.internetworldstats.com/.

million users; by 2010, it had 711 million users. Figures 3.14 and 3.15
reveal the differences in patterns of Facebook use. Surprisingly, Facebook's second largest audience is Indonesia, a Muslim country with the
fifth largest Asian presence participation in cyberspace. While Facebook's
expansion in China is prevented by the Great Firewall, observers generally agree that Taiwan and Hong Kong provide clues to its potential
popularity in China.[13]

Few would dispute the dramatic expansion of social media. The
growth of new Twitter users between December 2006 and April 2009 is
shown in figure 3.16 by country, and the inset signals the top ten user
countries. In the United States, the expected overall expansion of social
network users between 2008 and 2014 is shown in figure 3.17. The
precise numbers are far less indicative than the overall trend.

3.4   The Big Picture

From a global perspective, the big picture is clear: participation in cyberspace is growing at a remarkably rapid rate. Table 3.1 provides the most
recent Internet use statistics and a view of potential constituencies (or
players) in the domain of cyberpolitics. This does not mean, however,
that such participation will be effective or that all voices can or will be
taken into account. Rather, as with all politics, whether in kinetic or in

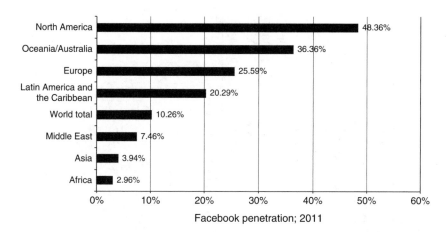

Figure 3.15
Facebook penetration by geographic regions, June 2011.
Source: Internet World Stats. © 2001–2012 Miniwatts Marketing Group. www
.internetworldstats.com/.

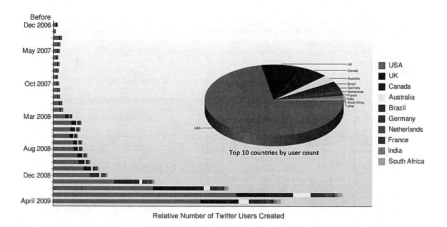

Figure 3.16
New Twitter users by state.
Source: Inside Twitter: *An In–Depth Look Inside the Twitter World.* © 2005–
2012 Sysomos Inc. All rights reserved.

Table 3.1
World Internet usage and population statistics: March 31, 2011

World regions	Population (2011 est.)	Internet users, Dec. 31, 2000	Internet users, latest data	Penetration (% Population)	Growth 2000–2011 %	Total users % of
Africa	1,037,524,058	4,514,400	118,609,620	11.40	2527.40	5.70
Asia	3,879,740,877	114,304,000	922,329,554	23.80	706.90	44.00
Europe	816,426,346	105,096,093	476,213,935	58.30	353.10	22.70
Middle East	216,258,843	3,284,800	68,553,666	31.70	1987.00	3.30
North America	347,394,870	108,096,800	272,066,000	78.30	151.70	13.00
Latin America / Carib.	597,283,165	18,068,919	215,939,400	36.20	1037.40	10.30
Oceania / Australia	35,426,995	7,620,480	21,293,830	60.10	179.40	1.00
World total	6,930,055,154	360,985,492	2,095,006,005	30.20	480.40	100.00

Source: *Internet World Stats*. http://www.internetworldstats.com. Copyright © 2001–2011, Miniwatts Marketing Group.

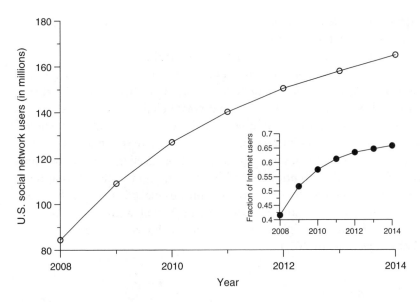

Figure 3.17
U.S. social network users.
Source: US Network Users, 2008–2014 (millions and % of Internet Users), as reported by eMarketer. © 2012 eMarketer Inc. All Rights Reserved.

virtual domains, the dynamics of interest articulation and aggregation, in conjunction with the locus of concentration of power and capabilities, will shape the authoritative allocation of values pertaining to who gets what, when, and how.

In view of the foregoing, it is not difficult to anticipate some critical contentions that might evolve throughout the years. Depending on how some potentially powerful trends play out, they could have major impacts on effective access to and uses of cyberspace. Here we note only some of the most obvious. For example, if the structural differentials noted in this chapter continue to create impediments to cyber access and use, they will reinforce the cyber cleavages, which appear so far to mirror the traditional international fault lines. Another pertains to the role of the state, particularly the efforts of some governments to control cyber access as well as content. Such trends reflect states' efforts to extend the sovereignty accorded to them by international law to a new arena of interaction, one constructed long after the creation of "sovereignty," "law," or other fundamental concepts of social order. The third potential trend follows: we can anticipate the emergence of new policy dilemmas, with attendant problems, contentions, and conflicts, along with new demands for management and control of cyberspace.

On all counts, however, the delineation of the new "spaces," records of conduct within cyber domains, and evolving norms for future interactions are all under construction. As cyberpolitics begins to take shape, they will become more pervasive and create challenges because of concurrent realities, namely, ubiquity, on the one hand, and fundamental fault lines and inequalities on the other. While there is not, as yet, a leveling of the playing field, there may already be a leveling of the opportunities and the vulnerabilities created by participation in the playing field. This in itself may well accelerate pressures to place issues of cyberspace governance, control, and security on the global agenda. Figure 3.18 presents trends in the global population and Internet users since 1995, with projections to 2020.

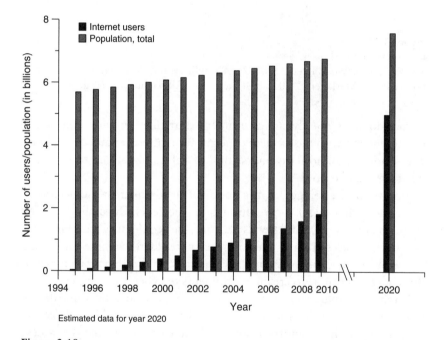

Figure 3.18
Trends and projections.
Source: Data from the World Bank: World Development Indicators; www.Future Timeline.net.

4

Cyber Content: Leveraging Knowledge and Networking

If there is a phrase that most aptly characterizes world politics today, it is "the global race for knowledge."[1] Winston Churchill is reputed to have said, "The empires of the future are the empires of the mind." To shape or control the content of knowledge is itself an exercise in power. The previous chapter looked at patterns of participation in the new space. But cyber access alone tells us little about the substantive uses of cyber venues or about cyberspace's enabling functionalities. As a venue for communication and interaction, cyberspace highlights the importance of knowledge in politics. In this context, cyber access becomes both a cause and a consequence of the global race for knowledge and thus points to the power underpinnings of world politics and the competitive edge in the world economy.

This chapter focuses on knowledge and networking as fundamental features of the new cyber reality. Once the practical applications of knowledge emerge, issues of valuation are not far behind. When such issues arise, contentions surrounding alternative ways of assigning value to knowledge follow. This is true in both kinetic and cyber domains. Matters of relative power, capacity, influence, and persuasion all come into play, as do the abilities to articulate and aggregate interests and to pursue political goals.

4.1 The Knowledge Factor

In the early years of the twenty-first century, it became common understanding that the global economy was increasingly knowledge-driven. Today, knowledge is no longer considered a residual, a companion to the technology effect in the production function; rather, it is central to economic activity and in some cases to the very performance of individual sectors. With advances in information technology, the growing density of cyberspace, and greater efficiencies in information management, handling knowledge is rapidly assuming the status of a core competency for firms, a key to the effective performance of national governance, and central to efficacy for individuals. The potential for strategic uses of knowledge has in turn shaped new modes of knowledge management, and this situation has given rise to what is now known as knowledge networking—a verb, a noun, an adjective, and a new mechanism for creating added value. All of this reinforces the enabling power of knowledge.

If knowledge is power, as is commonly said, then the global economy at the beginning of the twenty-first century is increasingly reliant on cyber-based facilities to accelerate the transformation of knowledge into power. This source of power is contingent on the *content* of knowledge and the *value* of knowledge—and both are significantly enhanced by knowledge-networking practices made possible through innovative uses of mechanisms for cyber access. We also see the liberating potentials for individuals and groups in ways that were not possible earlier.

The explicit theoretical connections of knowledge to power, influence, capability, war, and peace are seldom clearly articulated in the study or practice of international relations. Knowledge has served mainly as an implicit variable in relations among nations and has been accorded little if any importance. With the exception of Karl W. Deutsch (on cybernetics), Ernst B. Haas (on institutional learning), and Peter M. Haas (on epistemic communities), among a small group of scholars, the field has not focused on the role or the politics of knowledge to any significant degree. Robert C. North was among the first scholars to look at automated content analysis and the "measurement of meaning" in international relations.[2] Knowledge in any context is largely unobserved. As an economic good or a political asset, its elements are heterogeneous and for the most part "dispersed and divided" (Foray 2004, 18). A review of developments in growth theory summarizes the emerging centrality of knowledge thus: "Scarcity was indeed a cardinal principle of economics, but it was not the only cardinal principle. The economics of knowledge was about abundance. And for the previous several centuries, at least, abundance had routinely trumped scarcity" (Warsh 2006, 298). This highlights the importance of learning about knowledge and its content, as well as how to generate knowledge and how to enhance its use and reuse as needed. Today the knowledge economy is seen as a forceful driver of power and influence.

The knowledge economy is one in which "the proportion of knowledge-intensive jobs is high, the economic weight of information sectors is a determining factor, and the share of intangible capital is greater than that of tangible capital in the overall stock of real capital" (Foray 2004, ix). By definition, it is also one in which there is enhanced access to knowledge and knowledge bases. Accordingly, the knowledge economy constitutes "a qualitative innovation in the organization and conduct of modern economic life—namely, the factors determining the success of firms and national economies are more dependent than ever on the capacity to produce and use knowledge" (ibid., x).

Profit-seeking enterprises in both industrialized and developing countries appreciate the importance of learning about knowledge, how to generate knowledge of relevance, and how to bring knowledge to market. Generally, however, knowledge per se is not yet a fully recognizable commodity. Reviewing Organisation for Economic Co-operation and Development research on the knowledge economy, Bergling Ásgeirsdóttir (2006, 19) has argued that "*the development of the knowledge economy is dependent on four main 'pillars': innovation, new technologies, human capital, and enterprise dynamics*" (italics in the original).

The idiom of the marketplace reflects the emergence of new demands, new suppliers, and a competitive framework within which interactions converge around the need for "reregulation," accompanied by competition for the authoritative value-framing of the contentions over who gets what, when, and how. None of this is neutral with respect to cyberspace access. The ability to engage in cyberpolitics is the ability to shape the nature, scale, and scope of competition over "loyalties"—that is, to determine the content of the value around which competition takes place.

Conventionally, *value* is defined by *Merriam-Webster's Collegiate Dictionary* (2008) as "a fair return or equivalent in goods, services, or money for something exchanged." It also means worth of some kind, as well as being of some importance. But the terms and conditions of that value and its units of measure are not implied in the core concept. Value in this context has different meanings in private and public settings. For example, in private contexts it is connected to economic gain and market prices and conditions; in public settings it is viewed in terms of facilitating the provision of services for meeting social needs and implementing policies to improve social and public well-being.

Especially relevant is Paul Romer's argument that "knowledge grows through conscious investment in knowledge . . . [in contrast to Solow, who] had taken technological knowledge as a given . . . [and who believed that] knowledge came from things that were independent of economics, like basic science" (quoted in Easterly 2002, 148). Not unrelated is the feature that *"knowledge leaks"* and that *"new knowledge is complementary to existing knowledge"* (ibid., 150, italics in the original). More often than not, knowledge comes with some degree of uncertainty attached. When uncertainty itself becomes politicized, it may be wiser to assume more rather than less uncertainty.

Further, the value of knowledge is not neutral with respect to the content of knowledge. In political terms, harnessing content and deploying it in the pursuit of the authoritative allocation of value means that content viewed as neutral in one situation may be seen as highly politicized in another. The "knowledge value chain" reflects the addition of greater value at each segment of the process (or transaction) as specific activities transform raw information or observations into more knowledge-intensive elements, thereby increasing the value of the knowledge to the user. In other words, the knowledge value chain, depicted in figure 4.1, shows what can be done so that greater value is derived from enhanced content.

When interactions are undertaken in the cyber arena, it increases the value of knowledge to the actors. Conversely, if the connectivity is interrupted or is inefficient, ineffective, or irrelevant, then the value-enhancing effects are damaged accordingly.

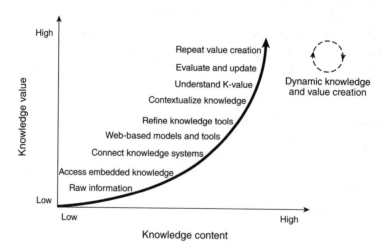

Figure 4.1
The knowledge value chain.
Source: Choucri, "Value of Knowledge–Project Report." *MIT: Alliance for Global Sustainability,* 2004.

Some might argue that the nature of the supply chain has changed as a function of the increasing role of knowledge (McGee 2003). With increased knowledge intensity of economic activity, the knowledge value chain becomes correspondingly important, a potential partner of the supply chain. In the context of the production, manufacturing, and delivery of goods and services, efficiencies in the supply chain are important in reducing costs and enabling more rapid transformation of raw materials into manufactured goods.

In practice, knowledge is increasingly generated through collaborative group activity rather than through the more traditional individual scholar-researcher model. This sociological shift in itself reflects important adjustments in research modes. When combined with new communications technologies, the practice of knowledge networking (and meta-networking) is a mechanism to create new knowledge. The knowledge value chain itself can be central to the formation of global markets, real and virtual.

Cyberspace and Knowledge Markets

We begin with an overarching view of the market in which both real and virtual are represented in the mode of exchange (i.e., trade), as well as in the good or service exchanged. In examining the evolving structure of markets in cyberspace, it is necessary to use idioms from the kinetic real-world, physical exchange of goods and services to characterize transactions undertaken in cyber venues.

In general, *e-commerce* refers to the usual market interactions between buyers and sellers, as well as the attendant information gathering, facilitating methods, efficiencies, and quest for economies of scale—all performed in the virtual reality of cyberspace. This was evident well over a decade ago. "It is almost impossible nowadays to open a newspaper without encountering a story about e-commerce" (Huberman 2001, 83). Closely related is the practice of *e-business*, which generally refers to the provision of services through this medium by firms or enterprises. The distinction is becoming less relevant since many if not most commercial transactions now involve some type of e-exchange.

By the turn of the twenty-first century, it was apparent that the value chain in e-commerce (irrespective of the substance of the transaction) could not easily be defined within the conventional classifications of economic activities. The value chain for electronic commerce consists of "the many activities necessary for the delivery of a final good" (Foray 2004, 213). It is too highly fragmented, it changes too rapidly, it is dominated by intangibles, and documentation is usually limited. However, we are gradually improving our understanding of the *process* of the creation of value. Some aspects are obvious, such as lower transport costs and ease of interconnections. Others are more contentious insofar as the interconnections are not located with any single firm's individual domain. The potential exists that firms may intentionally seek to create bottlenecks in order to exert greater control (Greenstein 2000, 152–157). What is clear, however, is that the explosion of e-commerce invariably contributes to the diffusion of knowledge across national borders in commercial as well as noncommercial forms.

The *market for knowledge* is still something of a nascent notion and an emerging practice. Yet, as is commonly agreed, "Never before has there been such growth in market transactions in connection with knowledge" (Foray 2004, 213). In this vein, the knowledge value chain spans the conceptual space and the empirical domain within which we can situate the potential role of *networking* in global knowledge markets, including networking as an institutional enabler for the development of new knowledge. Figure 4.2 depicts the network dynamics.

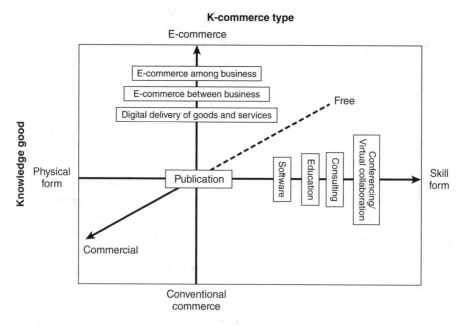

Figure 4.2
Markets for Knowledge.

Almost all indicators of knowledge production, such as patents, copyright, and income from licensing, are on the rise. For the most part these trends are seen as reflections of a knowledge-based market economy (Foray 2004, 213–223). To date, e-commerce in knowledge is concentrated in traditional forms of knowledge activity, namely, training, consulting, and to some extent publishing. By contrast, the rapidly growing practice of knowledge networking is creating new value, new modes of activity, and new sources of power.

4.2   The Power of Networking

The concept of a network has achieved common currency in a wide range of disciplines despite often subtle variations in its meaning and uses, theoretical and empirical. The role of networks is aptly summarized by Manuel Castells (2000), who stated, "Networks constitute the new social morphology of our societies . . . and [modify] the operation and outcomes in processes of production, experience, power, and culture" (496). The transformational impact is generally acknowledged to be one of the most important features of networks.

All transmission mechanisms, whether human or machine, involve networking activities predicated on some implicit or explicit networking principles. More definitive is Yochai Benkler's observation that "networked information economy has upset the apple cart on the technical, material cost side of information production and exchange." Enabling this impact is the multiplier effect, which we discuss later. Clearly, the "fundamental elements of the difference between the networked information economy and the mass media are network architecture and the cost of becoming a speaker" (Benkler 2006, 57, 212).

The Network Factor

The relevance of networks—social, computational, and political, among others—is generally recognized in international relations but has not been fully exploited.[3] A notable exception is the role of epistemic communities in the diffusion of policy-relevant knowledge. Introduced in a study of international relations by Ernst B. Haas (1990) and developed further by Peter M. Haas, "epistemic communities" are the conjunction of "knowledge" and "community" created by networking practices.[4] Social learning, by definition, rests on the consolidation of knowledge through shared practices of knowledge networking.

Access to cyber venues creates new social networks and reinforces old ones. More specifically, in world politics, Anne-Marie Slaughter (2004, 14) sees the network as "a pattern of regular and or purposive relations much like government units working across the borders that divide countries from one another and that demarcate the 'domestic' from the 'international' sphere." Focusing on the real (kinetic) world, she argues that networks are critical drivers of global governance and important enablers of linkages across institutions at different governance levels, with only passing reference to cyber venues.

By contrast, Seymour E. Goodman and Herbert S. Lin, (National Research Council 2007) take explicit account of cyberspace and its enabling possibilities in the formation and performance of networks. They highlight different types and modes of networks in business and industry and stress the role of people, location, technology, and cyber venues in shaping the network structure. It may not be an overstatement to note, as James N. Rosenau and J. P. Singh (2002, 3) do, that "all conceptual frameworks now speak of networked organizations." Stated succinctly, "the ultimate goal of the study of the structure of networks is to understand and explain the workings of systems built upon those networks" (Newman 2003, 244).

To date, however, in the study of international relations relatively little attention has been devoted to the role of cyber venues from the perspective of mathematical network theory (also known as graph theory). Many of the current insights pertaining to networks, as well as to the evolution of network theory and its applications in the social sciences, are rooted in the *small world phenomenon* first delineated by political scientist Ithiel de Sola Pool and mathematician Manfred Kochen in the 1950s. Pool and Kochen (1978) made the bold assertion that through various social connections, any two individuals anywhere are joined by some minimum number of links, as aptly summarized by Lloyd Etheredge (2006).

When Albert-László Barabási (2002) and Duncan Watts (2003) showed the relevance of network links in a variety of different contexts, they contributed to the growing interest in networks in both real and virtual arenas. Among the most powerful discoveries was the "scale-free network," characterized by power law distributions. Attributed initially to Derek J. de Solla Price (1965), this specific distribution confirmed an earlier finding by Herbert A. Simon (1955), termed descriptively "the rich get richer" (cited by Newman 2003, 213); it means that the powerful enhance their power, those that have advantages increase their advantages, and so forth. Simple as this observation might seem, it is especially relevant because it enriches the logic of who gets what, when, and how in any strategic exchange.

Knowledge Networking Dynamics

The dynamics of knowledge networking generally involve core elements of a knowledge system or a knowledge market. At a minimum, these consist of:

• *Basic assets*   The initial requisites for e-commerce, namely, cyberspace access, (capacity), networking facilities (connectivity), and substantive materials (content), the 3C's.

• *Knowledge e-tradables*   The products and the processes (in terms of goods and services) that are exchanged, P&P.

• *Forms of commercial value*   The size and terms of value added (e.g., size of market share or profits).

• *New demands for knowledge-e-tradables*   Added desire to pursue further exchanges of e-knowledge because of new market participants or the activities of current participants.

• *New demand for basic assets*   Added e-trade and networking traffic, in turn, create pressures to expand the basic assets in place.

These are generic features of a knowledge market, irrespective of the specific knowledge in question, and they span the virtual (cyber) and the kinetic (physical) domains. The network itself is distinct from the elements (or actors) that constitute it. Figure 4.3 shows in simplified form the feedback dynamics of a knowledge networking system.

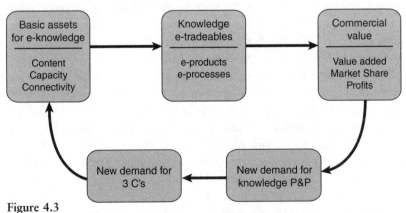

Figure 4.3
Feedback dynamics in a knowledge networking system.
Note: 3C's refers to content, capacity, and connectivity. P&P refers to products and processes.

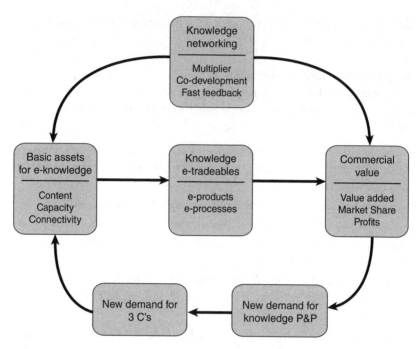

Figure 4.4
Multiplier effects in a knowledge networking system.
Note: See figure 4.3 for 3Cs and P&P.

Missing from figure 4.3 is a fundamental feature of an *effective* knowledge market, the multiplier effects that reinforce and expand the value of knowledge. Figure 4.4 signals the operation of multiplier factors through two distinct transmission routes—one enhancing the basic value of these assets, the other enhancing their commercial value. Multiplier effects generally influence market size and managerial and infrastructure requirements. We return to these issues later on.

Figure 4.4 also shows some added properties of effective networking dynamics. The relationships in the top part represent the basic *system assets*, and the relationships in the lower part represent the *demand for new properties* in assets or relationships. Since barriers to e-commerce in knowledge and to systemwide effects can (and do) emerge at various stages (or points) throughout these processes, the strategic challenge is to minimize impediments, remove barriers, and facilitate overall efficiency. If impediments to the general flows emerge and persist, they will reduce the value accrued of connectivity. However, if effective correctives can be made, then the value of connectivity will be restored and even protected. The directionality of influence is itself an empirical question, contingent on the nature of emerging cyberspace configurations at any point in time and in any location.

Depending on the issue area, the difference between knowledge and networking can become blurred. The digitalization of economic activities is particularly perplexing in its elusiveness. What is the commodity or service embedded in a digital image? Who owns what? Who will regulate the new e-exchanges?

4.3   Contentions over Rights and Regulations

The speed, scale, and scope of cyber access and advances in uses, coupled with the explosion of content transmitted, contribute to the development (and profitability) of new businesses and new e-services (e.g., browsers, e-commerce, search tools, and a range of new applications). Users demonstrate a wide range of interest and influence (e.g., in information generation, knowledge sharing, distributed and collaborative ventures) and contribute to the consolidation of new interests and constituencies.

To be efficient, markets must operate within a stable regulatory framework in which the role of the state is clear, the conditions for intervention in the market are specified, and the reach of instruments and influence is understood, credible, and stable. In principle, these conditions must also hold in knowledge markets, but the intangibility of knowledge, coupled with the increasing penetration of the virtual into the real domain, creates new challenges for some of the most important institutional cornerstones of modern society. For example, the fluidity of cyberspace affects the institution of property rights—most notably intellectual property—with potentially pervasive implications for the firm, the state, the economy, and the society.

In today's world, states inevitably encounter difficulties in applying instruments that regulate physical (kinetic) domains to interactions in virtual (cyber) contexts. Newcomers to cyberspace as well as some segments of the cyber established community are often reluctant to conform to the rules of the game supported by the dominant players. In fact, they do not necessarily buy into the advanced countries' views of the rules or of the nature of the game itself. The increasingly strident contentions over matters of valuation and models of value are only the tip of a robust iceberg of conflict and contention of impressive proportions. This is not to dismiss the salience of well-established norms and rules such as intellectual property rights. Rather, it highlights new constraints on the implementation of established norms, particularly those forged by the historical trajectory of the advanced industrial states.

In many ways, we see shifts in the frontiers of rights and regulations, exchange, and codification, in theory and possibly in practice. These shifts may result in new modes of behavior or adaptation to emerging ones. Indeed, the entire playing field may be changing. In this connection, we now turn to the emergence of alternative models of knowledge rights and knowledge regulations.

Knowledge Rights: Alternative Cyber Models

Many of the reasons to address the contours of cyberpolitics surrounding the value of knowledge are articulated by Yochai Benkler (2006) and Ernest J. Wilson (2004), as well as by a number of other scholars and analysts who have written on various facets of these increasingly contentious issues. Benkler provides the most insightful inquiry into proprietary and nonproprietary markets as well as current predicaments of ownership, production, and distribution in a networked society, while Oran R. Young (2002) reminds us of the two-stage process of bargaining in an institutional context: negotiations relate not only to the nature of the outcome itself but also to the rules according to which (the contending parties agree) the substantive bargaining will take place. In the first instance, the critical issue pertains to the product, while the second is a matter of process.

If we draw on the arguments and analysis of Benkler (2006), who talks of alternative institutional ecologies, on the one hand, and of Young (2002), who formulated the concept of institutional bargaining, on the other, we can readily discern the characteristic features of three general models of knowledge value. These are the dominant and traditional market-based model, anchored in proprietary principles; the nonproprietary value model, which includes open access and the knowledge commons variants; and the value-in-networking model.

Each of these models is characterized by different assumptions related to the nature of value markets and institutions and legitimacy in cyber venues. All of them refer to configurations of capacity, connectivity, and content. Not only do they represent different views pertaining to who gets what, when, and how but, most pressing, they articulate fundamentally different modes of behavior based on different underlying principles considered to be authoritative for shaping the allocation of value.

Property Rights

The range of legal and institutional instruments designed to protect the creations of the human brain and mind, such as inventions, works of arts, software, literature, and the like, are known as intellectual property rights. Property rights remain among the most contentious issues surrounding knowledge and its deployment in cyber venues. The nature, scale, and scope of rights considered as authoritative differs substantially among the relevant players, as does recognition of the legitimacy of such rights. The conventional rights model is that of "propertized knowledge," defined as "intellectual property capable of commanding a monopoly rent—made its appearance for the first time in the kind of aggregate analysis that constituted mainstream economics" (Warsh 2006, 298).

The concept of a right to intellectual property is well established, with a general understanding on the relative legitimacy of various devices, such as copyrights, patents, trademarks for industrial designs, collective marks, and certification marks. In light of the changing parameters of the cyber arena, it should come as no surprise that the intellectual property rights issue in itself has become a subject of considerable contestation.

Nonproprietary Rights

Summarizing the basic claims related to property rights issues, Benkler (2006) argues that the importance of proprietary strategies in information production systems is overstated. The expansion of property rights places a burden or tax on nonproprietary models in favor of proprietary ones. Basic technologies and software make nonproprietary rights very attractive, including peer production and collaborative production—and all of this stands in major contrast to standard economics of information production (Benkler 2006, 460–461).

Nonproprietary models of knowledge rights are connected to, even derived from, issues central to the "tragedy of the commons," a concept introduced by Garrett Hardin half a century ago. These issues revolve around the matter of rules and rights, anchored in theoretical principles of fairness, and have profound political and economic implications. In the knowledge arena, viewed broadly, there is no agreed-upon frame of reference or standardization of concepts and terms. For example, some analysts refer to "information commons" (David 2006) while others tend to use the term "knowledge commons" (Hess and Ostrom 2007). Despite the shared use of the term commons, the meaning differs. David considers open access broadly defined as the core feature, whereas Hess and Ostrom distinguish between open access and the knowledge commons.

Foray notes that the fundamental properties of knowledge potentially create a "combinatorial explosion" generating increasing returns to scale, clearly an important feature of any economic activity (Foray 2004, 16). Of the many properties noted by Foray, the most important for the purpose of this book is that knowledge is "dispersed and divided" (ibid., 18), and that this, and other factors, contribute to the formation of a knowledge commons. Interestingly, Graciela Chichilnisky (1998) argues that the market itself can be utilized to enable the deployment of knowledge and the Internet as global public goods through the use of compulsory licensing systems.

By contrast, Hess and Ostrom take an uncompromising position and view knowledge as a global commons that transcends concepts and behaviors in a market. In *Understanding Knowledge as a Commons,* they build on Elinor Ostrom's earlier work (Ostrom 1990, 2005; Ostrom and Buck 1998), and proceed from the view that "a commons is a shared resource that is vulnerable to social dilemmas" (Hess and Ostrom 2007, 13). To this we add that such dilemmas are more often than not accompanied by political contention. Indeed, the definition of a commons motivates particular theoretical and political precepts and an implicit, if not explicit, orientation toward institutional development.

Value in Networking

This model of knowledge rights is based on the gains to knowledge obtained from networking multiplier effects. Networking enables the creation of new knowledge—that is, knowledge about matters that were not previously salient—or new understandings of earlier knowledge. Networking gives the participants the rights to knowledge gains made possible by networking.

Since the diffusion of networking makes it possible to engage in multiparty, asynchronous, and multidirectional interactions, it facilitates the flow of content (knowledge) from lower levels of aggregation (at the bottom) to higher levels (at the top), both within and across societies. Access to interactive knowledge networking empowers stakeholder communities to project their preferences into the decision-making process and, conversely, gives decision makers access to multiple stakeholder communities. Transcending these interactions and are powerful feedback dynamics whose characteristics are not fully understood.

Multiplier effects reinforce two mutually supportive outcomes: the globalization of knowledge through greater diffusion and the localization of knowledge by means of the representation of distinct local, technical, and linguistic factors. In both cases, knowledge networking is a critical enabler for harnessing the value of knowledge—across borders, cultures, disciplines—and for transforming knowledge into practical applications and implementations.

In sum, the value-added multipliers are fundamentally those tied to access, uses, diffusion, and expansion of knowledge. Multiplier functions are shaped by the interaction between the content of knowledge and the value of knowledge. Both are significantly enhanced by interactive practices made possible through the innovative use of cyber venues.[5]

Regulation and Extensions of "Code and Commerce"

The increased interactions and transactions taking place in cyberspace are pushing the frontiers of public policy debates and policy deliberations surrounding matters of property rights, and calling into question the assumptions that have prevailed to date. The legal ambiguities surrounding rights on cyber venues are compounded by the absence of a regulatory framework predicated on some notion of sovereignty and guaranteed by a sovereign entity. Increasingly, access control is being achieved through technological means rather than legal ones. The proliferation of filtering software that prevents access to targeted cyber sites has already introduced some practical regulation and even control.

In *Code and Other Laws of Cyberspace,* Lawrence Lessig (1999) identifies four modes of regulation: the law of the land (the state), the nature of the market, the architecture of the Internet, and the norms of interaction and communication. Each mode has the potential for imposing constraints that shape emergent communications and interactions, as well as future possibilities. Lessig argues that the future will be shaped by regulation and control in two areas of human activity, commerce and code making. This duality could either exacerbate prevailing cleavages or, alternatively, dampen them, depending on the management for code and for commerce. Lessig's argument is provocative in that it helps to unbundle some of the hidden politics and to differentiate among positions (or locations) in the code/commerce contentions and realities. This logic has notable implications for international relations theory as it allows us to situate different policy and political positions on matters of e-code and e-commerce in a common space.

Our purpose here is to extend Lessig's duality of code and commerce in order to explore some underlying features and hidden politics. Accordingly, figure 4.5 differentiates among modal types of control for code and for commerce. The individual quadrants in the figure, each with high or low signs, indicate the salience of regulation and control. Our intent

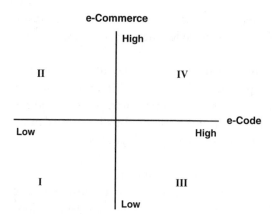

Figure 4.5
Models of regulation and control.
Note: See text for discussion of issues and quadrants.

here is to highlight the differences in core principles surrounding who gets what, when, and how across these four types of conditions, not to assign any one of Lessig's regulatory modes to any of the four cells. Accordingly, each quadrant illustrates an ideal or archetypical situation along with its distinctive modes of control and regulation; jointly they highlight fundamentally different possibilities.

Quadrant I captures the least formalized and routinized sets of interactions where there is relatively little institutionalization of commerce and code, and ad hoc interactions dominate. This case is perhaps closest to the proverbial laissez-faire situation with respect to low regulation of e-code and e-commerce.

Quadrant II represents low regulation of code and high regulation of e-commerce. We would expect that symmetry or asymmetry (i.e., balances or imbalances) in the regulation of e-commerce and e-code not to be neutral with respect to their political effects. More complex in their underlying premises are cases in quadrant III, with convergence around regulation principles in e-code but divergence in the domain of e-commerce. Embedded in this divergence are the social costs of alignment for synergy. Finally, cases in quadrant IV reflect the heavy hand of the state, with high regulation of both e-code and e-commerce.

Although figure 4.5 is a somewhat stark extension of the original code-is-law thesis, it can help articulate contentions over who gets what, when, and how in the structuring of the new arena of interaction. We can even consider a range of derivative possibilities based on Lessig's articulation of alternative regulatory modes—the legal, normative, market, and code modes. For example, we can envisage the gradual emergence of iterative adjustments (and reactions) taking place among all four modes. Alternatively, one could explore the conditions under which different states (or a coalition of states) would prefer to operate under one or more of these modes.

4.4   Global Demand for New Knowledge

Well over fifty years ago, Harold Lasswell reminded us that "in epochs of rapid development, there is need to reassess the relevance of intellectual effort" (Lasswell 1958, v). While the politics of wealth-enhancing growth were and continue to be the dominant social value in almost all countries of the world, the legitimacy of this legacy is being seriously challenged, as we noted in chapter 1 when we discussed the convergence between cyberspace as a new arena of interaction and sustainability as an alternative to the traditional economic growth model. The policy community worldwide has already embarked on a mission to pursue transitions to sustainability, but the concept of sustainability remains underspecified. Its knowledge base is under development. It is difficult to argue for limiting growth in developing countries, and few would argue for limiting the growth of the private sector or for constraining financial or other gains. Aside from the innovative work of a handful of individual scholars—including most notably Dennis Pirages (1977, 1978), Pirages and Ken Cousins (2005), and Choucri, Mistree, et al. (2007)—the issue area of sustainable development is not a central concern for international relations theory.[6] Increasingly important in sustainability thinking is the issue of the potential trade-offs that are embedded in the competing objectives of states, firms, and other actors whose impacts at the local level may reverberate throughout all levels of interaction, including the all-encompassing global system.

   Increasingly, enhancing the sustainability-related content with "knowledge" based on some form of legitimacy or legitimizing process is a mechanism for choice of desired knowledge as well as its politicization.[7] In practice, knowledge generation is "a process in which subjective and objective elements inevitably meet" (Deutsch 1963, 6). Subjectively, norms and values shape the type and composition of demands and their various manifestations in empirical terms. Objectively, meeting demands is constrained or enabled by the capabilities available to individuals and collectivities.

We end this chapter with an important caveat: the dominance of knowledge per se will not necessarily make an economy more sustainable. Moreover, the knowledge economy may not necessarily be a sustainable economy.[8] The challenge is to transform the vicious cycle of continued threats to social systems into a "virtuous cycle" of social resilience. The global demand for an integrated and coherent knowledge base to support transitions to sustainability is on the agenda of international institutions.

The recognition of sustainability science as a formal domain of scientific inquiry legitimizes the quest for alternatives to growth and is an important milestone in the sociology of knowledge. We return to these issues later in the book when we explore the synergy between cyberspace and sustainability, and its implications for the emerging global agenda.

II

Cyber Venues and Levels of Analysis

5

The State System: National Profiles and Cyber Propensities

Part II of this book explores in some detail the interactions of the traditional real-kinetic world and the new cyberspace features of structure and process in international relations. It follows closely the levels of analysis logic introduced in chapter 2, in terms of the state system, the international system, and the global system, known also as second, third, and fourth images. Recall that this logic extends the traditional three-level view of international interactions presented by Kenneth Waltz (1959) by defining a fourth image, the global system, and by expanding the scope, taking into account the environmental system and the cyber system. Throughout, we consider the individual level, the first image, as relevant to the issues addressed.

This chapter focuses on the state system, drawing on the concept of the state profile as the major organizing device in order to explore the real (kinetic) and the cyber features of the second image in international relations. The logic of lateral pressure theory holds that the profile concept, defined by the master variables—population, resources and technology—provides the basis for connecting a state's core internal attributes and characteristics with propensities for manifestations of different external behavior and activities.

We begin with the basic parameters of the second image and examine trends over time in the master variables (and some derivatives), as well as carbon emissions as an indicator of impacts on the natural environment. In this way we can provide a rough mapping of the state system in terms of relative power and capability, as well as environmental effects over time. We then turn to the cyber domain and explore the key enablers of cyber access and participation. Largely technological in nature, these variables are good signals of propensities for cyber participation. Finally, we focus on the uses of cyber venues for governance within the state as well as effectiveness in the conduct of government functions.

5.1   Profiles of States

A country's location in any profile group at any point in time is a function of its own master variables (relative to each other) and to those of all other countries.[1] This profile inquiry contributes to international relations theory in three ways, by (1) providing an empirical base for the proof of concept, (2) yielding some insights into variations among states within and across profiles, and (3) illustrating patterns of cyber propensities and performance in the state system today.

Trends over Time

We begin with the long-term trends in the distribution of states across profiles in the international system since 1960. As noted in chapter 2, profiles 2 and 3 are population dominant and usually characterize developing and less-developed states. Profiles 1 and 4 are resource dominant and characterize a diverse set of countries, some developed and some developing. Profiles 5 and 6 are technology dominant and applicable to the more industrial countries. Figure 5.1 shows the profile distribution for 2009 on a world map. Appendix 5.1 (at the end of this chapter) identifies the specific countries in each profile group defined by (a) their master variables at any point in time relative to the global total for each of the master variables, and (b) the results displayed according to the inequalities that define the profile groups (see table 2.1) This approach allows us to track the changing landscape overall, as well as the locations of states within it.

Since the location of a country in a particular profile is a function of that country's master variables and the master variables of all other states in the international system, profile locations are variable rather than fixed. Figure 5.2 tracks the number of states in each group over time, and figure 5.3 shows each profile group as a percentage of all states in the international system. These trends concern sovereign states and their shifts in profile relative to other states. For example, over time there is a small decline in the number of profile 1 states (resource dominant and technologically constrained) and a growth in the number of profile 2 states (population dominant and technologically constrained). However, we do not show the shift of individual countries across profiles, only a shift in the overall proportion of countries in each profile group over time.

Empirical investigations have yielded a more nuanced view of profiles and their path dependence over time (Choucri and North 1993; Lofdahl 2002). However robust the historical trajectory may be, the theoretical claim is dependence, not determinism, and contingency rather than

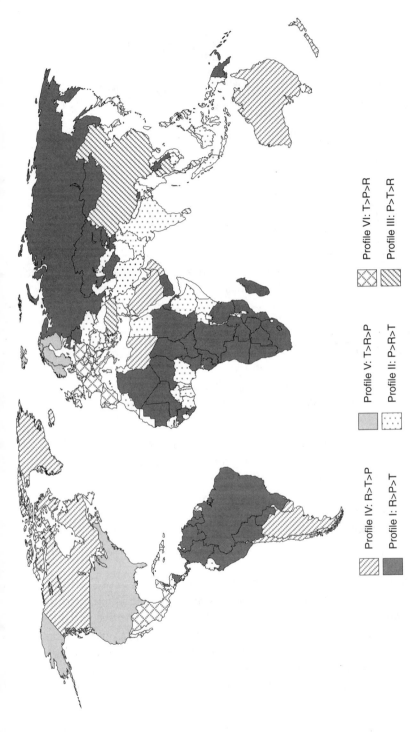

Figure 5.1
State profiles, 2009.
Note: See appendix 5.1 for list of states in each profile group.
Source: Based on data from the World Bank: World Development Indicators.

Profile IV: R>T>P

Profile I: R>P>T

Profile V: T>R>P

Profile II: P>R>T

Profile VI: T>P>R

Profile III: P>T>R

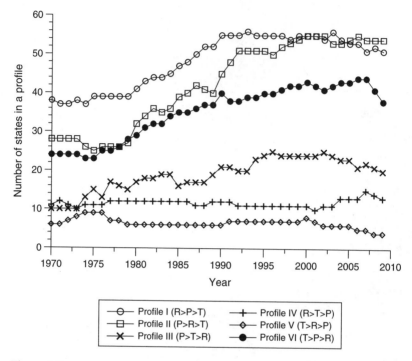

Figure 5.2
Number of states in each profile group over time.
Source: Based on data from the World Bank: World Development Indicators.

inevitability.[2] It is increasingly recognized that interactions and feedback relations create interconnections among the master variables, and that these critical drivers are almost always affected by policy interventions, as well as by the impacts of earlier actions. As James N. Rosenau (1969, 61) reminds us, linkage occurs when an action in one part of a system or organizational boundaries affect conditions in another system or part of a system.

Comparative Analysis
This inquiry begins with real (kinetic) parameters and explores the master variables—population, resources, technology—and their environmental impacts (carbon emissions), as well as select derivative variables of low politics (e.g., life expectancy at birth) and high politics (e.g., military expenditures). On empirical grounds, we would expect notable variations across profiles in terms of basic attributes and behavioral patterns, differences that are congruent with changes in the master variables

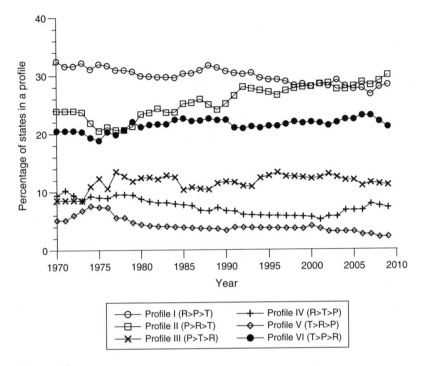

Figure 5.3
State profiles over time: 1970–2010.
Source: Based on data from the World Bank: World Development Indicators.

and yield good evidence of transformations of societies over time. The profile differentiation is considerably more nuanced than the usual rich/poor or developed/less-developed categories.[3] We do not infer a causal connection across the distributions in the figures below. Our purpose is more limited: we seek only to highlight the diverse traces of human activities on the natural and the social systems.

Population and Environment

In figure 5.4a we see the familiar global distribution of population size in relation to *carbon dioxide emissions*, a well recognized as a by-product of human activity. The distribution of states is entirely consistent with a core feature of lateral pressure theory, namely, the close connection of the social system and the natural system. In figure 5.4b the same variables are disaggregated according to state profile. The patterns are also familiar, with few surprises.

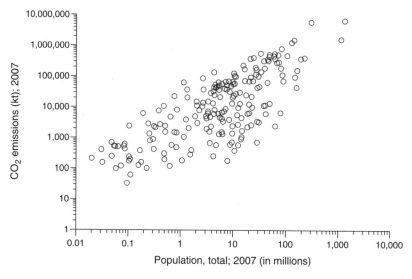

Figure 5.4a
CO_2 emissions and population, 2007.
Source: Data from the World Bank: World Development Indicators.

Life expectancy at birth is often used as an indication of overall well-being in a society. Figure 5.5a shows the overall distribution of life expectancy as a function of GDP per capita for 2009, and underscores a well-known pattern: technology-intensive countries enjoy a higher level of life expectancy. The companion inference is that as economic conditions improve in other countries, their life expectancy also improves.

Interestingly, when we decompose the global or cross-national aggregate view into the profile groups (figure 5.5b), we note a highly structured differentiation. Put simply, we can see the individual pieces of the overall developmental puzzle. As countries in profiles 1, 2, and 3 develop, we would expect them to attain greater life expectancy, as shown in profiles 4, 5, and 6. Again, this is in line with common understandings.

GDP and Environment

The cross-national distribution of GDP in relation to carbon emissions for 2007 is shown in figure 5.6a. The distribution of state profile types in figure 5.6b is entirely consistent with global patterns of human impacts on the natural environment. Although we have not taken into account the composition of economic activity, figure 5.6b, the cross-national distribution into profile groups shows the same close coupling of GDP

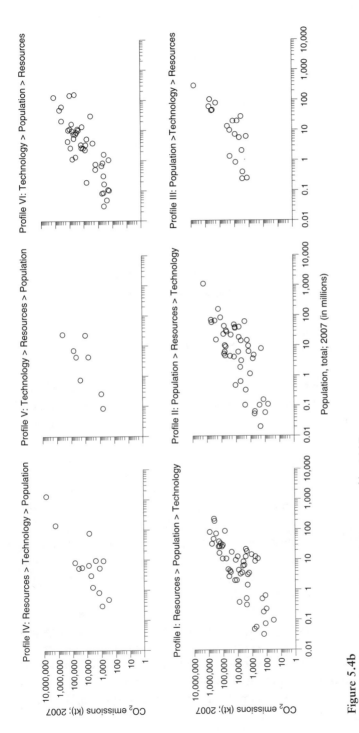

Figure 5.4b
CO_2 emissions and population by state profile, 2007.
Source: Data from the World Bank: World Development Indicators.

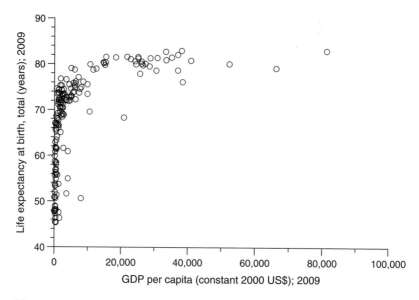

Figure 5.5a
Life expectancy at birth and GDP per capita, 2009.
Source: Data from the World Bank: World Development Indicators.

and carbon emissions across in each profile group. If there is a regularity linking human activity and environmental impacts, this one is among the most robust to date.

Energy and GDP
Given the high positive correlation between energy and GDP—and despite recent changes in the energy intensity of economic activity—we are gradually coming full circle as we consider each of the master variables. Figure 5.7 shows the cross-national aggregate energy use per GDP for 2008. Were we to extend our search for regularities—laws—of human environmental impacts, the energy-GDP connection already has a claim to that status. As to be expected, the profile-based distributions (not shown here) mirror those of figure 5.6b.

In the past, this type of evidence was relegated to the realm of low politics, marginal to daily affairs. But now almost everyone acknowledges the environmental effects of energy use, especially with respect to carbon dioxide emissions. Some of the most contentious political debates in the scientific and policy communities worldwide involve energy and the environment. Despite the usual political conflicts and discord, the inter-

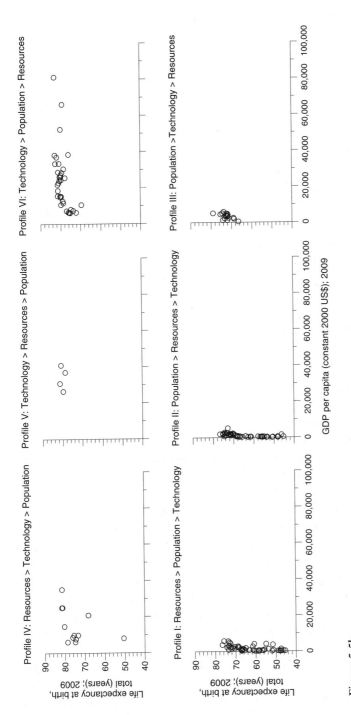

Figure 5.5b
Life expectancy and GDP per capita by state profile, 2009.
Source: Data from the World Bank: World Development Indicators.

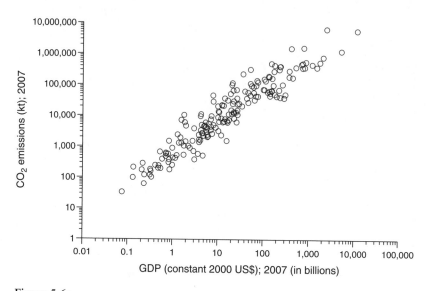

Figure 5.6a
CO$_2$ emissions and GDP.
Source: Data from the World Bank: World Development Indicators.

national community is, once more, preparing to take another step toward coordinated action.

Per Capita Distributions

Figure 5.8a shows the impacts of population and graphs the overall cross-national data on carbon dioxide emissions per capita against GDP per capita for 2007, and Figure 5.8b decomposes the cross-national view into the six country profiles. The overall perspective reveals a familiar pattern, again entirely consistent with general expectations, and the country profile patterns are consistent with those noted above.

The distributions of countries for profiles 1 and 2—the most technologically constrained—are at variance with those of the remaining four profiles, reinforcing the disparities between rich and poor in the world.[4] The profile patterns in figure 5.8b point to changes among poorer states as they generate economic output. This reinforces the view that these countries will follow the historical trajectory of the more industrial states, whose profiles show greater technology intensity.

To state the obvious: the rich produce more and pollute more, and through their industrial activities they stress life-supporting resources in significant ways; the poor produce less and pollute less, yet they also

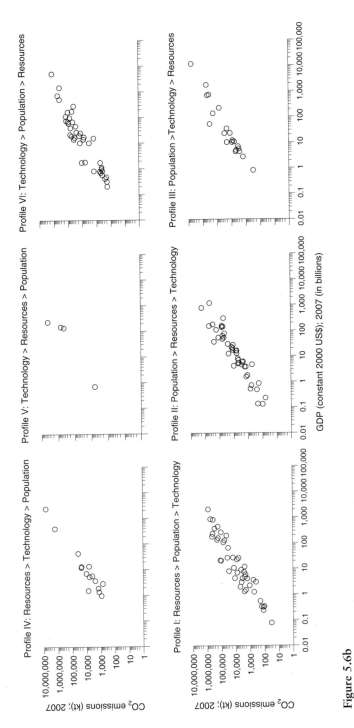

Figure 5.6b

CO_2 emissions and GDP by state profile, 2009.

Source: Data from the World Bank: World Development Indicators.

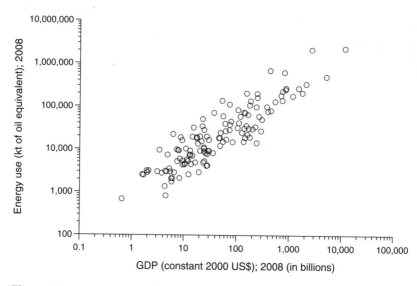

Figure 5.7
Energy use and GDP, 2008.
Source: Data from the World Bank: World Development Indicators.

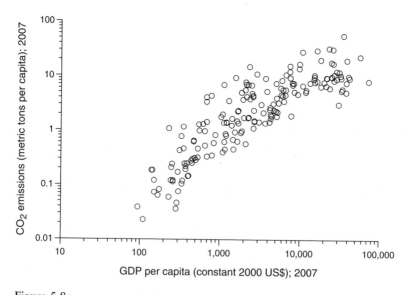

Figure 5.8a
CO_2 emissions and GDP per capita, 2007.
Source: Data from the World Bank: World Development Indicators.

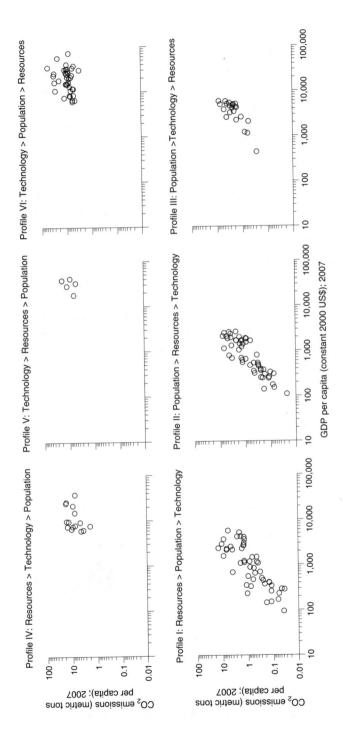

Figure 5.8b

CO_2 emissions and GDP per capita by state profile, 2007.

Source: Data from the World Bank: World Development Indicators.

place some stress on life-supporting resources, though in different ways. These considerations raise the usual traditional questions: What happens when the poor become richer? Can these factors be managed, and can sustainability substitute for growth? If so, what are the implications of the substitution? If not, what are the effects on environmental variables? As we factor in cyberspace, the connections between the new domain and these traditional questions will become more apparent.

Military Expenditures

Military expenditure is clearly a decision variable in the realm of high politics. Figure 5.9a presents the aggregate global distribution of military expenditure relative to country GDP and the inset shows this distribution as a percentage of GDP for 2009. These patterns are not similar to each other, and they are very different from those we observed for life expectancy; especially notable is the absence of observable differences across profiles (fig. 5.9b).

Funding for the military is often seen as detracting from the achievement of basic national wellbeing and developmental objectives and as a waste of scarce resources in both human and financial terms, not to mention the opportunity costs. The similarity across profiles supports the realist view in international relations that all states consider "self-

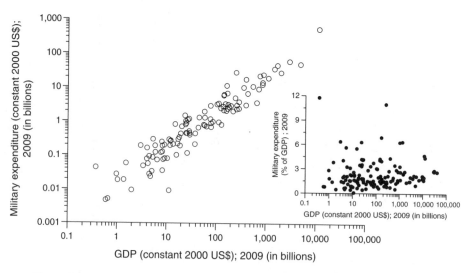

Figure 5.9a
Military expenditure and GDP, 2009.
Source: Based on data from the World Bank: World Development Indicators.

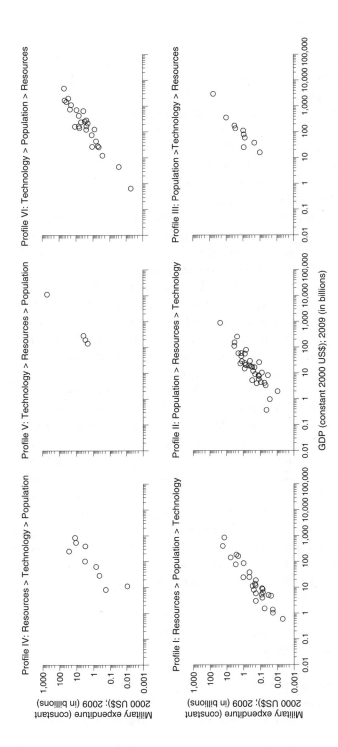

Figure 5.9b
Military expenditure and GDP by state profile, 2009.
Source: Based on data from the World Bank National Accounts and OECD National Accounts; World Bank: World Development Indicators.

help"—signaled by their allocations to the military—fundamental to their security and survival. Furthermore, the experience of industrial countries shows that the military sphere is often a source of innovation and technological change.

To summarize: the profile view of states, the second image in its real, empirical guise, shows the distribution of countries at one point in time and the transformation of this distribution over time. For example, today, the United States holds a location at an advanced level of economic output. By contrast, a less-developed country such as Chad is located at a lower left side level of industrial performance at the global level, and in the corner bottom for profile 1. Such trajectories help us track and understand the patterns of growth, development, and evolution of states (and empires), from their beginnings through their rise, decline, and eventual disintegration or collapse, as well as contemporary forms of transformation and the attendant environment and sustainability challenges.

Such patterns lead us to ask what options are available to a country such as Chad. Could this country proceed along a trajectory of greater development (however we define that term) without reproducing the environmentally damaging industrial trajectory of the United States and other industrial economies? Is it possible to improve people's quality of life without generating a commensurate level of carbon emissions? How much of this issue is within the realm of current industrial and technical performance? How much is manipulable and amenable to policy design?

The state profile logic is strictly empirical in nature; it records a state's location relative to all other sovereign states at a point in time. Some countries may "slide back" toward a less technologically oriented profile than was observed at an earlier time. However, even by standing still a state may slide back with respect to the overall performance of all other states in the system. So far we have considered the empirical observations of the master variables as given, without focusing on drivers of change. It would be reasonable to ask, for example, are changes in population due to changes in fertility, to immigration policies, to the large-scale expulsion of people, or to changes in territorial boundaries? Could altering these drivers of change alter a country's profile in respect to other countries? Is there any role for cyberspace in these contingencies? These are all provocative questions.

Cyber Supports for the State System

In chapter 3 we highlighted major patterns of cyber access in the international system in the first decade of the twenty-first century. We noted the increased upward trend in cyber access everywhere, coupled with notable but declining disparities and differentials in cyber participation. We now explore the ways in which the state system has accommodated to two different technological venues for cyber access, mobile cellular devices and fixed telephone lines.

For contextual and comparative purposes, we use GDP per capita as the common denominator throughout this discussion. This variable helps connect the state attributes examined in the previous section with various mechanisms for cyber access, traditional as well as novel. Accordingly, we begin with the aggregate distribution of Internet users relative to GDP per capita for two points in time, 1999 and 2009 (figure 5.10). Over this time period, there is evidence of increased access to the Internet. The overarching trend in the number of Internet users is indicative in its own right, but it provides no information about the venue of use.

For this and other reasons, we now turn to users of mobile telephones and show in figure 5.11a the distributions at two points in time, 1999 and 2009. These observations are entirely consistent with the evidence introduced in chapter 3. Figure 11b disaggregates this pattern into profile groups.

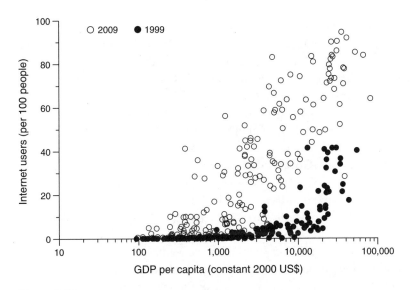

Figure 5.10
Internet users per 100 people and GDP per capita, 1999 and 2009.
Source: Data from the World Bank: World Development Indicators.

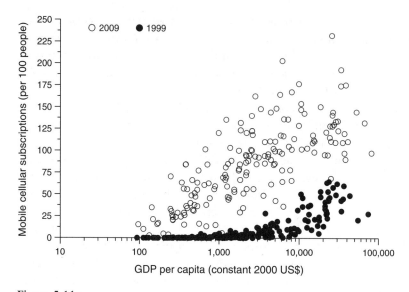

Figure 5.11a
Mobile cellular subscriptions per 100 people and GDP per capita, 1999 and 2009.
Source: Data from the World Bank: World Development Indicators.

We consider next the traditional link to cyber access in the state system, namely, fixed telephone lines and GDP per capita for two points in time, 1999 and 2009. Figure 5.12a shows the aggregate trends for these two years. Figure 5.12b shows the disaggregated profile groupings of the same variables for 2009.

The evidence in figures 5.10 to 5.12 provide a context for exploring cyber supports for governance and highlighting the determinants of e-Government.

5.2   Enablers of e-Government

The growing propensity to use cyber venues for the provision of government services is a novel feature of the twenty-first-century state system. Many countries are moving toward e-governance, and with this move there is a growing politicization of cyber venues. Drawing on the UN's method for measuring readiness for e-governance in the state system, we now explore patterns of e-governance at the second level in international relations and examine aggregate features as well as profile-specific manifestations. Figure 5.13 provides a graphical representation of the e-Government Readiness Index, (labeled as e-Government index) and its constituent elements. The details for 2009 are presented below.[5]

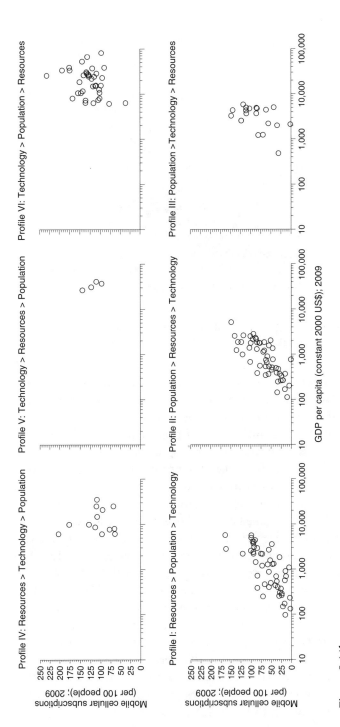

Figure 5.11b
Mobile cellular subscriptions per 100 people and GDP per capita by state profile, 2009.
Source: Data from the World Bank: World Development Indicators.

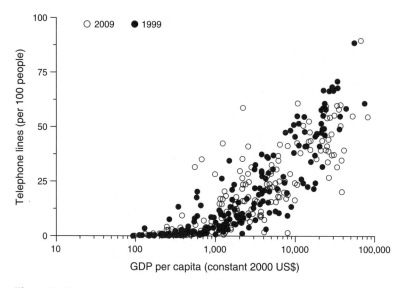

Figure 5.12a
Telephone lines per 100 people and GDP per capita, 1999 and 2009.
Source: Data from the World Bank: World Development Indicators.

For contextual purposes, we begin with the worldwide distribution of readiness for e-Government index and GDP per capita for 2008 (figure 5.14a). When the observations at the global level are disaggregated by profile type (figure 5.14b), we note a general positive relationship: the higher the GDP per capita, the greater the propensity for e-governance. Despite the paucity of data for some of the profile groups, this relationship is supported by the observations in figure 5.14b.

Against this background we now turn to the direct or most immediate constituent variables that make up the e-Government Readiness Index—namely, the indices of *human capital, online services,* and *telecommunications infrastructure,* shown on major branchings in figure 5.13. Our purpose is to explore their respective relationships with GDP per capita and to observe variations across state profile groups. While all three indices reflect similar patterns, there are some subtle differences of potential interest that might be further demonstrated at the profile group level.

The *human capital index* shows a notable relationship between the distribution of GDP per capita and the e-Government Index at the aggregate level (figure. 5.15a). The differences across profiles are visually compelling, with the more affluent states showing greater propensities for e-government (figure 5.15b).

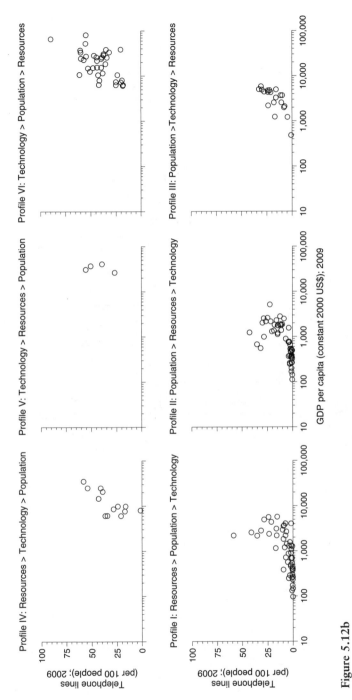

Figure 5.12b
Telephone lines per 100 people and GDP per capita by state profile, 2009.
Source: Data from the World Bank: World Development Indicators.

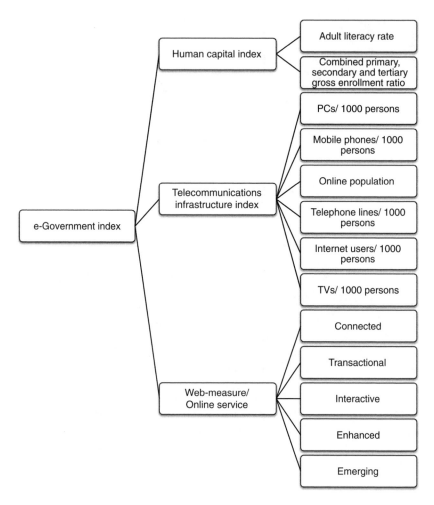

Figure 5.13
The UN e-Government readiness index.
Source: Based on narratives and analysis in United Nations 2008b, 12–18.

Web-based online services as a direct component of the e-Government Index in relation to GDP per capita (figure 5.16a) shows a somewhat diverse pattern subsumed under an overarching linear trend. The view by profile group, shown in figure 5.16b, clarifies the nature of the disaggregation.

The *infrastructure index*, the last of the constituent variables of the readiness for e-Government Index, is shown in figures 5.17 (also for 2008). When we disaggregate the overall trend into profile groups, we observe a propensity toward greater differentiation between profile 1 and 2 states, on the one hand, and profile 5 and 6 states on the other. This is not surprising, for the aggregate pattern indicates that with more infrastructure capability there is also more e-government. While not surprising, it does reinforce the general propensity toward greater e-government subject to the capacity-in-place.

5.3   Performance and Perceptions of e-Governance

Consistent with the international community's appreciation of good governance as an important precursor of development, security, and stability, the World Bank developed a series of Worldwide Governance Indicators (WGI). Drawing on a wide range of materials—thirty-five data sources from thirty-three organizations worldwide—the WGI captured perceptions of governance across six specific dimensions for two hundred countries (and territories) from 1996 to 2008. The discussion that follows is based on the 2009 WGI results.

The World Bank Institute defines governance as "the traditions and institutions by which authority of a country is exercised" (World Bank Institute 2009, 1). In contrast to the UN's e-Government Readiness Index, which is based on quantitative variables, the WGI reports seek to capture the cognitive reactions to government performance in terms of participation and accountability, political stability, government effectiveness, regulatory quality, the rule of law, and control of corruption.

Based on the UN data for e-government and the WGI for perceptions of government effectiveness, the evidence shows relatively strong associations—positive correlations—between each of the individual dimensions of e-government (perceptions) and the e-Government Index (metrics). In this context, the WGI dimension with the highest positive correlation with the e-Government Index is "Government effectiveness" (figure 5.18), defined as the quality of public services, the capacity and independence of the civil service, and related features. The dimension showing the

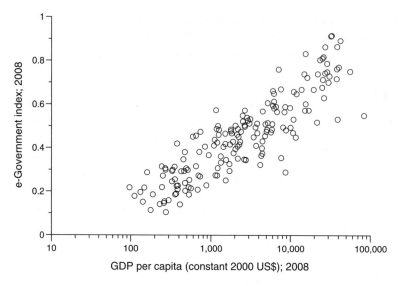

Figure 5.14a
e-Government readiness index and GDP per capita, 2008.
Source: Data from the World Bank: World Development Indicators; United Nations 2008b; UNPAN: Data Center.

lowest positive association with perceptions of e-governance is "political stability" (figure 5.19).[6]

5.4   The Real and the Cyber: Some Inferences

The empirical observations in this chapter support seven sets of inferences and observations pertaining to the propensities for cyberpolitics.

1. The record points to the diversity and density of actors and interests worldwide and growing cyber participation as increasingly salient features of contemporary structural realities. More and more, aggregations of individuals, interests, and networks are transcending the state in the conduct of purposive action in the international arena—real as well as virtual. And states, too, are extending their activities and influence into the cyber domain and engaging in various forms of cyberpolitics.

2. A closer look at real (kinetic) physical indicators of states, without engaging in statistical inference analysis, shows at least four features that are recognizable simply by observing the distributions of state profiles. These are (1) the usual clustering of less-developed states on the lower left side of the figure, (2) the semi-arc emanating from this cluster toward

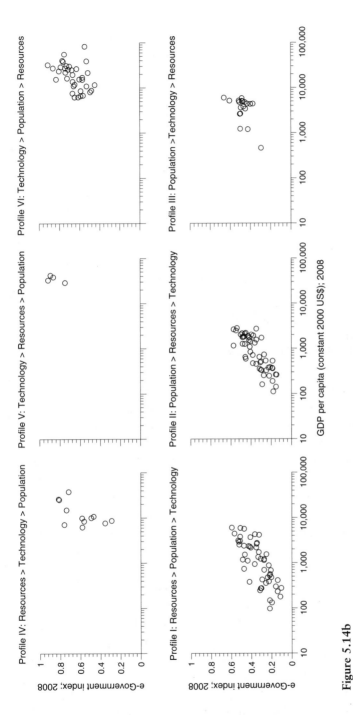

Figure 5.14b

e-Government readiness index and GDP per capita by state profile, 2008.

Source: Data from the World Bank: World Development Indicators; United Nations 2008b; UNPAN: Data Center.

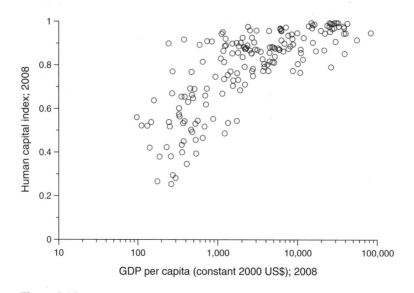

Figure 5.15a
Human capital index and GDP per capita, 2008.
Source: Data from the World Bank: World Development Indicators; United
Nations 2008b; UNPAN: Data Center.

the top center of the figure, (3) the common regression line predicated
on linear assumptions, and (4) the recognizable S-shaped curve arising
from the lower left cluster, growing, and then indicating potential satura-
tion around the $4,000 GDP per capita point. These are all empirically
based descriptions subject to statistical inquiry for rejection, reinterpreta-
tion, or verification, as the case may be.

3. Despite some differences across state profiles, there is evidence that
the state system as a whole is tending toward greater engagement in cyber
venues. This observation is based on trends in cyber-enabling variables,
where we see greater convergence among states than we do for real
indicators.

4. We note the propensity toward e-Government. If we consider government and governance as core to politics of the state system, then it is not
too difficult to infer that the enablers of cyberpolitics are on the rise.
This evidence is particularly relevant as it taps into the relationship
between the government and the governed, so fundamental to who gets
what, when, and how.

5. In light of the relatively strong positive relationship between evidence
of the performance of e-Government and the perceptions of government

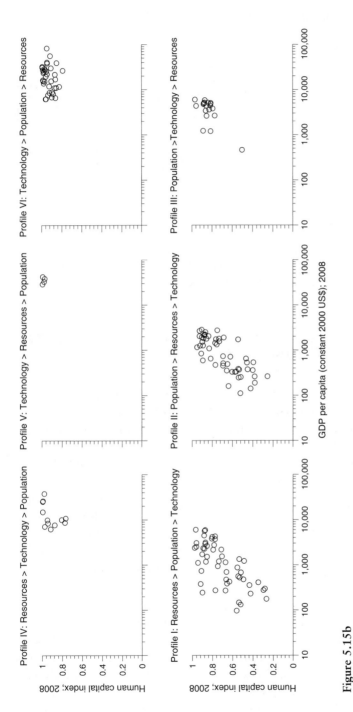

Figure 5.15b

Human capital index and GDP per capita by state profile, 2008.

Source: Data from the World Bank: World Development Indicators; United Nations 2008b; UNPAN: Data Center.

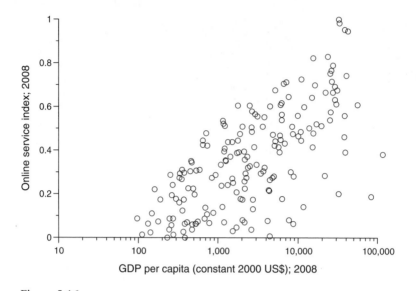

Figure 5.16a
Online Service Index and GDP per capita, 2008.
Source: Data from the World Bank: World Development Indicators; United
Nations 2008b; UNPAN: Data Center.

effectiveness, we can infer that the enabling factors supporting e-
Government do in fact have an impact on the ground.

6. The notably low positive relationship between e-Government and perceptions of political stability is somewhat puzzling. One would expect
political stability to facilitate government performance and thus to
shape perceptions of government effectiveness. Alternatively, the distribution of cases in figure 5.19—which shows the relationship between
political stability in relation to e-Government score—reflects the wide
variation in perceptions of political stability, which are likely to track
empirical realities rather closely. This figure conveys a message that is
more informative about political stability than about its connection to
e-Government.

7. While we tend to concentrate on aggregates, it remains the case that
individuals shape real kinetic world parameters and individuals participate in cyber venues. In the traditional view of international relations
and international law, individuals and aggregate populations have no
standing in the international system separate from the state to which they
belong. However, more and more we see aggregations of individuals,
actors, interests, and networks transcending the state and its norms
in the conduct of purposeful action in the international arena. These

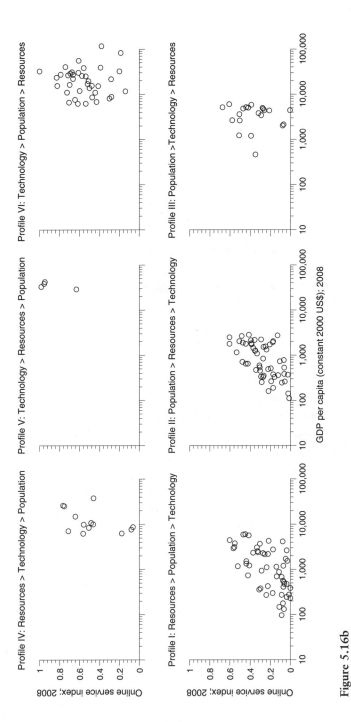

Figure 5.16b
Online service index and GDP per capita by state profile, 2008.
Source: Data from the World Bank: World Development Indicators; United Nations 2008b; UNPAN: Data Center.

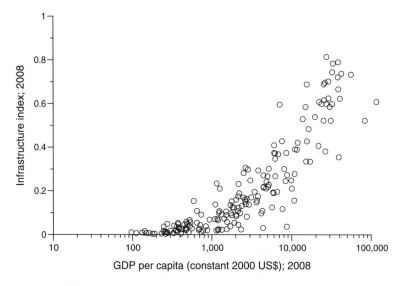

Figure 5.17a
Telecommunication infrastructure index and GDP per capita, 2008.
Source: Data from the World Bank: World Development Indicators; United Nations 2008b; UNPAN: Data Center.

aggregations are almost always bottom-up processes that are anchored in the power and influence of individuals. The first image is no longer constrained or contained within the boundaries of the state. It is taking on dynamics of its own, becoming an increasingly salient feature of international relations.

All of these observations and explorations constitute the tip of an inherently complex iceberg whose properties are increasingly important in the study of international relations.

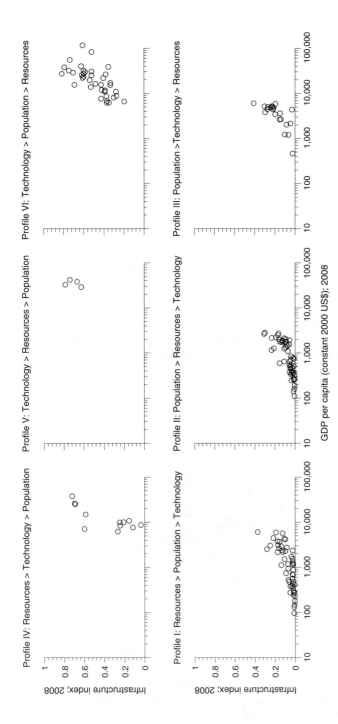

Figure 5.17b
Telecommunication infrastructure index and GDP per capita by state profile, 2008.
Source: Data from World Bank: World Development Indicators; United Nations 2008b; UNPAN: Data Center.

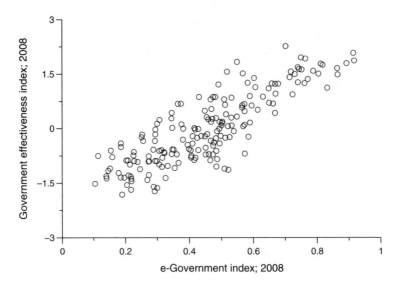

Figure 5.18
Perception of government effectiveness and e-Government readiness index, 2008.
Source: Data from UNPAN: Data Center; United Nations 2008b; Kaufmann, Kraay, and Mastruzzi 2010; World Bank: Worldwide Governance Indicators.

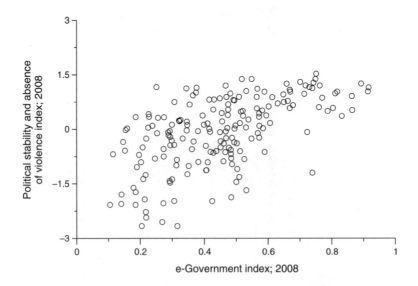

Figure 5.19
Political Stability and e-Government readiness index, 2008.
Source: Data from UNPAN: Data Center; United Nations (2008b); Kaufmann, Kraay, and Mastruzzi 2010; World Bank: Worldwide Governance Indicators.

Appendix 5.1
Distribution of states in profile groups, 2009

Profile 1 R < P < T	Profile 2 P < R < T	Profile 3 P < T < R	Profile 4 R < T < P	Profile 5 T < R < P	Profile 6 T < P < R
Algeria	Albania	Bangladesh	Argentina	Bahamas*	Andorra
Angola	Armenia	China	Australia	Finland	Antigua and Barbuda
Belarus	Azerbaijan	Costa Rica	Canada	Norway	Aruba*
Belize	Benin	Cuba*	Chile	Sweden	Austria
Bhutan	Bosnia and Herzegovina	Dominica	Equatorial Guinea	United States	Bahrain
Bolivia	Bulgaria	Dominican Rep.	Estonia		Barbados*
Botswana	Burkina Faso	El Salvador	Greenland		Belgium
Brazil	Burundi	Grenada	Iceland		Bermuda
Cameroon	Cambodia	Jamaica	Libya		Brunei*
Central African Rep.	Cape Verde	Hungary	New Zealand		Channel Islands*
Chad	Comoros	Malaysia	Oman*		Croatia
Colombia	Côte d'Ivoire	Maldives	Palau		Cyprus
Congo, Dem.	Egypt	Marshall Islands	Saudi Arabia		Czech Republic
Congo, Rep.	Ethiopia	Mauritius	Uruguay		Denmark
Djibouti	Ecuador	Micronesia			France
Eritrea	Gambia	Philippines			Germany
Fiji	Georgia	Sri Lanka			Greece
Gabon	Ghana	St. Lucia			Hong Kong
Guinea	Guatemala	St. Vincent and the Grenadines			Ireland
Guyana	Guinea-Bissau	Thailand			Isle of Man*
Iran, Islamic Rep.	Haiti	Turkey			Israel
Kazakhstan	Honduras				Italy
Kyrgyz Republic	India				Japan
Laos	Indonesia				Korea, Republic
Latvia	Iraq				Kuwait
Liberia	Jordan				Lebanon
Madagascar	Kenya				Liechtenstein
Mali					

Profile 1 R < P < T	Profile 2 P < R < T	Profile 3 P < T < R	Profile 4 R < T < P	Profile 5 T < R < P	Profile 6 T < P < R
Mauritania	Kiribati				Luxembourg
Mongolia	Kosovo				Macao
Montenegro	Lesotho				Malta
Mozambique	Lithuania				Mexico
Namibia	Macedonia				Monaco
Nicaragua	Malawi				Netherlands
Niger	Moldova				Poland
Panama	Morocco				Portugal
Papua New Guinea	Nepal				Qatar
Paraguay	Nigeria				San Marino*
Peru	Pakistan				Seychelles
Russian Federation	Romania				Singapore
Solomon Islands	Rwanda				Slovak Republic
South Africa	Samoa				Slovenia
Sudan	Senegal				Spain
Suriname*	Serbia				St. Kitts and Nevis
Tajikistan	Sierra Leone				Switzerland
Tanzania	Swaziland				Trinidad and Tobago
Turkmenistan	Syria				United Arab Emirates
Vanuatu	Timor-Leste				United Kingdom
Venezuela	Togo				
Yemen	Tonga				
Zambia	Tunisia				
Zimbabwe	Uganda				
	Ukraine				
	Uzbekistan				
	Vietnam				

*Most recent data since 2002.

6

The International System: Cyber Conflicts and Threats to Security

Cyberpolitics at the international level is evolving, complex, and dynamic in scale and scope; it is also increasingly diverse in its various modes and manifestations. This chapter explores different types of cyber conflicts and their various manifestations. We recognize that realities on the ground and in cyber venues can change very rapidly, and that both catalogue and the characteristics of conflict may take on new features. We also expect that, over time, the nature of cyberpolitics will be charted more fully and its key elements and parameters will be better understood. Our purpose here is only to map cyber conflicts and contentions early in the twenty-first century and to provide a baseline for future analysis.

In general, the cyber domain broadly defined cannot be devoid of the inevitable contentions that arise when competing interests consolidate around different principles and priorities and then collide when actors with different intents and capabilities seek to pursue their objectives. In the best of all possible worlds, we would import theories of conflict that have proved useful in understanding the traditional "real" kinetic international system. Here we are reminded once more of the famous question posed by Kenneth N. Waltz, "Where are the major causes of war to be found? . . . . The answers can be ordered under the following three headings: within man, within the structure of the separate states, within the system" (1959, 12).

6.1 Complexities of Cyber Conflicts

Earlier in this book we noted that, until recently, traditional international relations theories generally focus on state interactions in the social and the organizational contexts. Traditional theories of conflict are also state-centric (even when the focus of inquiry is on alliances and counter alliances). They assume that the adversaries are known, that power and capability are the critical drivers, and that decisions and policies can reduce the prospects for war or, conversely, accelerate the antagonizing behavior.[1]

In recent years, we have seen a growing interest in the power of non-state actors in international relations. If we consider terrorism, and other forms of non-state violence, the state is no longer the actor of first and last resort. The instruments of the state are delinked from the capabilities or identities of individuals and aggregates thereof. In such cases, the focus shifts away from the state (the second image) to encompass other levels of analysis. In situations of this sort, traditional theories will carry only modest analytical and explanatory power—perhaps even limited policy relevance. When the conflicts and contentions take place in the cyber domain—with the characteristic features noted in table 1.1—then traditional theory is particularly disadvantaged.

Despite differences in cyber access, as well as in uses of cyberspace, there is considerable creativity in the manipulation of this new space for political purposes. While many states try to control access to connectivity and others seek to control access to content, both the range of political expression and the volume of participation in cyber venues are on the rise. In all political systems, regardless of the degree of participation, the formation of a critical mass for political action is usually contingent on interest articulation and interest aggregation. As noted in earlier chapters, cyber access facilitates both the aggregation and the articulation of interests, goals, and preferences.

This chapter explores three broad types of cyber contentions and conflicts: contentions over the architecture of the internet and the management of cyberspace, conflicts in the pursuit of political advantage and economic gain (legal and illegal), and cyber threats to national security. Table 6.1 lists examples of each type of conflict in order to illustrate their manifestations as well as some of their characteristic features. Each type is rooted in different sources (and motivations) and often has different consequences (and impacts). Each is about the struggle over the authoritative allocation of value and the control over who seeks to get what, when, and how across a set of issue areas.

Cyber contentions of the first type take place over the architecture of the Internet and the rules that shape the cyber context. These conflicts are rooted and anchored in low politics. In recent years, however, they became more politicized as new contentions arose over the management of cyber venues. Migrating to the realm of high politics, such conflicts draw on using power and leverage in the real domain to shape the parameters of cyberspace (see figure 1.1).

Table 6.1
Cyber conflicts and threats to security

	Types	Cases
I.	Contentions over architecture and management of cyberspace	End-to-end argument Layers principle Network neutrality "Code is Law"
II.	Cyber conflict for political advantage and profit	State power for political control Cyber challenges to the state Competitive politics via cyber venues Cyber crime and cyber espionage
III.	Cyber threats to national security	Militarization of cyberspace Cyber warfare Cyber threats to infrastructure Cyber terrorism

Cyber conflicts of the second type are about the uses of cyber venues for political advantage in the traditional real domain and/or for profit and gain. These conflicts are usually dominated by second image concerns. They become international when the use of cyber leverage threatens to alter the distribution of power. (Again, see the influence trajectories in figure 1.1).

Cyber conflicts of the third type revolve around matters of national security. They consist of threats to cyber supports of fundamental infrastructures and to cyber capabilities, broadly defined. This type of conflict is a distinctly state-based, second image concern—with the exception of terrorism, which can also be seen as a first image activity with diffusion effects.

Following the presentation in table 6.1, the remainder of this chapter explores these modes of cyber conflicts and their various types or manifestations.[2] Each type reflects different values, leading to different forms of politicization of players and positions. Each represents, implicitly or explicitly, different principles and political values as well as visions of preferred futures.

6.2 Contentions over System Architecture and Management

Early in the history of cyberspace, the debates over architecture choices and decisions were driven largely by a vision of open vistas, the cyber commons, to be realized by deliberate design. David D. Clark, a creator of the Internet, is reputed to have said, "We reject: kings, presidents, and voting. We believe in rough consensus and running code" (quoted in Goldsmith and Wu 2006, 24). There was a tendency to view cyberspace as the great leveler, enabling widespread participation in virtual arenas. Implicit in this view was the eventual possibility of large-scale political democratization.

To date, this space has been dominated by the U.S. private sector's power of innovation. If the vision of an open space is to be realized, then supportive political factors, empowered with all relevant instrumentalities to uphold this vision, must be in place. While technology per se could very well push toward leveling the playing field—whereby gains at the frontier of new spaces become increasingly available to individuals around the world—the politics became increasingly dominated by contentions over the management of the cyber domain.

Although type 1 disputes are played out largely in the context of the United States, they have implications in the world cyber arena. As is said of politics broadly defined, those who make the rules control the game. So far, only a select number of players have been able to participate in the deliberations over the rules that shape the core features of cyberspace. Few anticipated early on that the very nature of the new space would itself become the subject of significant political discord. We are increasingly observing challenges to U.S. dominance as other states, especially China, begin to exert their influence on cyber matters.

We now turn to the different manifestations of type 1 cyber conflict. Three sets of debates are interconnected and reflect different aspects of disagreement over system design and, as relevant, what operators are allowed to do; the fourth set presents a stark definitional perspective about the nature of the playing field.

End-to-End Argument

The "end-to-end argument" refers to the Internet architecture. To simplify: as conceived, designed, and implemented by the original system architects, the set of protocols known as Transmission Control Protocol/Internet Protocol (TCP/IP) that defines the Internet consists of four functional levels, described as "layers" that "stack up" to generate the built environment enabling interactions in cyberspace. The end-to-end argument is about a core feature of the TCP. It holds that communication protocol operations features are justified only in the lower layers of the system. In this connection, Blumenthal and Clark (2001) signal that, in principle, the end-to-end argument provides three important advantages in a rapidly expanding cyber arena, namely, reduced complexity of the network at its core, improved venues for added applications, and increased autonomy of applications.[3]

The Layers Principle

The layers principle is related to and provides a broader context for the end-to-end argument. This principle concerns itself with the lower layers and focuses on regulations appropriate to the layered structure of the Internet. As Solum and Chung (2003) observe, if we view the Internet as a system of communication among ranges of users, the layers provide different services and value to users.[4] Knowledge and information enter the system as content; the database is digitized and customized to meet the layer-defined specifications and move laterally to the designated destinations; at that point, the content ascends vertically to its terminal. The layers principle, examined by many others—notably Michael L. Dertouzos (1998), Manuel Castells (2000), and Thomas S. Wurster (1999)—led to the thesis that "the law should respect the integrity of layered Internet architecture" (Solum and Chung 2003, 3).

The structure of this system, as Solum and Chung also note, provides the foundation for interventions by Internet regulators. They argue that if regulation is required (demanded, or desired), then it should be done in a way that does not violate the layered architecture. Otherwise, regulatory initiatives may generate a range of consequences that could undermine not only the intent of the regulator, but the viability of the system itself, not to mention the possibility of unintended or collateral damage. The elegance of the argument rests on the well-known importance of fit between the ends of regulation and the means employed.[5]

Network Neutrality

Also connected to the foregoing is the neutrality principle. *Network neutrality* means there should be no discrimination or restrictions by Internet providers to users access to applications or content. This non-discrimination clause is at the center of debates over the management and control of the cyber playing field. It is a normative idea that reflects a political preference rather than an engineering necessity. At issue is whether network architecture should take into account elements (issues, factors, concerns) other than those directly connected to transport, transmission, and connectivity. In this case, semantics do matter, and the term "neutrality" may well be misleading, especially in light of evolving uses and changing meanings of the concept itself.

At this writing, some features of the network neutrality debate—irrespective of the position taken by the proponents or the preferred definition of the term—converge on how and where control of access should be exerted. This convergence is moving the debates closer to the issues of why, when, and by whom. All of this is about competing values and alternative distributions of anticipated gains.

"Code Is Law"

Distinct in its framing and close to the idiom of politics is the position expressed in *Code and Other Laws of Cyberspace* by Lawrence Lessig (1999). Lessig reminds us that what we call cyberspace was manufactured by human ingenuity and is distinct from nature. Moreover, the engineering that constructed cyberspace was the outcome of innovative architecture rather than the result of bargaining and negotiation among competing interests in society, nationally or internationally.[6] As such, the architecture defines the configurations of the system at any point in time and becomes the reference for future configurations.

Lessig's declaration that "code is law" may well be seen as a baseline of sorts, one that captured prevailing conditions early in the history of the Internet but may be superseded by new conditions. The layers that made cyberspace possible determine what can and cannot be done; they serve as the home for (and of) the code that enables communication and interaction. So far, the general tendency is for users to proceed in good faith, with the expectation being that technical proficiency determines the nature of the design, the architecture, and its implementation.

"Code is law" is an argument about where the actual power is located. To Lessig, power is located in the architecture and its code. Given that cyberspace is a constructed space, we know that, with expanded human interaction and new opportunities and possibilities, regulation is seldom far behind. Lessig's map of regulatory paths (discussed in chapter 4) consists of four modes of regulation—state regulation, market-based regulation, regulation via the Internet architecture, and the norms of interaction and communication—each designed to meet specific needs.

The political elements become more explicit when Lessig points out (correctly) that the state, through its laws, regulates the implementation of activities enabling cyberspace. Imperfect as these regulations may be, the instruments used are generally available to and developed for the regulation of real behavior in kinetic or physical domains.

Correlates of Cyber Conflicts Type 1

The fact that there are conflicting views about system design and architecture, buttressed by seemingly well-reasoned arguments, reflects not only the politicization of the new space but the emerging cleavages about the normative principles (and attendant gains) associated with much of the above. Interestingly, it is also somewhat challenging to characterize these contentions in value-explicit terms. Accordingly, we now consider several overarching, more pervasive, correlates or concerns related to type 1 cyber conflicts and their various manifestations.

The first correlate is about the prevailing contradiction, perhaps even paradox, created by the success of the layer design and its implementation. On the one hand is the claim that the Internet cannot be regulated; it is a jungle with anarchic tendencies. On the other hand is the view that various regulatory modes can be used to manage the anarchy. Contentions about whether we should or should not regulate the Internet—in terms of content, connections, flows, and directionality—bring into play issues of freedom, access, rights, and responsibilities.

The second correlate is about the value foundations of the Internet. These are diverse in nature and can be often be contentious. Some argue that the Internet is not and was not neutral in its architecture, as it facilitated one set of applications (such as data transmission) at the expense of others (such as voice and video), and that the specificity of applications should be recognized and built into the networks; others argue that the Internet should provide only transmission or transport services and not cater to the customized requirements of specific applications.

The third correlate is that the close coupling of politicization in cyberspace with the uses of regulatory instruments that have been effective in kinetic domains. In other words, the increasingly political nature of the cyber domain generally contributes to a growing propensity to use traditional regulatory instruments and leverages.

The fourth, a generalized concern associated with the consequences of the politicization of cyberspace, is captured by the portability assumption, namely, that traditional instruments of leverage in the physical world can be effective in the cyber domain. While there are commonalities between the two realities, there are also differences that might limit the extent of portability. Regulations in effect at this time operate indirectly rather than directly, and the modes noted by Lessig are hardly obsolete. In the future, if norms, laws, codes, or markets change, if new instrumentalities are developed, if new challenges to the open vista are effective, or if powerful interests converge to create new norms, then we may see new ways of regulation.

The fifth set of correlates is rooted in the empirical situation and the power of change. We have seen that, over time, the original vision of the architecture was challenged by an increasingly complex cyber domain shaped by the rapid growth in uses and users, the expansion of consolidated interest articulation and aggregation over how to manage the Internet—and the growing number of stakeholders, private and public, who recognized the potential for influence and control.

In this context as in many others, change is seldom a negotiated driver of the human condition. Reflecting on the nature of cyber realities twenty years after the initial creation of the new space, Blumenthal and Clark (2001) focused on emerging evidence of changes in the cyber landscape, not only in terms of increased density but, more pressingly, in terms of the growth and diversity of user motivations. Further, they observe, "The consequences of untrustworthy end-points on the Net include attacks on the network as a whole, attacks on individual end-points, undesired forms of interactions such as spam email, and annoyances such as Web pages that vanish due to end-node aberrations. The situation is a predictable consequence of dramatic growth in the population of connected people with a wider range of motivations for using the Internet, leading to uses that some have deemed misuses or abuses" (ibid., 72).

Closely related is a sixth correlate, namely, the usual disconnects between the fact of change and recognition thereof. The impacts of change often appear long before any agreement is reached about the formal definition of the changes themselves.[7] Technological innovations are rarely framed in a social vacuum; individuals or groups that gain from the prevailing authoritative allocation of values will protect their interests and prevent fundamental changes. Underlying such issues is the power of legacy systems and attendant interests—in political, economic, and institutional terms.

While Blumenthal and Clark may have been correct in referring to these changes as "predictable," the events of September 11, 2001, all but ensured increased control and new interventions in response to threats to national security. And while Lessig and others point to the driving role of the state, the dominant players shaping the technical nature of the playing field are private entities, non-state actors. Supported by the U.S. government and the resources at its disposal, the architecture, operations, and design of the Internet were in private hands. It seems unlikely that the rest of the world will continue to unanimously accept the choices made by the dominant power at the turn of the twenty-first century.

For the most part, the conflicts and contentions are still framed in technical terms, despite the recognition of new challenges in the real world that cannot be ignored in future cyber system architectures. Continued technological advances in cyber venues invariably ensure that the cyberpolitics of the playing field will continue to shape future directions and create new contentions, along with struggles to control the outcomes. Ultimately, it is through political mechanisms, rather than technical ones, that the old and the new interests will find ways of collaborating, coexisting, converging, or dominating.[8]

6.3   Cyber Conflicts for Political Advantage and Profit

The second type of cyber conflict has to do with the use of cyberspace for political advantage and for profit. This mode includes the ways in which interactions in the new domain are controlled, managed, prohibited, or utilized as a weapon or instrument in the pursuit of real-world goals on either side of prevailing law. Central to this mode of cyber conflict is the commonly accepted distinction between power as an attribute and power as a relationship. They are interlinked, but to exercise power, attributes must already be in place. In these cases, the stakes or "utilities" are in the domain of real politics, and the actors resort to cyber venues as arsenals for purposive action.

The differentials in cyber access highlighted in chapter 3 explain much of the uneven deployment and effectiveness of cyber conflict for strategic advantage. The players are very diverse, with different degrees of power and capabilities (technical and managerial) and different levels of infrastructure development enabling cyberspace access. The most notable players are generally states that seek to control Internet access within their borders. But opponents of the state may also be leading players, depending on their capacity, infrastructure conditions, organization, and other factors.

State Power and Control

The enabling power of cyberspace for the individual (the first image) may be limited by the strong hand of the state (the second image), which can exert control over the content of the communication as well as the behavior of the communicator. If the state seeks to manipulate access, regulate content, manage information availability, and constrain its citizens' use of cyber amenities, then control of cyber access is simply an extension of control in the real domain.

There is considerable evidence of government control through filtering and other mechanisms, but it is difficult to assess the impacts on the ground. Interestingly we also observe shifts in control strategy. The OpenNet Initiative, which monitors government controls of cyberspace over time, shows that early phases were based on denial of access.[9] *Access Denied* (2008), edited by Ronald Deibert and colleagues, tracks how countries implement sophisticated ways of denying their citizens access to cyberspace. In a comprehensive and detailed examination of the OpenNet Initiative, Deibert and collaborators summarize the central tendencies in filter activities as well as the outliers, in terms of practices, policies, and country activities. While the general claims are undisputed, the challenge is to keep up with the changes in scale, scope, and impact of different controls, as individuals with different incentives and motivations find ways to avoid the instruments of the state.

Different countries deny access to different degrees and for different reasons, but some common patterns are observable. For example, in Yemen, Internet providers are state controlled, with strict guidelines pertaining to content. Tunisia, Iran, and the United Arab Emirates use made-in-America filtering software. In these cases, the targets of government control are more cultural in nature than political—at least at first blush. In Bahrain, one of the most open societies in the region, government control of cyber access appears to have declined somewhat. At the same time, Bahrain's legal system provides legitimacy for a considerable degree of government oversight of cyber access, just as it does for other media.

Of the countries covered by the OpenNet Initiative early on, two in particular exhibit especially high degrees of government control, Saudi Arabia and China. The former can be fairly described as a closed society, where tradition dominates and deviations are seldom tolerated. The most aggressive forms of control are exerted against sites whose content relates to pornography, drugs, and gambling—all considered to be strongly at variance with the country's values. While little reference is made to the filtering of sites communicating messages of political opposition, most threats to traditional values are defined as political in nature. China is generally reported to have a sophisticated and extensive form of filtering, which is usually executed at specific control points in addition to the usual venues. This, combined with its complex systems of laws and regulations that control cyber access, creates a powerful arsenal that enables

Chinese control of Internet usage. Overall, the OpenNet Initiative concluded that the practice of control, in one way or other, is extensive worldwide.

Access Controlled, the follow-up study, focused on evolving shifts in government strategies, from access denial as the first response strategy to access control designed to filter out specific types of content. This shift illustrates the growing attention to the content of the message and efforts to control the message (and possibly the messenger as well). We draw on the narrative cases presented in *Access Denied* to develop a closer look at the shift in focus. Their investigations explore filtering practices to control access to four types of content: political, social, conflict and security, and Internet tools.[10] Here we consider only the political and social motivations for filtering.

Table 6.2 summarizes the patterns of *political filtering*. Political filtering focuses primarily on websites that express views in opposition to those of the government, in addition to those concerned with matters of human rights, freedom of expression, minority rights, and religious movements.[11]

In chapter 5, we presented the distribution of states across profile groups and explored their cyber features. We now extend this analysis and show in figure 6.1 the distribution of states across two indicators, the World Bank's World Governance Indicator of voice and accountability and the UN's e-Government Index, and locate the states listed in table 6.2 that engage in pervasive filtering. As the table shows, countries with a history of or a tendency toward pervasive filtering of information score low on the voice and accountability index and the e-Government Index. By contrast, states with no evidence of filtering score high on the e-Government Index and on the voice and accountability index.

Similar patterns are evident when we consider the World Bank's rule of law index, which captures perceptions of the extent to which agents have confidence in and abide by the norms of society, and have confidence in the institutions of governance. Most of the states involved in political filtering score low on the rule of law index (figure 6.2).

Turning to *social filtering*, that is, denying access to materials considered socially unacceptable, we show in table 6.3 the distribution of countries according to the degree of filtering (including materials related to sexuality, gambling, the illegal use of drugs and alcohol, and other topics that may be socially sensitive or perceived as offensive) in relation to the e-Government Index. The table points to pervasive social filtering in the distribution of states across two indices, the UN's readiness for

Table 6.2
Political filtering and state profile, 2009

No evidence of filtering	Suspected filtering	Selective filtering	Substantial filtering	Pervasive filtering
Egypt (2)	Pakistan (2)	Azerbaijan (2)	Armenia (2)	Burma (*)
France (6)		Belarus (1)	Saudi Arabia (4)	China (3)
Germany (6)		Georgia (2)	United Arab Emirates (6)	Iran (1)
Italy (6)		Kazakhstan (1)		Syria (2)
South Korea (6)		Kyrgyzstan (1)		Tunisia (2)
Ukraine (2)		Moldova (2)		Turkmenistan (1)
United Kingdom (6)		Russia (1)		Uzbekistan (2)
		Tajikistan (1)		
		Turkey (3)		

Note: Parentheses refer to state profile.
*Missing data.
Source: Developed from the narrative and analysis reported in Deibert et al. (2008) and reported in Zittrain (2008).

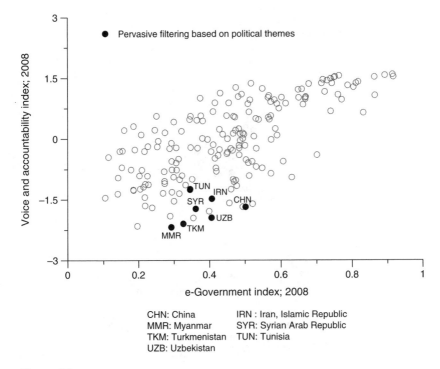

Figure 6.1
Political filtering for voice and accountability, and e-Government readiness index, 2008.
Source: Data from UNPAN: Data Center; United Nations 2008b; Kaufmann, Kraay, and Mastruzzi 2010; World Bank: Worldwide Governance Indicators; Data on pervasive filtering based on political themes are derived from the narratives and analysis in Deibert et al. 2010.

e-Government Index and the World Bank's voice and accountability index, both for 2008. States that limit citizens' participation in selecting their government, freedom of expression, freedom of association, and freedom of the media also engage in high degrees of social filtering, that is, filtering information based on social criteria (figure 6.3). (The filtering patterns for political accountability are very similar.)

Finally, we show in table 6.4 the distribution of states according to degree of filtering based on conflict and security criteria and matters related to Internet tools.

State intervention in the denial of content is not restricted to authoritarian or traditional societies. Many democratic states seek to manage content to reduce obscenity and pornography and to control sources of

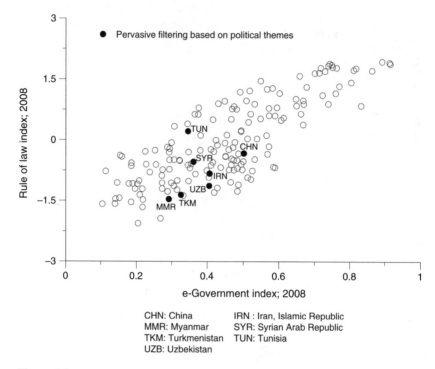

Figure 6.2
Rule of law and political filtering, 2008.
Source: Data from UNPAN: Data Center; United Nations (2008b); Kaufmann, Kraay, and Mastruzzi 2010; World Bank: Worldwide Governance Indicators; Data on pervasive filtering based on political themes are derived from the narratives and analysis in Deibert et al. 2010.

threat and reduce the potential for political and other disruptions. The world's largest democracy, India, is also putting cyber controls in place. In 2006, India was reported to impose "a puzzling silence on some Web services."[12] Overall, it is difficult to determine a net balance when comparing effective control by government, on the one hand, and growth in the number of users and uses on the other. The underlying dynamical process is not so much the action-reaction of an arms race as it is a game of hide-and-seek.

Cyber Challenges to the State

The entry points through which the state can exert its influence—notably Internet service providers, information service providers, financial service providers, and the domain name system—are potential targets for con-

Table 6.3
Social filtering and state profile, 2009

No evidence of filtering	Selective filtering	Substantial filtering	Pervasive filtering
Egypt (2)	Armenia (2)	Burma (*)	Iran (1)
France (6)	Azerbaijan (2)	China (3)	Saudi Arabia (4)
Georgia (2)	Belarus (1)	Pakistan (2)	Tunisia (2)
Germany (6)	Italy (6)	South Korea (6)	United Arab Emirates (4)
Moldova (2)	Kazakhstan (1)	Uzbekistan (2)	
Tajikistan (1)	Kyrgyzstan (1)		
Ukraine (2)	Russia (1)		
United Kingdom (6)	Syria (2)		
	Turkey (3)		
	Turkmenistan (1)		

Note: Parentheses refer to state profile, computed by the author. See chapters 2 and 5 for concept of profiles.
*Profile not listed due to missing data.
Source: Developed from the narrative and analysis presented in Deibert et al. (2008) and reported in Zittrain (2008).

trolling behavior deemed troublesome. The cyber action or event is often identifiable. But determining provenance, the attribution of action at the source, is far more difficult.

At the same time, opposition groups in many democratic and non-democratic states have learned how to employ cyber strategies to spread their message. Even in countries where surveillance, filtering, and access controls are extensive, we see evidence of opposition to the regime leaking through cyber venues.[13] Thus, the interest articulation and aggregation functions of politics are greatly enabled through cyber processes, whereby the individual message generates multiplier effects. This process starts at the individual (first image) level but, once engaged, the dynamics of interest recognition, articulation, and aggregation take over. Gradually, the lone individual becomes an affiliated participant, supported by intermediaries and the increasingly important functions they perform. (This is not contingent on a particular type of content, location, or message.)

Tunisia's Jasmine Revolution of January 2011 and its peaceful character are particularly noteworthy in that the uprising was the first event of its type in the modern history of the Arab world. The suicide of an

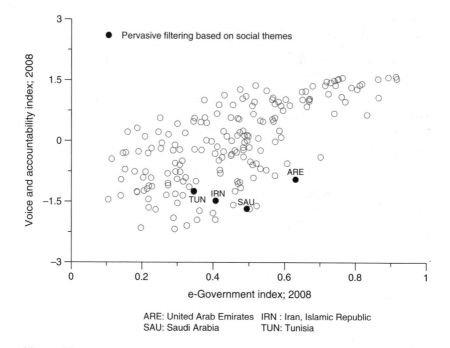

Figure 6.3
Social filtering for voice and accountability, 2008.
Source: Data from UNPAN: Data Center; United Nations (2008b); Kaufmann, Kraay, and Mastruzzi 2010; World Bank: Worldwide Governance Indicators; Data on pervasive filtering based on political themes are derived from the narratives and analysis in Deibert et al. 2010.

educated, unemployed peddler in response to policy injustice and insult triggered a national response that spread across the country with the goal of removing the country's president after twenty-three years of repressive government. This event was a tipping point that unleashed powerful sentiments throughout the region and an expansion of political commentary through the accelerated uses of social networking sites and other cyber venues.

No one had expected to see revolutionary moves or spillover effects in other countries of the region. The Tunisian revolution was, in itself, a major event of historic proportions. More likely, however, is the potential demonstration effect based on the logic that holds, "if it can happen in Tunisia, it can happen anywhere."

Shortly thereafter, calls for political change in Egypt flooded Facebook and other social networking websites. As one observer noted, cyber protest is not protest in the streets, but protest in the streets can be

Table 6.4
Filtering for conflict and security and Internet tools, and state profile, 2009

	No evidence of filtering	Suspected filtering	Substantial filtering	Pervasive filtering
Conflict and security	Azerbaijan (2) Egypt (2)	Armenia (2) Belarus (1)	Burma (*) Iran (1)	China (3) South Korea (6)
	France (6) Germany (6) Italy (6) Kazakhstan (1)	Georgia (2) Saudi Arabia (4) Tunisia (2) Turkmenistan (1)	Pakistan (2) Syria (2) Uzbekistan (2)	
	Kyrgyzstan (1)	UAE (6)		
	Moldova (2) Russia (1) Tajikistan (1) Turkey (3) Ukraine (2) United Kingdom (6)			
Internet tools	Azerbaijan (2) France (6)	Armenia (2) Belarus (1)	Burma (*) China (3)	Iran (1) Saudi Arabia (4)
	Georgia (2) Germany (6) Italy (6)	Pakistan (2) Turkey (3) Turkmenistan (1)	Uzbekistan (2)	Syria (2) Tunisia (2) United Arab Emirates (6)
	Kazakhstan (1) Kyrgyzstan (1) Moldova (2) Russia (1) South Korea (6) Tajikistan (1) Ukraine (2) United Kingdom (6)			

Notes: Numbers in parentheses refer to state profile. See Appendix 5.1 for state profiles.
*Profile not listed due to missing data.
Source: Developed from the narrative and analysis presented in Deibert et al. (2008) and reported in Zittrain (2008).

reinforced by cyber protest. At a minimum, these processes could, in the case of Egypt, be seen as a release of pent-up frustrations. They could, also been seen as a mechanism for social communication, creating and reinforcing cohesion. Overall, however, the revolution was relatively devoid of large-scale violence.

Concurrently, protests broke out in Yemen, where the leadership tried to reach an accommodation with protestors. The results remain inconclusive. In Bahrain, one of the most stable countries in the Gulf region, demands for a constitutional monarchy were coupled with demands for overarching political change. In Saudi Arabia, the royal family found it necessary to extend additional benefits to its citizens, a move that met with little success. All of these cases were largely nonviolent. Observers and analysts alike disagree as to the relative influence of the Internet and the various uses of cyber venues.

Then the Libyan eruption began. A strong reaction followed, with the use of power, force, and violence by the incumbent government. It is difficult to argue that the events on either side of Libya's borders, to the west and the east, had little influence on the onset of protest. It is also difficult to assign specific responsibility to cyber venues or social networking websites. Unlike in Tunisia or Egypt, Libya's Internet infrastructure and cyber culture were relatively less developed. It is difficult, however, to ignore the role of access to new information and communication technologies.

In this connection, it is useful to recall the trends identified in chapter 3 indicating low levels of cyber access in the Arab states and, by contrast, very rapid rates of growth of users. There is no long tradition of cyber-based discourse, social networking, blogging, or other forms of cyber interaction. By contrast, the revolutions in Tunisia and Egypt were accompanied by unexpected and surely unprecedented effective uses of cyber venues, social media, and other forms of communication to challenge the authority and legitimacy of the regime.

Competitive Politics via Cyber Venues

For advanced industrialized countries with competitive political systems, interaction and communication in cyberspace have become natural extensions of normal politics. In the United States, for example, a cursory look at the uses of cyberspace for specific political purposes shows some distinct patterns. In terms of day-to-day politics, communication by means of cyber venues is well established, large, growing, and with few observable constraints. People use email to discuss political events and send links to information of relevance. Many try to influence their friends and engage in political discussions on blogs where users can share ideas and debate topics. Political groups solicit donations on their websites, and supporters can transmit donations through credit cards online. Political groups can also organize meetings and rallies with expectations of greater efficiency over the Internet. By using email and websites, campaign organizers can coordinate their efforts across the entire country.[14] For the most part, cyber statistics are outdated soon after they are compiled, so estimates of use are rough at best.

Observers have noted that the Democrats first used the Internet when they controlled neither the White House nor Congress, and cyber venues provided new opportunities to express their views. Republicans resorted to cyber venues because they believed the conventional mass media (newspapers and TV news stations) to be more sympathetic to the other side. They used cyber functionalities more as a way to post opinions and editorials that supported their causes than to post official party platforms.

People obtain their news from the Internet for various reasons. For example, they may feel the conventional media are biased and believe it is easier to find a neutral source online. Alternatively, they use the Internet to obtain news from a source that is known to support their views. The practice of Internet polling is now a part of everyday life. To the extent that they have access to cyber venues, people in different parts of the world can compare their living conditions with those in other countries. If citizens learn that their government is not providing comparable services and benefits, they may demand change. Some analysts note that the growth of the Internet will seriously inhibit effective propaganda and government control, while others argue that the potential for government control remains unlimited.

A useful reminder by Chappell Lawson (2007), however, is that the rate of cyber penetration and participation in a country is not a particularly important predictor of future political mobilization. Referring to evidence from Singapore and Malaysia, Lawson notes that the predictive power of penetration is limited at best. Such inferences, of course, must be weighed in relation to government filtering activities and their effectiveness.

Cyber Crime and Cyber Espionage
It is difficult to gauge which is growing faster, the reports of cyber espionage and cyber crime or innovations in modes and methods to commit

them. The growth of malware is difficult to ignore, as is the speed of innovation. One example among many is as the well-known "drive-by downloads," tools that install malware on the systems of visitors to websites, which then run automatically (Provos et al. 2008). Neither the identity of the perpetrator nor the routing path of the damage can be identified.

It is nearly impossible in most cases to attribute the espionage—political or commercial—to a particular state, government, or firm. Jason Franklin and colleagues (2007) noted an important shift from "hacking for fun" to "hacking for profit." This type of experience has created a new vocabulary. For example, the term "worms" has been used to refer to malicious, self-expanding, network-based threats (Organisation for Economic Co-operation and Development 2008b, 10–11). Various sources point to China, whose hackers appear increasingly active and effective, but they can only speculate about the extent, if any, of state support.

In sum, new modes of malware, new tools for inflicting cyber damage (such as botnets among others), and new types of threat appear almost daily. The proliferation of cyber harm is near-instantaneous and pervasive. It is difficult to estimate the level of damage, but a general consensus is billions rather than millions of dollars. Not to be overlooked are the illegal service providers.

It is not easy to characterize the Google China case. However viewed, it was clearly a case of high politics. In 2009, Google claimed it was the target of a cyber attack that originated in China and was designed to steal intellectual property. Google informed the U.S. government, made its charge public, and announced it would no longer comply with China's filtering laws. Charges and countercharges flew; the U.S. Secretary of State reiterated support for the free flow of information. This three-way contention seemed more and more like a clash of Titans, with every indication that it would not be an isolated incident. We are likely to see many more in the future.

6.4   Cyber Threats to National Security

At the most general level, cyber threats to national security span the spectrum from fears of unauthorized access to classified proprietary materials, at one end, all the way to the use of cyberspace for strategic and military purposes at the other. Within this range are increasingly complex problems that transcend more familiar ones (such as the right to privacy).[15] Terms such as "hackers" appear increasingly quaint in light of the potentially powerful disruptions posed by cyber threats. Figure 6.4 shows the dramatic growth of three facets of cyber threat for the United States, namely, malicious code signatures, percentage of attacks on the United States by source country, and the percentage of U.S. organizations affected by type of attack.

In 2005 the International Telecommunication Union completed a comparative review of state-based perspectives on cyber security and institutional responses. The review showed that threats to security and attendant damages are defined in different ways by different countries, and the response strategies differ as well. Using data from this survey, table 6.5 shows the various definitions of cyber security and the type of organizational response for thirteen countries. None of these or related initiatives have been integrated into an overall national security framework.

In recent years the policy deliberations surrounding cyber security in the United States have become increasingly politicized, involving diverse government agencies, private contractors, and consultants through the various mechanisms by which decisions are made and assume an authoritative nature, notably with respect to the allocation of resources required. The growing politicization of cyberspace contributes to a perception of a tight coupling between the real and virtual domains. For example, the Patriot Act, adopted by Congress in response to the tragic events of September 11, 2001 includes provisions enabling the government to monitor Internet communications without obtaining prior permission from the Justice Department. The presumption is that cyberspace provides potential terrorists with a clear venue for undermining the security of the United States.

The Obama administration's efforts to bring cyberspace into the policy domain are an important step toward integrating cyberspace oversight into the overall calculus of national security. Unprecedented in scale and scope, the U.S. government's Sixty Day Review and the Cyber Initiative are major landmarks in the evolution of cyber-centered public policy. The creation of the Cyber Command in the U.S. armed forces—in addition to the commands for land, air, oceans, and space—is a major step whose full implications are yet to be realized.

At the same time, the challenges associated with, or created by, the growing use of cyber venues in a wide range of security-related domains—such as the "big data problem," when the volume of security-related materials exceeds the capacity of existing mechanisms to process these materials—are likely to increase rather than decrease over time.

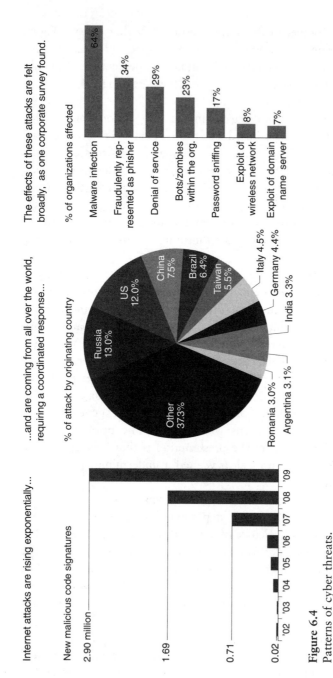

Figure 6.4
Patterns of cyber threats.
Source: Graphic Design by Tommy McCall/Infographics.com from David Talbot, "Moore's Outlaws," *Technology Review* 113 (4) (2010): 43. © 2012 Technology Review, Inc. 90558:612JM

Table 6.5
Comparative analysis of state positions, 2005

Country	Cyber security definition and institutional response
Australia	Cyber security is a counterterrorism effort. Organizations involved: Australian Security Intelligence Organization, Defense Signals Directorate, and Australian Federal Police
Austria	Cyber security is a data protection effort. Organizations involved: Official Austrian Data Security Website, Austrian E-Government Program, and the Pilot Project Citizen Card
Canada	Cyber security is an emergency preparedness effort. Organizations involved: Public Safety and Emergency Preparedness Canada, Civil Emergency Planning
Finland	Cyber security is a data security effort. Organizations involved: Committee for Data Security, Emergency Supply Agency, Communications Regulatory Authority, and Board of Economic Defense
France	Cyber security is an information society and high-tech crime issue. Organizations involved: Secretary-General of National Defense
Germany	Cyber security is an information security effort. Organizations involved: Federal Office for Information Security (under the Ministry of the Interior)
Italy	Cyber security is an information security effort. Organizations involved: no single group; Ministry for Innovation and Technologies is a group recently set up (as of 2005)
Netherlands	Organizations involved: Ministry for Interior and Kingdom Relations
New Zealand	Cyber security is an infrastructure protection effort. Organizations involved: The Centre for Critical Infrastructure Protection, Domestic and External Secretariat
Norway	Cyber security is a civil emergency planning issue. Organizations involved: Directorate for Civil Defense and Emergency Planning, Ministry of Justice and Police
Sweden	Cyber security is an emergency preparedness issue. Organizations involved: Swedish Emergency Management Agency (under the Ministry of Defense)

Table 6.5
(continued)

Country	Cyber security definition and institutional response
Switzerland*	Organizations involved: the Reporting and Analysis Centre for Information Assurance, and various public-private partnerships.
United Kingdom	Cyber security is a national infrastructure protection effort. Organizations involved: National Infrastructure Security Co-ordination Centre
United States of America	Cyber security is an infrastructure protection effort. Organizations involved: Department of Homeland Security, various public-private partnerships

* No definition of cyber security.
Source: Based on the analysis presented in International Telecommunication Union (2005, 15–16).

(Parenthetically, this problem is akin to the "explosion of materials" noted in chapter 3.)

We now turn to three interconnected modes of cyber threats to national security, namely, the militarization of cyberspace, cyber warfare, and cyber threats to critical infrastructures.

Militarization of Cyberspace

Heralding the use of cyberspace for military purposes, Ronald Deibert (2003) refers to the militarization of cyberspace as a "quiet" extension of defense policy. This logic falls squarely in the domain of realist international relations theory. The military use of cyberspace is a "natural" extension of the deployment of advanced information technologies, along with the requisite expansion of institutional and organizational capabilities. Deibert is correct in stating that "theory has definitely trailed behind practice in this case" (ibid., 13). It may also be trailing behind effective scrutiny in legal terms as well. The full range of military cyber threats is growing more rapidly than their semantics.

The militarization of cyberspace is an increasingly powerful requisite for national security, and any efforts to impose constraints on such practices will be counterproductive at best, and possibly considered seditious in some quarters. Under such conditions, we can readily anticipate the development of cyber threats and counter threats similar to the traditional tit-for-tat moves that characterize actions and reactions in arms race contexts.

Cyber Warfare

Clearly, sustained attacks on networks could effectively impede the communications systems of the military. The notion of cyber warfare covers a set of cyber-based activities designed to protect the state and its interests. It is closely related to net-centric notions but is more all-encompassing in its concentration on the range of network support systems to facilitate military activities.[16]

The characterization of cyber warfare as offensive or defensive parallels to a large extent the same type of spectrum in physical space. In each space the means, ends, actors, agents, and instruments may differ to some extent—and sometimes greatly. At the same time, however, the underlying generic properties of offense and defense, so salient in the domain of high politics, are particularly relevant in the domains of cyber security and cyber warfare.[17] For example, James R. Gosler (2005) points out that in the virtual domain, "the contest between the offense and the defense is dreadfully mismatched, with the advantage strongly in the offensive corner." Few would dispute such an assessment, for the "technology used by the U.S. public and private sectors is virtually identical to that of our allies and our enemies" (ibid., 96–97). More to the point, however, is that major damage to networks can be inflicted even under assumptions of inequalities in technology levels and capabilities. When placed in the broader context of information gathering and analysis for security purposes, as seen in Loch K. Johnson and James J. Wirtz's (2004) notable anthology *Strategic Intelligence,* this type of assumption shapes the various ways in which response strategies are being framed.

In considering the potential for cyber threats to security and the responses to such threats, Gregory J. Rattray (2001) uses the term "strategic warfare" to refer to the nature of the problem and to a class of cyber-based solutions. The issues highlighted in *Bombs and Bandwidth* (2003), edited by Robert Latham, span a range of potential threats and some of their implications. It is difficult to say whether these threats represent a worst-case scenario, are statements about the average expected damage, or suggest notable deviant possibilities. What appears persuasive, however, is that irrespective of contextual specification, the dislocations will be extensive.

Most telling in this connection is the U.S. General Accountability Office's (2007) assessment that the Department of Homeland Security (DHS) "has not fully addressed any of the 13 key cyber security-related responsibilities that we identified . . . and it has much work ahead" (noted

Table 6.6
Venue and target of potential cyber attack

	Physical target	Cyber target
Physical means	• Cutting telecommunications wires or cables • Breaking a computer or network server by hitting it with a hard object	• Using radio-frequency devices to control various components of a network or a system • Undermining the networks in different ways
Cyber means	• Penetrating a network or system that controls an electric grid or water treatment plant • Imitating an air traffic control system to direct flights	• Penetrating an important computer network or system • Creating Trojan horses or other malicious viruses and sending them throughout a network

Source: Based on the analysis presented in International Telecommunication Union (2005, 10).

by Urstadt 2005–2006, 80). While this does not negate the many initiatives undertaken by DHS, it does emphasize the magnitude and diversity of the challenges.

An overview of the major venues and targets of cyber attacks, based on the analysis presented by the International Telecommunication Union (2005, 10), is presented in table 6.6. The clear implication is that cyber warfare is here to stay. Several incidents of cyber attacks are acquiring near textbook status. One is the Estonia case, in which the country experienced a distributed denial-of-service attack over several weeks. Everyone agreed that the attacks came from Russia, but there was considerable disagreement about exactly who in Russia was responsible: the state, some individuals, the nongovernmental sector, other? Another case involving Russia was the military conflict with Georgia over South Ossetia's moves toward independence. But unlike in the Estonia case, this cyber attack was part of a larger, on-the-ground military initiative.

In *Cyber War*, Richard A. Clarke and Robert Knake (2010) argue that owing to its salience and seriousness, cyber warfare cannot be managed by any one individual country. They conclude that international collaboration is an essential requirement for building effective responses to emerging and powerful cyber threats. This argument is an important reminder that international conflict is almost always accompanied by a degree of cooperation between the adversaries, and international cooperation generally involves a degree of conflict or contention even among the closest allies.

Cyber Threats to Infrastructure

Cyber threats to infrastructure are of two broad types: threats to communications and information infrastructures per se and threats to all other forms of infrastructure that are contingent on robust communication systems. In the absence of agreed-upon policy-relevant activities and technologies at the interface between information systems and infrastructure systems, it is easy to envisage the potential for damage.

Closely connected are the "normal" vulnerabilities in advanced industrial societies created by the complexities of information systems and infrastructure networks. With or without malicious intent, such vulnerabilities can never be discounted. With even the slimmest shadow of malicious intent, the vulnerabilities are compounded by potentials for cyber threat. But with malicious intent, perceptions dominate, and the impacts can be all-pervasive. As Arnaud de Borchgrave and colleagues (2001, xvii) remind us, the Internet has become a backbone of backbones, with all that this implies. The combined stakes and vulnerabilities of the public and private sectors render such threats particularly pernicious.

The International Telecommunication Union 2005 report, noted earlier in this chapter, differentiates threats to infrastructure according to target, physical or cyber, as shown in table 6.6. The Stuxnet case, a particularly bold initiative, shows the complexities associated with cyber attacks designed to damage particular components of an industrial control system. This is a case of several powerul players—none formally recognizing the source or consequence of the attack—notably the United States and Israel (the potential source), Iran (the potential target), and countries such as Bulgaria (the unintended target of potential collateral damage). Overall, the entire script, so to speak, was driven by the Iranian nuclear policy. The details, however, remain contentious.

The concept of resilience has gradually crept into this domain of inquiry. The focus is less on preventing threat than on ensuring that the systems that could be threatened are not excessively vulnerable and that some form of resilience is built into their design and construction. Important here is the shift from a concern about vulnerability per se to the quest for creative ways to minimize the scale and scope of an attack, thereby enhancing the ability to recover from or manage the impacts of damage.

Cyber Terrorism

There is a whole range of ways in which terrorism can affect cyber domains, just as there is a range of ways in which terrorists can use cyber access and capabilities.[18] Our purpose here is not to enumerate all the known ways and means but rather to highlight some behavioral uses of cyber access and the potential gains to be derived from such access by groups designated as terrorist.

Terrorists have learned to use cyber capabilities to their advantage; many of the most prominent groups—and the lesser ones as well—have an established presence in the cyber arena, and their usage patterns appear quite sophisticated. In recent years they have recognized the potential of cyber access to provide instant communication and anonymity. They have also learned of its potential for psychological warfare and for political recruitment, mobilization, training, fundraising, and even instructions on how to build a weapon to behavioral tips on how to conduct surveillance, assassinations, and sabotage.

It can legitimately be argued that cyber terrorism can be seen as a form of information warfare in which political messages and counter messages are expressed in violent ways.[19] The cyberpolitics thereof are exemplified by the symbiotic growth of the international cable news media, cyberterrorism, and websites (and blogs) on terrorism. Cyberpolitics may well have amplified the significance of terrorism by several orders of magnitude. The nature of the discourse—and the very existence of cyber communication and expression—is highly politicized in democratic societies, especially when civil rights come into conflict with state efforts to intercept communications and disrupt terrorist networks.

Not unrelated to the above is the increased strength, ingenuity, and resilience of various forms of hackers—not formally designated terrorists— and their seemingly unlimited ability to bypass state regulations. The creative strategies of cyberspace "freedom fighters" involve moves and countermoves as they attempt to undermine regulations that are perceived as devoid of legitimacy.

In the absence of alternatives, the tendency is for states to deploy in cyberspace policy responses that regulate interactions in traditional international relations, and to apply the same instruments and measures. Indeed, the degree of fit or misfit between the real and the cyber may itself create a new set of challenges to theory and policy generated by configurations of cyberpolitics and the quest for coordinated action in the search for order in international relations, in real as well as cyber terms.

On a closing note, the cases of cyberpolitics in this chapter are all characterized by already defined political spaces in which actors, stakes, contentions, and potential outcomes are delineated, at least at the start—even if the identity of all of the actors is not known. More complex, however, is the nature of politics, in kinetic or virtual domains, when the conflicts and contentions are about defining the issue area itself and the value of the stakes. In such cases the political discourse is about the very nature of and the mechanisms for defining value and for its authoritative allocation.

If the issue area is not well defined, uncertainty and ambiguity often reflect an emerging "market for loyalties," a "period of re-regulation or remapping occurs when existing modes of control...can no longer maintain its position of civil authority" (Price 2002, 231). If the contours of an issue are obscure, then clarifying meaning and value becomes the core of the contention. Far from being a matter of semantics, this definitional phase is fundamental in shaping the playing field in terms of power and influence.

7

The International System: Cyberpolitics of Cooperation and Collaboration

A persistent challenge in international politics is how to navigate the critical disconnects between the "demand" for managing the global agenda and the "supply" of authoritative mechanisms. This chapter on the international system explores alternative ways in which cyberspace is used to pursue collaborative values and practices worldwide and, more important, to articulate the nature and legitimacy surrounding newly developed norms.

7.1 The Collaboration Challenge

The large literature on coordinated international actions addresses a wide range of collaborative mechanisms and their implementation, but it is disparate and contingent on alternative theoretical precepts.[1] Our purpose here is not to review the literature but to focus on how the construction of cyberspace creates new complexities for international cooperation.[2]

A significant aspect of such complexity relates to the variety of actors and agents whose interactions are subject to international management. In the real (kinetic) international system we recognize that nation-states, international corporations, nongovernmental organizations (NGOs), regional agencies, and local actors are among the most salient of these entities. In the cyberspace context, new international issues that require management and new groups are emerging, with new demands and new propensities for both conflict and collaboration. These new international realities are discernible but often ephemeral, as are the various kinds of collaboration, formal and informal. The logic for worldwide collaboration rests on three key questions, generally known as the *why, when,* and *how* of international accord:

- Why collaborate?
- When to collaborate?
- How to collaborate?

In general, countries collaborate either (1) in the pursuit of common interests or (2) in the management of common aversions. In the first instance, states seek to collaborate as a way to pursue jointly some objective they might not be able to attain individually. In the second, collaboration is driven by the recognition that states face shared adverse conditions that require coordinated action for the most effective management.

While interpretations of interests and aversions may differ, as might the underlying realities, the important factor here is the willingness to engage in joint international action. The mode may be one of coordination or one of collaboration. The end product is reaching an agreement on the type of action. The follow-up requirements will likely generate an entirely new and often complex set of processes at both national and international levels. The duality—the joint pursuit of goals or protection against common aversion—begs the question of content or substance:

- *What* is being pursued or must be avoided?
- *Who* is engaged in such avoidance or pursuit?
- *What* would be the impacts of success or failure?
- *How* would any of this make a difference?
- *When* might this matter most?

This logic presumes that states can both identify their specific preferences and objectives and perceive their vulnerabilities and sensitivities. It also presumes that countries can determine the conditions under which unilateral action is not appropriate or bilateral operations will not be effective. By definition, collaboration imposes constraints on national sovereignty, both internal (states must refrain from taking actions that have negative national consequences) and external (states must refrain from generating negative effects for other states).

Why does institutionalization take place? At the international level, institutionalization takes place (1) to consolidate and implement new norms, (2) to coerce states that resist the new norms and pressure them into conformity with the collective understanding, (3) to reduce uncertainty in processes, outcomes, and information, and (4) to generate and maintain shared modes of communication, understandings, and explanations. In addition, institutionalization is believed to (5) facilitate mediation among conflicting actors and (6) enhance the overall prospects for problem solving.[3] The mechanisms for institutionalization are diverse in mode and in effectiveness.

On a worldwide basis, we see increasing awareness of the ways in which international institutions utilize cyber venues purposefully and systematically to articulate, forge, and pursue new courses of action or to shape a new domain of interaction. We are reminded by Ernst B. Haas (1990) that such institutions are created by states and, in principle, are designed to pursue objectives agreed upon by states. However, like all organizations and bureaucracies, international institutions develop interests of their own and pursue objectives tied to these interests.

Haas's *When Knowledge Is Power* (1990) presents a set of propositions pertaining to the institutional management of content (particular knowledge) in interactions in real (kinetic) domains and thus illuminates the nature of conventional international interactions. By distinguishing between adaptation, on the one hand, and learning on the other, Haas raises an issue relevant for all modes of cyberpolitics as well and helps us understand institutional interactions in virtual domains. He defines adaptation as behavior that persists as new activities are pursued, without any alteration of original beliefs. Learning, by contrast, involves questioning the underlying theoretical premises that shape behavior and support programs of action.

Haas's conception of adaptation versus learning is presented in the context of international institutions created by agreement among states and hence can legitimately be regarded as a form of situational logic. Nonetheless, the distinction is sufficiently generic that Haas's insights can be imported into the cyber domain. Over time, we should be able to determine which of these logics is most relevant by asking, for example, whether access to cyberspace and the deployment of cyber tools lead to adaptation in behaviors and beliefs, or alternatively, whether access and deployment create conditions for learning.[4]

The remainder of this chapter examines the three modal types of cyber collaboration and illustrates each type with specific cases, as shown in table 7.1. Cyber collaboration of the first type consists of cyber-enabled *governance* at various levels of organization. Some empirical trends were noted in chapter 5. Cyber collaboration of the second type focuses on *global norms and public goods*. Political goals can often be diffuse and difficult to characterize, but many norms can be tied to a particular cause, such as fostering civic society, supporting human rights, or protecting the security of individuals and of groups. Here the focus is

Table 7.1
Cyberpolitics of cooperation and collaboration

Types	Cases
I. Cyber governance	Networked e-governance
	Institutions for cyber management
	Institutions for cyber security
	International cyber treaties
II. Global norms and public goods	Politicizing cyber rights
	Facilitating knowledge provision
	Consolidating global norms
III. Toward a global agenda	Internationalizing cyber supports
	Developing new cyber norms and behaviors
	Exploring precedents
	Supporting sustainability

on behavior in cyber venues. The third type of cyber collaboration relates to the *global agenda*—a wide range of consensus-seeking collaborative international activities undertaken to define global priorities and, to the extent possible, the parameters of permissible behavior.[5] Included in this type are the uses of cyber venues for the pursuit of traditional real objectives.

7.2   Cyber Governance

Practices of government and governance are about the rules and regulations for managing social interactions in ways that are sanctioned by social and legal convention. In principle, government involves the implementation of outcomes determined by the political process, as occurs in societies with high levels of political participation or societies defined as democratic in form. In many parts of the world, however, government itself constitutes the political process.[6] As discussed in chapter 5, many countries have already moved into the arena of cyber-enabled. governance.

Networked e-Governance
In *A New World Order*, Anne-Marie Slaughter (2004, 1) argues that "These government networks are a key feature of world order in the twenty-first century, but they are underappreciated, undersupported, and underused." By distinguishing between vertical and horizontal networks,

she paints a vision of a world dense in networks and concludes that the state "is not disappearing; but it is disaggregating" (ibid., 18). By contrast, Philip G. Cerny (1995) puts forth a different argument, namely, that the state is repositioning itself.

For the most part, however, networked governance has been addressed in conventional rather than in virtual terms. Even Slaughter's insightful inquiry does not address e-governance per se. For our purposes, networked e-governance refers to cyber-based interactions between government units, and usually within national boundaries. Increasingly, however, we are seeing the formation of cross-jurisdictional and cross-border e-governance initiatives.

The view from the bottom, those at the recipient end of government e-practices, provides empirical evidence about the mechanisms for e-governance as well as the impacts to date. We may also infer that greater cyber usage generates more evidence of actual performance and hence, almost unavoidably, some measure of transparency. Whether this transparency is politicized, enters the political process, or has any observable impacts on the nature of politics, virtual or kinetic, remains to be seen.

Institutions for Cyber Management

The effective operation of interactions in cyberspace rests on the effectiveness of the various institutions established to manage all aspects of this new reality—the physical infrastructure, the organization of identifiers and access functions, the various logical and related services, and the participation of actors in the overall space. The U.S. government's leadership, vision, and support for the creation of the Internet was followed shortly thereafter by its formation of the Internet Corporation for Assigned Names and Numbers (ICANN), the private entity enfranchised to provide entry-point credentials, the domain name system. Within a short time a large number of affiliates were developed that jointly represent the overall governance of the Internet. To date, the core governance structure is still within private authority. We return to the management of cyberspace in chapter 9 when we consider the emerging contentions surrounding Internet governance and the evolution of international institutional responsibilities on the twenty-first-century global agenda.

Institutions for Cyber Security

With the expansion of Internet use, many governments have recognized that cyber vulnerabilities threaten not only the security of their own networks but also the security of their citizens going about routine activities on a daily basis.[7] With the noted absence of coordinated industry responses or efforts to develop cooperative threat reduction strategies, a governance gap became apparent as a growing set of cyber incidents, large and small, alerted governments to the potential impact of their failure to address the emerging threat. As a result, governments in various ways mobilized substantial national and international resources toward the creation of a broad cyber security framework and coordinated institutional responses.

Recognizing overlapping responsibilities, we highlight only the major entities by way of illustrating the high level of cyber security concerns.[8] Table 7.2 presents a broad but not exhaustive accounting of the cyber security institutional ecosystem, a complex assortment of national, international, and private organizations. Since only national governments possess the proper legal tools and jurisdiction to prosecute attackers, an effective response to cyber crime is largely restricted to sovereign entities.

The current institutional landscape resembles a security patchwork that covers critical areas rather than an umbrella spanning all the known modes and sources of cyber threats. Because of the multiple contexts and diverse institutional motivations, we expect that responses will be driven more by institutional imperatives and reactions to crisis than by coordinated assessments and proactive responses.

We now turn to institutional mechanisms developed specifically in response to cyber crimes of various sorts, the Computer Emergency Response Teams (CERTs).[9] A distinctive addition to the dense network of international entities in the traditional kinetic arena worldwide, CERTs occupy an important place on the Internet security landscape. As defined by the CERT Coordination Center (CERT/CC), these teams are expected to organize responses to security emergencies, promote the use of valid security technology, and ensure network continuity. Although the majority of CERTs were founded as nonprofit organizations, many have transitioned toward public-private partnerships in recent years. They are also expected to reduce security vulnerabilities, enhance understanding of the nature and frequency of cyber threats, and improve methods of communicating and reporting these threats to other security teams and the general public.

While the CERT network is becoming increasingly organized, individual CERTs may differ considerably in their ability to effectively perform their mandates. At present, there are over two hundred

Table 7.2
The international institutional security ecosystem: Major entities

Institution	Role	Data availability	Example variables (if applicable)
Computer Emergency Response Teams (CERTs)			
AP-CERT: Asia Pacific Computer Emergency Response Team	Asian Regional coordination	High	Collation of security metrics from member CERTS in Asia
CERT-CC: Computer Emergency Response Team—Coordination Center	Coordination of global CERTs, especially national CERTs	Moderate	Vulnerabilities cataloged, hotline calls received, advisories and alerts published, incidents handled
FIRST: Forum for Incident Response and Security Teams	Forum and information sharing for CERTs	Low	Secondary data from conferences and presented papers
National CERTS (e.g., US-CERT)	National coordination; national defense and response	High	Varies—i.e, volume of malicious code and viruses, vulnerability alerts, botnets, incident reports
TF-CSIRT: Collaboration of Security Incident Response Teams	European regional coordination	N/A	N/A
International entities			
CCDCOE: Cooperative Cyber Defence Centre of Excellence	Enhancing NATO's cyber defense capability	N/A	N/A
Council of Europe	International legislation	Moderate	Legislation and ratification statistics; secondary data from conferences and presented papers
EU: European Union	Sponsors working parties, action plans, guidelines	N/A	N/A

Table 7.2
(continued)

Institution	Role	Data availability	Example variables (if applicable)
International entities			
ENISA: European Network and Information Security Agency	Awareness raising, cooperation between the public and private sectors, advising the EU on cyber security issues, data collection	Low	Awareness raising stats, spam surveys, regional surveys, country reports; qualitative data assessing the EU cyber security sphere
G8: Subgroup on High-tech Crime	Sponsored 24/7 INTERPOL hotline, various policy guidelines	N/A	N/A
IMPACT: International Multilateral Partnership Against Cyber Threats	Global threat response center, data analysis, real-time early warning system	N/A	N/A
INTERPOL: International Criminal Police Organization	Manages 24/7 hotline, trains law enforcement agencies, participates in investigations	N/A	N/A
ITU: International Telecommunications Union	Sponsors IMPACT. UN specialized agency for ICT. Release guidelines and standards, and supports seamless communication.	Moderate	Internet usage and penetration statistics; secondary data from conferences and presented papers
NATO: North Atlantic Treaty Organization	Responding to military attacks on NATO member states	N/A	N/A: classified
OECD: Organisation for Economic Co-operation and Development	Develops policy options, organizes conferences, publishes guidelines and best-practices	Low	Secondary data from conferences and presented papers
UNODC: United Nations Office on Drugs and Crime	Promotion of legislation, training programs, awareness, enforcement	N/A	N/A
WSIS: World Summit on the Information Society	Global summit on information defines priorities and monitors implementation through stocktaking efforts.	Low	Stocktaking database and Secondary data from conferences and presented papers

Table 7.2
(continued)

Institution	Role	Data availability	Example variables (if applicable)
U.S. national entities			
NSA: National Security Agency	Shares Director, General Keith Alexander with US CYBERCOM; specializes in cryptology services and research	N/A	N/A
CIA: Central Intelligence Agency	Defense of intelligence networks, information gathering	N/A	N/A: Classified
DHS: Department of Homeland Security	Protection of federal civil networks and critical infrastructure; information sharing and awareness; coordinating federal response and alerts	N/A	N/A: Unclassified data released through US-CERT
DoD: Department of Defense	Defense of military networks, counterattack capability	N/A	N/A: Classified
DoJ: U.S. Department of Justice	Federal prosecution	Moderate	Nonaggregated data: prosecuted cases, crimes by industry
FBI: Federal Bureau of Investigation	Federal investigation	Low	Total reported incidents, number of referrals to law enforcement agencies; annual surveys on corporate computer crime including: type and frequency of attacks, dollar loss, attack source
FTC: Federal Trade Commission	Consumer protection	N/A	N/A

Table 7.2
(continued)

Institution	Role	Data availability	Example variables (if applicable)
U.S. national entities			
IC3: Internet Crime Complaint Center	Cybercrime reporting and referral center	High	Total complaints, referred complaints, estimated dollar loss, complaints by industrial sector
NW3C: National White Collar Crime Center	Provides training and support to law enforcement agencies, helps administer the IC3 with the FBI	N/A	N/A: statistics released through IC3
FSSCC: Financial Services Sector Coordinating Council	By DHS mandate, identifies threats and promotes protection to protect financial fector critical infrastructure assets	N/A	N/A
Secret Service	Investigation of economic cyber crimes	N/A	N/A
US-CERT: United States Computer Emergency Response Team	Defense of federal civil networks (.gov), information sharing and collaboration with private sector	Moderate	Incidents and events by category, vulnerability reports
Non-U.S. national entities (frequent collaborative partners)			
GCHQ: Government Communications Headquarters (U.K.)	One of three of Britain's intelligence agencies responsible for information assurance and cryptology; Britain's leading authority on cybersecurity	N/A	N/A
National Cyberdefence Centre (Germany)	Recently opened agency for cybersecurity in Germany; responds to reports of cyberattacks on critical infrastructure	N/A	N/A
National Police Bureaus (for example: Taiwan, South Korea, Japan, France)	Investigation, enforcement	Varies	Cases, arrests, prosecutions, demographics

Table 7.2
(continued)

Institution	Role	Data availability	Example variables (if applicable)
Nonprofit entities			
GICSR: Global Institute for Security and Research	Conducts R&D with industry leaders, public-private sector, and academia to develop policy and strategy for cyberspace	N/A	N/A
Internet Society	Nontechnical branch of Internet Engineering Task Force (IETF); provides leadership in addressing policy issues that confront the future of the Internet	N/A	N/A
CyberWatch	Develops educational programs and curriculum to train next generation of cybersecurity experts	N/A	N/A
CAIDA: Cooperative Association for Internet Data Analysis	Gathers data that will increase situational awareness of Internet topology structure, behavior, and vulnerabilities.	High	Graphs and visuals of Internet traffic patterns

Table 7.2
(continued)

Institution	Role	Data availability	Example variables (if applicable)
Private sector			
MacAfee	Industry leader in antivirus software; computer security services	Moderate	White papers
PROINFO	Products analyze vulnerability dependencies and show all possible attack paths into a network	N/A	N/A
Raytheon	Cybersecurity Solutions division offers wide range of information assurance services	N/A	N/A
Lockheed Martin	Defense contractor that supplies many governmental cybersecurity G&S	N/A	N/A
Red Tiger Security	Investigates cyberattacks	N/A	N/A
HB Gary	Investigates cyberattacks	N/A	N/A
Versigen iDefense	Investigates cyberattacks	N/A	N/A
International Computer Security Association	Specializes in antivirus, antispam, and firewall services, among a wide array of other cybersecurity services	Moderate	Graphs of which countries sent the most spam per week

Source: Adapted from table 1 in Ferwerda, Choucri, and Madnick (2011).

recognized CERTs, with widely different levels of organization, funding, and expertise. In general, however, CERTs share a common structure and backbone, but with limited coordination among them, if any. The majority of CERT teams are defined according to guidelines originally published by CERT/CC, and many use common toolkits to establish their organizations (Killcrece 2004).[10]

Today, the CERT network has expanded beyond the scope and control of CERT/CC, although the organization continues to play an influential role in establishing national CERTs in developing countries and fostering CERT communication. Each individual CERT is embedded in its own institutional context. Figure 7.1 shows the governance coordination system for the CERTs, using Europe, Asia, and the United States as examples, and figure 7.2 shows the position of the U.S. CERT within the broader context of the nation's overall cyber security institutional network.

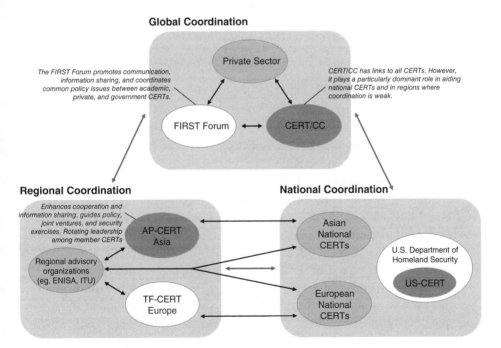

Figure 7.1
Illustrating coordination for cyber security and international CERTs for Asia, Europe and the United States—highlights.
Source: Ferwerda, Choucri, and Madnick 2011.

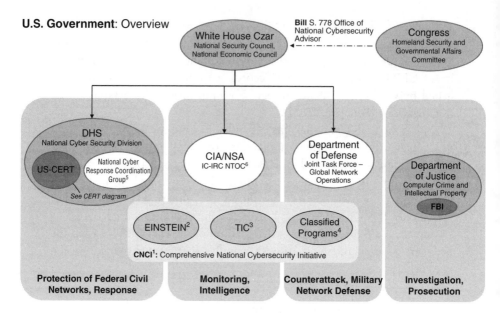

Figure 7.2
Highlights of institutional system for cyber security of the United States.
Note: The United States Cyber Command (USCYBERCOM), U.S. Department of Defense announced in 2009 was fully operational in 2010.
Source: Ferwerda, Choucri, and Madnick 2011.

International Cyber Treaties

The international community is still at an early stage on the path toward international cyber treaty making. A flagship initiative, the Convention on Cybercrime, drawn up by the Council of Europe, focused on crimes committed through the Internet and other computer networks, was established in 2001. Specifically, it seeks to harmonize national criminal law, develop national criminal procedural law power for the investigation and prosecution of offenses, and establish effective mechanisms for international cooperation. It also addresses computer-related fraud, child pornography, violations of network security, and lawful interception. By 2010 the total number of state ratifications or accessions stood at thirty, and the signatures without ratifications stood at seventeen. The U. S. ratification entered into force in 2007.

Far more pervasive is the World Conference on Information Technology (WCIT-12), December 2012, to review the 1988 treaty for worldwide communication, the International Telecommunications Regulations (ITR). Spear headed by the ITU, the WCIT-12 is an intensely political venue for contestation of ICT principles and practices worldwide.

7.3   Global Norms and Public Goods

One of the political issues being debated worldwide has to do with the provision of global public goods. The distinction between private goods and public goods, first articulated for modern readers by Adam Smith, has a long intellectual and political history. By convention, the economics and politics of public goods exist in the context of an economy, a market, or a jurisdiction. To simplify, the problem is this: if the market cannot provide public goods, then the government must do so. With public goods, unlike private goods, the gain accrued to an individual consumer is also available to others; further, its consumption by an individual does not reduce its consumption by others.[11] When benefits are extended to a constituency that transcends territorial boundaries and is global in scale and scope, however, some dilemmas arise. The fundamental issues involve each of the terms *global*, *public*, and *good*.

The politics surrounding global public goods—relating to definitions, decisions, provision, and implementation—are particularly complex, for several reasons. In chapter 3 we highlighted the differentials in cyber access and noted variations in the extent to which views are being expressed and voices heard. Exclusion, by definition, means nonparticipation. The United Nations Development Programme states that the "imbalances among states as well as those between state and non-state actors are not always easy to detect, because in many cases the problem is not merely a quantitative issue—whether all parties have a seat at the negotiating table. The main problem is often qualitative—how well various stakeholders are represented" (Kaul et al. 2003, 39). Only recently has the provision of global public goods become an issue area for international institutions such as the UN (2003a) and others that view such concerns as corollaries of globalization.[12]

Overall, the debates surrounding global public goods are usually framed with reference to real or conventional politics, yet they are increasingly manifested in the domain of virtual politics in notable ways. If we consider access to cyberspace as a global public good, then the good itself carries the central features (and label) of cyberpolitics. If we consider the contours of emerging global accord, we can point to the World Summit on the Information Society and access to advanced information and communications technologies worldwide as evidence of the politicization of cyber venues. In the context of the provision of global public goods, two ambiguities illustrate the emerging character of these initiatives. First is the nature of the public good itself, namely, the content or value whose authoritative allocation is at issue. Second is the limited attention to decision making about who gets what, when, and how. These elements are closely connected, even highly interactive, reflecting the complexities of collaboration.

Politicizing Cyber Rights

The diversity of the international community is reflected in equally diverse positions on the issue of rights, including political rights, human rights, and the protection of individual and group security.[13] In addition to these basic rights are some new ones that, to some extent, appear to be motivated by interactions in the new cyber arena. Issues relating to the scale and scope of rights are involved in the effort to define human security as a global value whose pursuit is legitimized through authoritative international processes.

In practice, however, the imperatives of *realpolitik* overshadow the matter of rights, individual or social. As suggested in chapter 6, it is not surprising that both industrial and developing countries are using cyberspace specifically for political objectives—to influence the authoritative allocation of value with respect to who gets what, when, and how. In some cases, governments invest in web portals to promote political support and elicit feedback to improve government-citizen connections. Competing politicians or political parties may draw on cyber facilities to express their views, appeal to their supporters, or criticize (even demonize) their opponents.

Since cyberspace facilitates new demands, fosters new types of conflict, and generates new contentions over regulation, it is a source of additional challenges for public policy. For example, political contention abounds concerning government secrecy and the extent to which the protection of civil liberties is being compromised. Privacy is a major issue in the area of cyberpolitics and of public policy in democratic societies, and deploying cyber tools for privacy protection is considered a corollary of cyber access. In chapter 6 we showed that many countries, notably nondemocratic societies, have engaged in deploying e-tools for invading privacy (recognizing that the term "privacy" may not hold in this context).

Facilitating Knowledge Provision

In many parts of the world knowledge is considered to be one of the most public and valued goods of all public goods.[14] In others knowledge is seen to be no more than a quasi-public good. The discussion in chapter

4, in which we considered different models of knowledge value, is especially relevant here.

At this writing, all the players in the cyber arena are affected, directly or indirectly, by the prevailing intellectual property rights regimes. Yet the nature, scale, and scope of such rights differ substantially across players, as does the extent of recognition and perception of their legitimacy. Not only are there contentions about the authoritative basis for the allocation of value to intellectual product, but, equally important, there are conflicts about the nature of the value in question. The provision of global knowledge as a public good—a major agenda item in international forums—is thus a highly politicized issue, especially when combined with access to cyber venues at all levels and in all locations around the world.

Consolidating Global Norms

The twentieth century is often seen as a period of growing demand for norms that span the entire global system and for consolidating related rights and responsibilities. It is difficult to overlook the symbolic effects rendered by images of human rights violations. Such images may be necessary to enhance awareness, but they are far from sufficient to transform human rights from a desired norm to an operational value. In 2006 the United Nations established the Human Rights Council to replace the UN Commission on Human Rights as the functional commission within the UN system. The assumption was that the change would carry more weight in the course of making human rights a value of global scale and scope.[15]

We can expect the demand for global norms to be maintained and even increased in the twenty-first century. This does not mean that these demands will be met or that the supporting pressures will result in acceptance and effectiveness. But we do expect greater propensities for norm articulation and consolidation. It is a rare leader, elected or otherwise, who argues against this value in principle, even if undermining it in practice.

In this domain, cyberpolitics serves to reinforce and enable the politics of norm consolidation performance of functions—at least at the conceptual level. More important, however, is improved access to information, communication, and visualization of the human condition when fundamental rights are threatened, if not destroyed entirely. In this way cyberspace reinforces the multiplier effects introduced in chapter 4. Nongovernmental organizations, various private entities, watchdog groups, and a wide range of human rights organizations all seek to use the full potentials of cyberspace to enhance their core values.

7.4   Toward a Global Agenda

Clearly connected to foregoing, but distinct in content, are emerging trends in international relations articulating a global (rather than an interstate) perspective and the related manifestations of cyber collaboration. This type of international initiative is arguably the most inclusive in its intended scale and scope but the least formalized in its operations and institutional infrastructures.

Internationalizing Cyber Supports

The internationalization of cyber support systems is one of the most important manifestations of collaborative cyberpolitics. Various initiatives have led to the proposal of a bundle of rights associated with development, rooted in the UN's Charter on Human Rights. The World Summit on the Information Society (WSIS) has provided a global venue for formalizing an agenda anchored in global norms, as we discuss further in chapter 9.

Buttressing the quest for knowledge, the WSIS Declaration of Principles (Geneva summit) made the commitment to build "a people-centered, inclusive and development-oriented Information Society" to enable all to "achieve their full potential in promoting their sustainable development and improving their quality of life" (WSIS 2003). The WSIS is an international forum organized specifically to aggregate and articulate contending interests and craft mechanisms for the authoritative allocation of responses and strategies pertaining to who gets what, when, and how. More specifically, at the end of the second part of the summit, in Tunis, two formal declarations were issued that directly connected freedom of access to information and human rights.

Since cyberspace is the targeted arena of international focus, the contentions and their eventual resolutions are all matters of cyberpolitics. The underlying objective is to expand access to cyberspace worldwide— as well as access to all information and communications technologies—in support of developmental objectives.

Developing New Cyber Norms and Behaviors

With the continued growth of uses and users worldwide, there is every indication of e-system overload in theory and in practice. David D. Clark has argued that the patchwork growth of technologies, uses, and users has become something of a "convoluted affair." It has created serious problems for the Internet such that we "might just be at the point where the utility of the Internet stalls and perhaps turns downward" (quoted in Talbot 2005/2006, 63). Clark and others believe that new ways of "pulling the pieces together" are needed to create a more viable system. More to the point, experts believe that there is not one but a myriad of problems, with cyber security and the authentication of communications being among the most basic.

An interesting turn of phrase illustrates a current sense of cyberspace, namely, that the architectures to be developed will be "battle tested with real world Internet traffic" (Talbot 2005/2006, 68). The scale and scope of vulnerabilities in virtual domains appear greater than society's ability to respond effectively; it is unlikely that they can be managed by a quick fix or a "killer app."

In many ways, users have been reactive rather than proactive, creating new challenges to and demands for technical protection. Ironically, the markets for such products will invariably grow, as will attendant investments in e-protective tools and more patchwork strategies. There is a broad consensus that something is needed, but precisely what that something is remains to be defined in conceptual, operational, and policy terms. Experience suggests that behavioral patterns are at least as daunting as the technological challenges for secure cyber communications.

The innovations required for improved uses of cyberspace are as much in the domain of the sociology of knowledge as they are the practical know-how of managing professional interactions in virtual domains.

Exploring Precedents

There is a long history of collaboration among states. Unclear, however, are precedents relevant to the cyber domain. Some point to the nuclear nonproliferation treaty as an appropriate precedent. Others note that a global consensus on cyber security could best be achieved by pursuing deterrence strategies. These arguments assume the portability of Cold War policies into the twenty-first-century cyber arena. In chapter 9 we suggest that environmental treaties, such as the Framework Convention on Climate Change, might be relevant in the cyber context since they deal with global phenomena.

Supporting Sustainability

A recent example of collaborative cyberpolitics is the effort to support transitions toward sustainable development. It is also, in principle, one of the most inclusive policy directions spanning states, non-states, transnational entities, commercial and noncommercial organizations, and so on. The objectives at the international level are to generate support and obtain a formal buy-in at all policy-relevant levels.

In chapter 4, we noted the emerging global demand for new knowledge, driven by the growing scientific consensus that human-initiated activities are altering the natural environment in potentially significant ways. "Sustainability science" is the response to this growing demand. Already, the quest for sustainability points to a policy trajectory different from any direction charted by theories, models, and practices of economic growth. The goal is different, as are most of the underlying assumptions. And whereas the international community is formally committed to a "sustainable future," a comprehensive knowledge base to guide this mission has yet to be created. It may be that some similar commitment is needed for the cyber domain. While a considerable amount of knowledge related to sustainability has been developed and continues to expand, a coherent body of knowledge, or even one whose foundations are fully codified, has yet to emerge.

8

The Global System: Pressures of Growth and Expansion

This chapter focuses on the global system—in conventional kinetic rather than cyber terms—to highlight the expansion of human activities and the resulting threats to the resilience of national and social systems. Our purpose is to provide the rationale for the gradual coevolution of cyberspace (a new arena of communication and interaction) and sustainability (a new policy imperative, on local to global scales). We identify some of the threats to the viability of the global system and the early responses by the international community. In the next chapter we extend the discussion to examine the synergy of cyberspace and sustainability and their convergence on the global agenda.

The global system itself is not a decision entity; there is no world government. But the global system is the overarching socio-environmental ecosystem and forms the broad playing field for human decision making and activities—transcending all jurisdictions, markets, and delineations. A large number of institutions and entities, not just the sovereign state, are active organized decision makers in this arena. Accordingly, we begin with the growth of the major decision entities, public and private, whose policies are increasingly global in scale and scope.

We then examine the growth of the global master variables—population, resources, technology—and their impacts worldwide. Because the master variables serve as drivers in lateral pressure theory, we would expect the growth and expansionist effects to be encroaching on the resilience of the life-supporting properties of nature, and possibly on the cohesion and stability of social systems.

More specifically, we illustrate how the most customary manifestations of growth and expansion of human activities alter the parameters of the global playing field to the extent that the loads on the overall system may exceed the capabilities available to manage these loads. Many of these effects are rooted in low politics but, when recognized as potentially constraining, become matters of high politics. Third, we high-light patterns of conflict and violence worldwide and, in less detail, evidence of environmental degradation. Traditionally, conflict and environment have been considered as separate if not independent issues in international relations. Increasingly, however, we recognize their inter-connections and mutually reinforcing effects.

The synergy between cyberspace and sustainability, examined in the following chapter, is an important case of cyberpolitics in international relations. We referred to this synergy in chapter 4, on emergent demands for new knowledge, and in chapter 7, on supporting sustainability on the global agenda. In chapter 9 we present the full logic, its political manifestations, and the underlying knowledge imperatives.

8.1   Global Actors and Decision Entities

The major decision entities, public and private, on the global landscape include but are not limited to the state, international institutions, the private sector and its agents, nongovernmental organizations (NGOs), faith groups, the institutional managers of cyberspace, and, increasingly, the global civil society. While all these entities interact within one global system, they have distinct if overlapping interests, as well as different capabilities and instruments of leverage. They are characterized by different types of asymmetries and have different views on what is real, what is important, and what can or should be done in the broad policy domain, from local to global. In many ways they are in a situation of mutual dependence on—or hostage to—each other's activities. Together they constitute the significant decision entities in the global system.

Our baseline year is 1945, the year of the creation of the United Nations following the end of World War II, and the reconstitution of the state system. The expansion in the number of sovereign states is one of the most critical features in the modern world. Some of these entities evolved into sovereign states over long spans of several centuries. Others arose as the result of the decolonization process after World War II and the dissolution of the Soviet Union and the end of the Cold War in the last decades of the twentieth century. Their activities, priorities, and deci-sions, and the outcomes of their decisions, all exist in a social context characterized by people, the resources they use, and the technologies they employ.

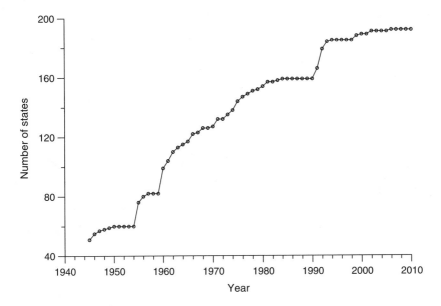

Figure 8.1
Growth in number of sovereign states, 1940–2010.
Source: Based on data from United Nations, "Growth in United Nations membership, 1945–present," 2011.

Among the responsibilities of the state are preventing the erosion of the social system, maintaining the relevance of institutions, and protecting the reutilization of basic functions required for survival and security. Because the international system consists of sovereign states, the larger the number of sovereign states, the greater is their diversity and the more varied the distribution of national interests—and hence the more difficult is the convergence on global accords. Figure 8.1 shows the state formation trend line since 1945.

The growth of intergovernmental institutions, also known as international organizations, is a structural feature of the international system that is widely recognized as one of the most significant features of the twentieth century (Kratochwil and Mansfield 1994). This growth is an indication of the increased state-based management of international interactions, on the one hand, and state-based challenges on the other. The trend shown in figure 8.2 reflects the growing bureaucratization of the provision of services to an increasing number of states and their constituencies. In the last several years a number of new international

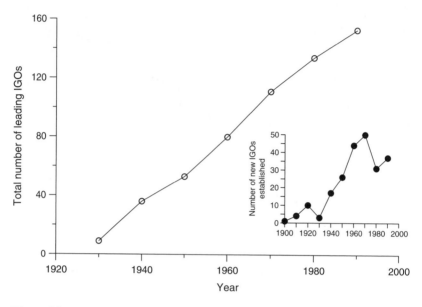

Figure 8.2
Growth in number of leading intergovernmental organizations, 1930–1990.
Source: Rourke 2001; inset: Rourke 2008. By permission of the McGraw–Hill Companies.

organizations have been established, raising the total number noted in the figure. The inset tracks the new institutions.

International relations theory reminds us that, once established, institutions define their own interests and develop constituencies aligned with those interests. By necessity or by default, international institutions have taken on the responsibility of compiling and to some extent of generating knowledge relevant to their own mission.[1] These institutional trends have resulted in a large body of scholarly research on requisites for and patterns of international collaboration. More recently, notions of global governance have appeared in both scholarly and policy-making circles.[2] We return to these issues in the next chapter.

The growing number of nongovernmental organizations that operate across national boundaries is also a notable feature of the global system. These entities operate without any necessary affiliation with the state system except for compliance with the requirements for their initial establishment and legalization. In principle, these institutions, which are formally defined as not-for-profit, are accountable to their stakeholders, but there are as yet few official mechanisms of accountability.[3] If we consider the absence of accountability an element of incomplete institu-

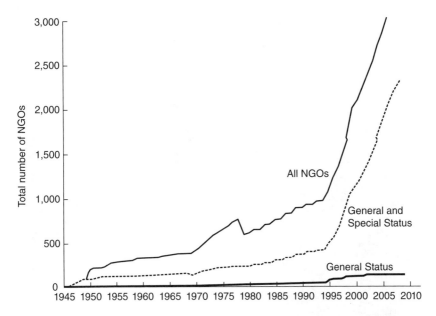

Figure 8.3
Growth in number of nongovernmental organizations, 1945–2010.
Source: Baylis, Smith, and Owens 2011, 335. By permission of Oxford University Press.

tional design, then we should anticipate the development of formal NGO accountability mechanisms in the future. Figure 8.3 shows the growth in these agencies over a sixty-five-year period.

Over time, NGOs have become a key forum for interest articulation and aggregation and a dominant arena for agreement on the authoritative allocation of value. They also play the important role of intermediation—and in some cases of anticipation and innovation—in framing the nature of the political field and the rules of the game. Critical in this regard are groups that organize specifically for the purpose of creating, supporting, and reinforcing the influence of civil society at the global level. (It goes without saying that cyber access significantly enables the aggregation process.) Such groups include, for example, Amnesty International, Doctors Without Borders, Make a Wish Foundation, Oxfam, and the Peace Corps.

Less well understood is the role in international relations of formal faith groups, increasingly important players in the global system. The historical narrative of modern civilizations usually takes note of dominant faiths and draws inferences about their implications for behavior in private and public spaces. The contemporary faith map in figure 8.4

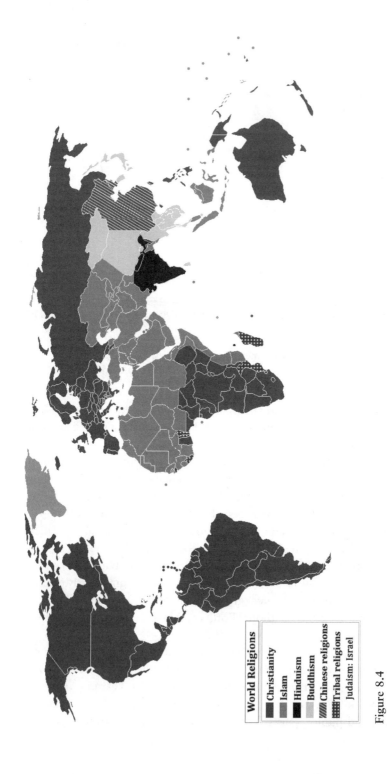

Figure 8.4
World distribution of major faith groups, 2011.
Source: 9th Doha Conference of Inter-Faith Dialogue. 2011. http://interfaith2011.qatar-conferences.org/map2.php.

shows the location of the dominant religious belief systems and highlights the diversity worldwide as well as the complexity of the patterns therein. It may well be that the politicization of religious groups can be considered either a "normal" feature of world politics or, alternatively, an aberration that requires remediation. Countries also differ significantly in their views on and policies pertaining to faith. Everyone agrees that cyberspace has served to amplify religious voices, irrespective of vision or mission.[4]

The power of multinational (or transnational) corporations in the global landscape is similarly undisputed. The remarkable growth during the last decades of the twentieth century is illustrative of corporate expansion. Between 1970 and 2000, the number of registered corporations worldwide increased from 7,000 to about 60,000, with the number of foreign subsidiaries amounting to 800,000 by the turn of the century (French 2000, 6). If the volume of sales is taken as an indicator of corporate power, by the end of the twentieth century, the top two hundred firms accounted for roughly 27.5 percent of the world's GDP (Anderson, Cavanaugh, and Lee 2000, cited in United Nations Conference on Trade and Development [UNCTAD] 2002, 90). If we compare sales volume to GDP,[5] considering each an indicator of economic performance, fourteen of the fifty largest economic performers were transnational corporations, while thirty-six were states. Early in 2008 there were close to 80,000 transnational or multinational corporations involved in international production. The total value of foreign direct investments (FDIs) exceeded $15 trillion. However, FDI figures do not necessarily reflect the total value of investments by these corporations, nor do they include the activities of affiliates, estimated at 790,000 in 2007, with a gross product valued at $6.1 trillion, compared to $0.06 trillion in 1982 (UNCTAD 2008).

A more detailed view of FDI inflows and outflows is shown in figures 8.5a and 8.5b, which list the top twenty host and home economies in 2008–2009. Although the data for the following years are not yet fully compiled; figure 8.6 shows the top host economies for FDIs in 2010 estimated to 2012.

Since these corporations conduct most of the world's economic activity—as producers, managers, and distributors of goods and services—their impact is significant in both the real international system and the natural, environmental system. They are technological innovators and agents of commercialization for new technology (organizational as well as mechanical) worldwide. These profit-seeking entities cannot remain insulated from the prevailing political winds and they have

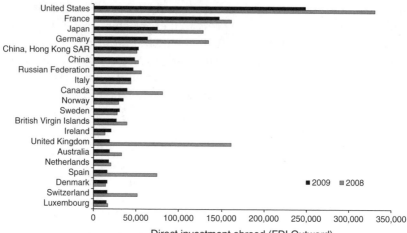

(a)

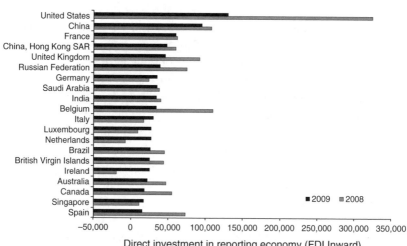

(b)

Figure 8.5
(*a*) Top 20 states making direct investments abroad (FDI), 2008 and 2009.
(*b*) Top 20 states receiving direct foreign investments (FDI), 2008 and 2009.
Source: Data from UNCTAD, Division on Investment and Enterprise.

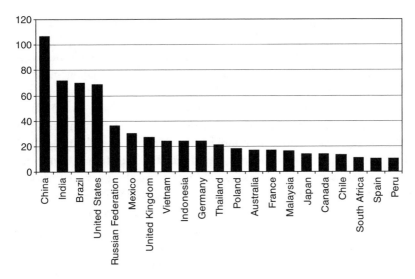

Figure 8.6
Top host economies for FDI in 2010–2012.
Source: United Nations Conference on Trade and Development (Geneva), *World Investment Report 2010: Investing in a Low-Carbon Economy*, 25 (New York: United Nations, 2010).

increasingly become involved in intergovernmental processes as indirect participants, but participants nonetheless. They are central players in all areas of information technology, and in recent years they have been called on by the UN to help facilitate management of the uses of cyber venues in connection with the world's developmental problems. In some ways they have contributed to the convergence of sustainability and cyberspace.

To this traditional accounting we must now add the managers of cyberspace. The construction of cyberspace was an activity of the private sector—with incentives from and the support of the U.S. government—and the structure of its management also rested in private hands. Because of its technological and political dominance and its position as the sovereign originator of the Internet, the United States set the principles and the terms of reference for governance. It is hardly news that the dominant state sets the rules of the game. The increased importance of the telecommunications industry and its associated services was seen as a driver of economic activity. The net impact was a shift in the U.S. position to support the view of liberalization and market-driven innovations as powerful engines of growth. Buttressed by the creation of private sector entities to provide management functions, cyberspace could now provide an arena for competition on many dimensions of industry and on a global scale.[6]

Of the many entities responsible for Internet governance and management, a few have lead positions in the operation and management of cyberspace. Especially critical to the operations of cyberspace is the Internet Corporation for Assigned Names and Numbers (ICANN), a private, nonprofit corporation created by the U.S. government in 1998 to take over a set of Internet-related tasks done on its behalf by other entities and thus to provide the foundational institutional requisites. ICANN's major responsibilities include managing the Internet Protocol (IP) address spaces, managing the top-level domain name space, and assigning address blocks to regional Internet registries. As a private entity, its mission is to protect the stability of the Internet and promote competition; it works largely through consensus building.

Figure 8.7 places ICANN, the pivotal Internet institution, in a broader organizational context. Currently ICANN derives its authority from the National Telecommunications and Information Authority (NTIA), a specialized entity in the U.S. Department of Commerce that controls the Internet. The figure also shows the Internet Assigned Numbers Authority (IANA) and its regional registries for Internet numbers in relation to ICANN and NTIA.

As an overarching institution, the Internet Society (ISOC) is a private, nonprofit entity designed to provide leadership in Internet-related standards, education, and policy and to facilitate Internet-related activities worldwide. It also serves as an organizational context for the Internet Architecture Board (IAB) and the Internet Engineering Task Force (IETF). The IETF is a worldwide network of network designers, operators, vendors, and researchers concerned with the smooth operations of the Internet and its evolution in the future. The IETF mostly concentrates on transport, routing, security, and the like. Figure 8.8 shows the connection between the IETF and ICANN.

Less well known is the North American Network Operators' Group (NANOG), a group of private individuals concerned with creating, maintaining, and operating IP networks. It is something of a trouble-shooter and a forum for the exchange of experience and problem-solving strategies. It locates itself at the intersection of the technical staff of leading Internet providers, network operations, standards bodies, and other technical groups and the research community.

These and other supporting entities reinforced the role of the private sector and facilitated the development and expansion of commercial and

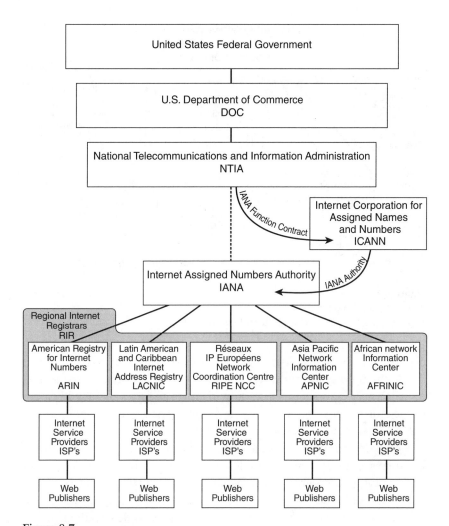

Figure 8.7
Highlights of cyber governance, 2006.
Source: CP80: Evolve the Internet to protect children. 2006. "Understanding Internet Governance." © 2012 The CP80 Foundation. All Rights Reserved.

ICANN Multi-Stakeholder Model

	Board of Directors	
President and CEO	■ ▪▪▪▪▪▪ ▪▪▪▪▪▪▪ ▪ ▪▪▪▪▪■	Governmental **G** Advisory **A** Committee **C**

ICANN Staff MDR–68 SV–9 Sydney-5 Other US-11 Other non-US-14	Nominating Committee Per ICANN Bylaws, Article VII, section 2	Technical Liaison Group **TLG**	Internet Engineering TaskForce **IETF**

ASO	GNSO	ccNSO	At-Large	Security and Stability Advisory Committee	Root Server System Advisory Committee
Regional Internet Registries AfriNIC APNIC ARIN LACNIC RIPE NCC	gTLD Registries gTLD Registrars IP interests ISPs Businesses Non-Commercial Interests	ccTLD registries (.us, .uk. .au, .it, .be, .nl, etc.)	Internet Users (At-Large Advisory Committee, in conjunction with RALOs) **ALAC**	**SSAC**	**RSSAC**

Figure 8.8
ICANN stakeholders.
Source: ICANN, "ICANN Multi-stakeholder Model."

profit-making opportunities. All of this strengthened entrepreneurship as the dominant organizational principle for the authoritative management of cyberspace access and shows how the private sector assumed responsibility for the governance of the new information and communications arena—as well as of its own self-governance.

Compared to other decision areas noted here, the governance of the Internet is among the most complex in structure and function. In chapter 9 we point to even greater complexity as cyber management intersects with the activities of international institutions and NGOs focusing on a central issue on the global agenda, namely, sustainable development.[7]

Cyberspace has enabled the creation and expansion of an increasingly significant decision entity, namely, vast networks of transnational fugitive groups, including criminal organizations, terrorist groups, and other non-legal entities. Generally referred to as "mafias," these entities are responsible for much of the world's underground profit-making activities.[8] Moreover, illegal activity is on the rise, and these groups become especially relevant if they are acting as proxies for a sovereign state. It is difficult to assign responsibility for malfeasance, which adds one more dimension of uncertainty to an already very uncertain world.

The past decades have seen the emergence of the global civil society, an aggregation of individuals and groups that has been greeted with varying degrees of enthusiasm.[9] The global civil society is the overarching constituency of the global commons in its environmental, social, and cyber dimensions. As such, it is not a decision entity or a formal constituency in the proper sense of these terms, but it has a voice in the world. The term *global citizen* is often used in this context. Connectivity to cyber venues greatly enhances the consolidation of civil groups into larger aggregates and facilitates political expression and political participation. We have already seen the enhanced politicization of the natural environment with the politics surrounding change.

Could cyberspace assume some features of the tragedy of the commons? The tragedy is that when more villagers put more and more cattle out to graze, the commons is destroyed. Classically, the responsible actors can be identified, and there is no doubt where the collective remedy must be sought. In contrast to the global analogy, however, the individual "villagers" in the cyber context may not be known; they have no legal standing other than through the state system. But there is some indication of potential spoilage of the cyber pastureland. As a man-made feature of the fourth image, it is rapidly becoming politicized. Serious political contentions arise concerning both the underlying problems and the potential solutions.

One of the distinctive modalities of cyberpolitics discussed in chapter 6 pertains to contentions over the architecture and management of cyberspace. Indeed, recently formulated notions surrounding the "command of the commons," as expressed in military and security circles, may be more readily applicable to the management or governance of cyberspace than as a reflection of an emergent cyber commons. But a critical reality remains: all of these actors, agents, and entities operate on the common global landscape, a landscape inhabited by populations, endowed with resources, and operating at different levels of technology. They are each driven by different motivations, have different goals and objectives, follow different rules of operation, and are subject to variable forms of regulation, if any. They all make decisions that can have an impact on others as well as on the global system.

We now turn to the master variables, the core drivers that lead to the propensity of countries to generate lateral pressure and extend behavior outside national boundaries. The differential growth and expansion of the master variables within and across states significantly alter the nature of the global landscape and the character of the playing field. These differentials also influence the relative power and capabilities of actors and decision entities and contribute to the dynamics of globalization.

8.2   Global Parameters and Globalization

Recognizing the interconnections among the master variables, we begin with population dynamics and then turn to resources and technology. To simplify, if there is one overarching global dilemma, it is shaped by the extent to which the problems exceed the current capacity or the willingness to manage them and the degree to which they constitute a threat to the social and the natural environments The core issue is the difference between two notional rates of change, noted earlier: changes in the loads on the global system and changes in the available capabilities to manage the loads. What are the critical loads? Where are the major capabilities?

Population Dynamics

By definition, the global constituency consists of all the people in the world. Population growth has been a characteristic feature of the global system throughout the twentieth century, even with declines in birth rates in industrialized countries. According to the Population Reference Bureau, "Each day the global population grows by 219,000 people" (Klesius 2002, 103). Figure 8.9 shows the well-known population trend

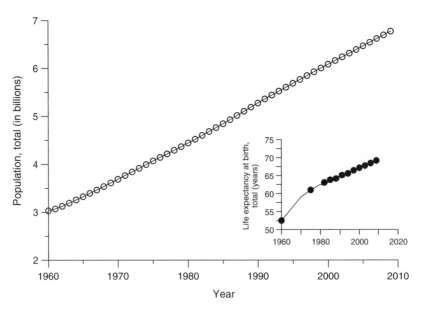

Figure 8.9
Global population and life expectancy at birth, 1960–2010.
Source: Data from the World Bank: World Development Indicators.

line for the years 1960–2010; less appreciated is the improvement in life expectancy over the same span of years, shown in the inset. But these improvements are far from compelling.

The parable of the tragedy of the commons has helped define the nature of the population-anchored dilemmas and the range of solutions, as well as provide a common context for discussion. Several interconnected population trends are relevant to the demographic realities of the twenty-first century, all legacies of the twentieth century. Among the most significant are the drop in birth rates, the increase in the human life span,[10] the youth factor,[11] and the aging of the global population. According to the UN, the number of people aged sixty years and over worldwide will almost triple between 2000 and 2050 (United Nations 2004b, 4).[12] Jointly, these trends shape the global demography.

The population across the globe (the demand side) and the resources required to meet that population's needs (the supply side) are unevenly distributed. This unevenness is accompanied by differences across societies in health and physical well-being.[13] The inverse relationship between level of consumption and unmet basic needs—illustrating the differentials worldwide—is evident in patterns of life expectancy at birth. When this variable is combined with other population variables within and across national boundaries, we can observe pathways through which changes occur in the overall demographic structure of the state and its profile, and hence of the overall state system.[14]

Since time immemorial, people have been on the move.[15] Cityward movement within territorial boundaries is an almost universal trend. At this writing, only three of the ten largest megacities in the world—defined as urban concentrations of 10 million or more—are located in industrialized countries.[16] The movement of people across territorial boundaries has already influenced the configuration of world politics, and in most advanced countries it has shaped the contours of domestic conflict and contention.[17] Many industrialized as well as developing states are beginning to consider cross-border migration issues and the skill set of migrants as central to overall foreign policy concerns[18]—thus illustrating that knowledge intensity and knowledge networking are increasingly significant of international relations.[19] The patterns of population movements in 2008, shown in figure 8.10, attest to the pervasiveness of the demographic globalization process itself.[20] Of the many correlates of international migration, one of the more salient pertains to the volume of remitted earnings of people working overseas. Not only do remittances demonstrate a steady upward trend, but by the middle of the 1990s, remittances were consistently greater than official capital flows.[21]

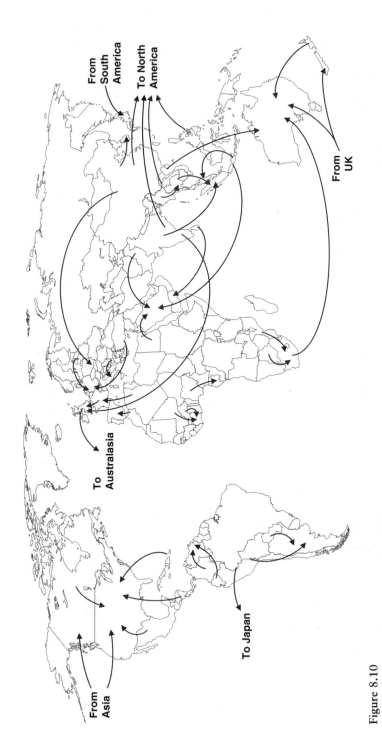

Figure 8.10
Patterns of international migration, 2008.
Source: Peter Stalker, "Interactive map of flows," *Stalker's Guide to International Migration,* 2008.

But people do not always move voluntarily. They also relocate because they are faced with direct threats to their security and survival—demographic dislocations impelled by necessity, not by choice.[22] By the turn of the twenty-first century the number of people so affected was close to 60 million. The erosion of life-supporting properties for any reason can be an immediate and proximate cause of migration, generating what are now known as environmental refugees. Invariably, these situations create pressures on the recipient states or communities. Even in circumstances of security and stability, the movement of people across borders almost always has multiplier effects.[23] Thus, depending on its scale and scope, international migration may influence the overall demographic dynamics, shape claims to resources, and alter the distribution of knowledge and skills. It may even change the profile of the state by precipitating changes in population variables relative to resource and technology variables. When many of the forces operate simultaneously, there may be devastating impacts on society and the environment. These range, for example, from decreased wages and increased inflation to insufficiencies of food, clean water, land, and fuel; from threats to local culture to racist backlashes against newcomers and civil wars; from undermining the political and economic stability of the host country to involving it in cross-border clashes with the refugees' country of origin (Dowty and Loescher 1996).

Most important of all, we must acknowledge the rise of the *virtual community,* composed of those who engage in e-based interactions motivated by shared values, affinities, and other linkages. There are real-world implications of this rise: Saskia Sassen (1991) and others have examined e-communities and their relevance to the globalization process. Because of the diffusion of social networking systems, cyberspace has enabled and empowered virtual communities across national boundaries. Virtual communities may reinforce communities on the ground, create new political entities, or extend the reach of political influence and political discourse.

In short, the demographic factors discussed represent a wide range of demands—directly or indirectly, formally or informally—and all make some claims on the resources of the global system.

Global Resources and Uses

Resources, defined as that which has value, are central to power and politics worldwide. Here we note only some of the more significant resources.

Water is a critical resource, necessary for the survival of all living things. Water itself is a non-substitutable resource, but the sources of water can be substituted. Sources of water include those related to geological conditions—deltas, aquifers, coastal zones, seawater—along with freshwater and reclaimed water, treated by desalination or purification processes.

The authoritative allocation of access to water may well be the starkest manifestation of what is at stake in arguments over who gets what, when, and how. Since the sources of water often cross-national boundaries, the contentions that arise are invariably internationalized. For the most part, scientific and technical solutions pertain to supply-side alternatives or demand-side management, a commonly understood way of thinking about managing water-related problems. The technical elements are fairly straightforward, but the accompanying social, regulatory, and economic strategies are more complex and often more contentious.

As a source of food, the *agriculture* sector reflects the interactions among population, resources, and technology. Agriculture encompasses such activities as cultivating soil, producing crops and fish, and raising livestock.[24] Common problems include deteriorating water quality, the destruction of aquatic ecosystems, potential climate-related impacts, and disappearing wetlands. The sustainability problems are well documented and increasingly understood. Sources of threats to these life-supporting activities include chemicals and pollutants, damage to ecosystems, and the socioeconomic dislocations that take place, including health effects, social impact, and often the unintended effects of the mismanagement or misuse of technology. Concurrently, a wide range of responses have been put forth in different contexts, along with innovative policy principles and policies.[25]

Forests and land use provide a wide range of uses, from producing sources of food and fuels to providing inputs for manufacturing and industrial activities. Recently there has been an increase in forest uses related to environmental and ecological systems, such as carbon dioxide absorption and ecosystem balancing.[26]

Forests and land use, as well as water sources and uses, have been the subject of international agreements, with varying degrees of specificity and actual implementation. For example, when the international community recognized that the loss of biological diversity was so great and that in "the catalog of global environmental insults, extinctions stand out as irreversible" (Pimm et al. 2001), negotiation processes were set in place that eventually to lead to the Convention on Biological Diversity, an international treaty for protecting the diversity of species on earth. [27] This convention has generated a number of reinforcing responses.[28] Notable among these is the attention given to the role of science and technology in the harnessing of biological resources and in their effective protection and management.[29]

As countries industrialize, they become more reliant on advanced technology for energy provision. At that point, access to *energy* rapidly becomes a matter of high politics. For advanced industrial countries, notably the United States, access to energy is closely connected to national security, and the objective features of the domain are increasingly skewed by subjective factors, such as perceptions of threat, which often dominate any assessment of the basic realities at hand. The connection between energy and security creates added complexities associated with debates over who gets what, when, and how.

For developing countries, the energy-security linkage is less salient than the more direct energy-survival connection. As Jose Goldemberg notes, for the less-developed countries, energy is "an essential ingredient of growth and development, which are the fundamental aspirations of 70% of the people who live in the poor countries of Africa, Latin America, the Middle East, and Southeast Asia. However such growth and development—irreversible features of our times —can be detrimental to the environment, and thus there is a basic potential conflict, . . . a delicate balance between economic paralysis, with its grievous consequences, and development has to be sought, and ways will have to be found to promote development while minimizing, but not completely avoiding, environmental problems" (Goldemberg 1995, 1058–1059).

The close coupling of energy and technology makes it nearly impossible to engage in a discussion of energy issues without also making assumptions about *technology*. This holds true for all sources and uses of energy, as well as for any attention to matters of efficiency or equity. The quest for alternative energy sources and alternative production technologies remains a priority for industrialized countries, and is generally pursued to some degree worldwide. But it not necessarily matched by investments in innovative technologies or financial commitments from public or private sources.[30] Figure 8.11 suggests that we are not likely to see dramatic departures from current energy source trends in the future.

Every source of energy has its own supporters and detractors, as the advantages are emphasized and the burdens of realization are obscured. Solar energy remains strong as a long-term source. Contentions relate to the costs in the short run, the uses solar energy can best serve, and the

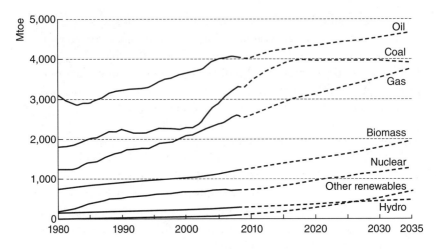

Figure 8.11
Alternative future energy sources.
Source: International Energy Agency, *World Energy Outlook 2010* ©OECD/
International Energy Agency, 2010.

constraints associated with infrastructure for effective distribution and utilization in industrial performance. At this time all options are being considered, some more seriously than others.[31]

If there is one powerful surprise, a legacy of the twentieth century, it is our realization of the environmental correlates of energy use. This is not a strategic issue in the conventional sense, nor can it be dealt with using traditional instruments of military force. The twentieth century did not prepare us for this contingency, a powerful parameter of the twenty-first century. At this writing, the idiom of the energy discourse has taken a sustainability turn. Concepts of sustainable energy are being developed and a wide range of innovative applications is being explored; problems have been identified and solutions proposed. Yet it is always useful to remember that today's solutions may create tomorrow's problems.

These observations are illustrative at best. They are highly selective, but they do reinforce the key point: human populations invariably call on available resources in trying to meet demands. Missing from this observation, however, is the enabling power of technology.

Technology: Applications of Knowledge and Skills

In chapter 4 we focused on knowledge as the underpinning of technology both at the individual level of analysis and at the aggregate level. From a global perspective, industry and manufacturing, trade and finance, and

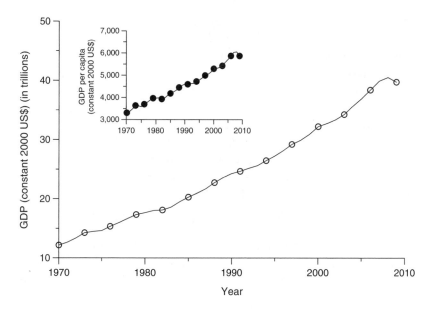

Figure 8.12
Trend in global economic output and per capita output.
Source: Data from the World Bank: World Development Indicators.

mobility and transport are three major technology segments of interest. Figure 8.12 shows the trend in global economic output, with the per capita output shown in the inset. Often, the more complex the mechanical feature of technology are, the greater are the requisite demands for organizational skills.

Industry and manufacturing generate various effluents. Since most of this activity is generated by burning fossil fuels, nitrogen oxides and sulfur oxides are released into the air as waste products, then deposited on the earth as wet or dry acids in a process colloquially known as acid rain. This is only one of the environmental hazards associated with industrial activity.[32] While there is a shift of location of such activities away from industrialized countries and toward developing countries, these shifts cannot necessarily be attributed to differences in environmental regulation. They could be related to policies of site exclusion: it appears that the greater the exclusion based on site characteristics, the more likely it is that industries will relocate "elsewhere."[33]

In general, the electronics industries, as well as all related activities bearing on information technology, are included as a subset of the industry and manufacturing sector in any accounting of economic performance. There exist no exact methods or metrics to evaluate the scale and scope of advances in information technology, but the available evidence suggests that the extent of the "energy-saving" properties of interactions in the new domain cannot be verified until the energy intensity of the infrastructure required for such interactions is known.[34]

Trade in raw materials of various types and from various sources is widely understood to contribute to a range of environmental dislocations. Interestingly, the very fact of trade is a source of uncertainty—perhaps even confusion—regarding attendant environmental implications.[35] For example, carbon dioxide emissions are associated with raw materials extraction, the production of intermediary inputs, the manufacturing of final products, transportation to destinations, final use by the consumer, and post-use disposal.

The challenge of untangling the metrics in this type of product-process interaction amounts to more than the usual statistician's nightmare. Increasingly, the linkage issue is framed as a potential (or real) trade-off between trade and environment—exacerbated by the contentions between the World Trade Organization and the United Nations Environment Programme. Figure 8.13 shows the expansion of world exports of goods and services over the period from 1970 to 2010.

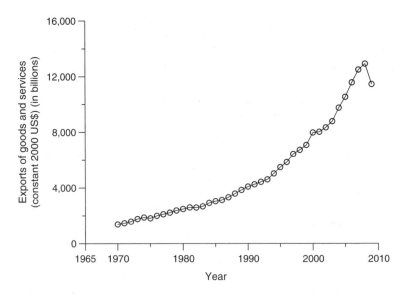

Figure 8.13
Trend in world trade exports.
Source: Data from the World Bank: World Development Indicators.

Finally, we note one additional feature of the world trading system, namely, trade through illegal venues or in illegal substances. The volume and composition of this trade are difficult to determine. By some estimates, counterfeiting and piracy account for 55 percent of illegal global trade and drug trade accounts for another 32 percent; human trafficking and trade in weapons, illegal consumer goods, and environmentally related goods account for the rest (Glenn and Gordon 2007, 35).

Overall, the remarkable growth and expansion throughout the twentieth century and the underlying globalization processes rooted in low politics—the routine activities that constitute day-to-day experience—can rapidly become matters of high politics. Concurrently, the shadow of threats to global sustainability and security borne of high politics further complicates policy debates and developments at all levels.

8.3 Violent Conflict and Threats to Security and Survival

We now turn to warfare,[36] a modal type of human activity with the potential to become all-pervasive in scale and scope. Violence and warfare inflict damage on both the social systems and natural environments. It is difficult to derive an accurate count of the number of conflicts under way at any one time, largely because of differences in the definition of conflict, differences in methods of counting, the duration of the conflicts (which may be episodic over centuries), and so forth.

Despite the large body of literature on incidences of conflict and warfare, there is as yet no fully authoritative source for quantitative indicators of conflict and violence.[37] Nor is there an agreed-upon understanding of the sources and consequences of international violence.[38] Among the concepts that contribute to our understanding of conflict and violence are the *conflict spiral* (e.g., Holsti 1972), the *arms race dynamics* (a term pioneered in Richardson 1960a), and the *security dilemma* (e.g., Herz 1950; Jervis 1997). Figure 8.14 shows the trends in global warfare for the period 1946–2009; see Pinker (2011) for an updated estimate. The annual number of interstate wars and societal wars rise and then decline. If the metrics are correct, there has been a downward trend in violence worldwide since about 1990. This observation is supported by the wide-ranging inquiry undertaken by Goldstein (2011), and supported by Pinker (2011). The decline in episodes of war is consistent with the observed decline in displaced populations. Figure 8.15 shows an upward trend in refugeeism over the period 1964 to 2008 followed a decline in

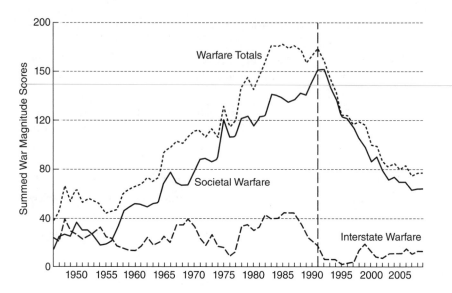

Figure 8.14
Trends in armed conflict, 1946–2009.
Source: Center for Systemic Peace. www.systemicpeace.org/conflict.

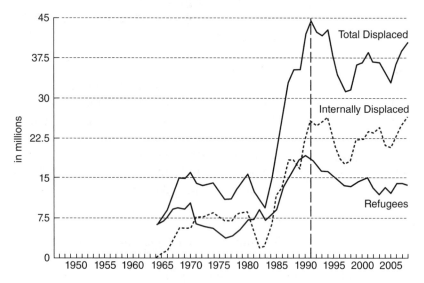

Figure 8.15
Trends in global refugees and displaced populations, 1964–2006.
Source: Center for Systemic Peace. www.systemicpeace.org/conflict.

1990, which is consistent with the decline in the global trends in armed conflict.

A critical addition to the repertoire of conflict and violence is terrorism, a non-state-based type of violence that is dispersed in form and diverse in manifestation. These characteristics make it especially difficult to identify the adversaries and to point to sources of actions and responsibilities for damage. It is also difficult to develop powerful defenses against terrorism.

Clearly, the extent of damage and destruction to the social system and the environment depends on the scale and scope of the violence. Over the past decade, more and more states have become unstable at rates that exceed available capacities to respond or even to retain the basic requisites of sovereignty. Figure 8.16 shows a recent accounting of countries whose populations are at risk due to civil conflict, the most common form of violence worldwide and the greatest source of refugees and displaced persons.

Former UN Secretary-General Kofi Anan is reputed to have warned that "environmental degradation has the potential to destabilize already conflict prone regions, especially when compounded by inequitable access or politicization of access to scarce resources" (Glenn and Gordon 2007, 84). Generally, environmental degradation and erosion of life-supporting properties originate in low politics but can rapidly become matters of high politics. Unsurprisingly therefore, we have also seen numerous instances of state failure. The security and sustainability of the global system as a whole are not neutral with respect to loss of state stability and the destruction of life-supporting properties.

Taking all of the above into account, there is really no simple way to capture the overall impacts of human activities. With appropriate caveats, carbon emissions provide something of an aggregate view of human impacts. Accordingly, we show in figure 8.17 the global trends in carbon emissions, the inset shows carbon emissions per capita.

The international community is now seeking to manage pervasive threats to the social and natural environments and, in so doing, is gradually shifting the policy focus away from traditional trajectories of growth—such as those depicted in this chapter—and toward those that could support transitions to a future characterized by sustainability. This is easier said than done. The proposed solution possibilities are extensive; the likely effectiveness is widely debated. A global consensus is easier to pursue than to reach, let alone turn into effective action.

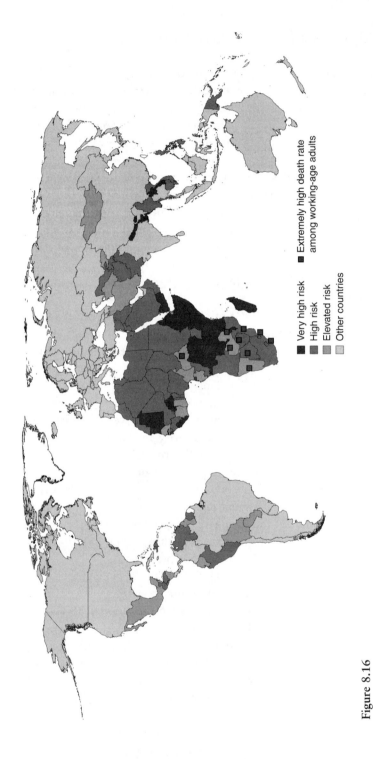

Figure 8.16
Global populations at risk of civil conflict.
Source: Population Action International, "A Decade of Risk, 2000–10: A Global Assessment of the Demographic Risk of Civil Conflict" (map), in *The Security Demographic—Population and Civil Conflict After the Cold War* (Washington, DC: Population Action International, 2003).

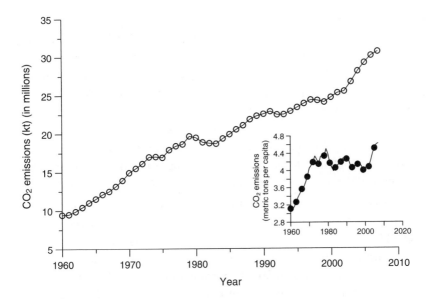

Figure 8.17
Trend in global carbon emissions.
Source: Data from the World Bank: World Development Indicators.

8.4   Management of the Global System

Although a world government does not exist, there is a very large institutional ecosystem designed to manage to the extent possible a specific set of shared problems, and there is a rich historical record of joint action among nations. The research community has long focused on *intents* and *impacts* in its effort to understand and contribute to strengthening current mechanisms and develop new and perhaps more effective ones.[39] Theoretical explanations of *how* and *why* to manage the global system in concert abound. But everyone agrees that international action is required when the problem is pervasive and eludes a unilateral solution.

Toward the end of the twentieth century there was a general consensus that collaboration becomes a global imperative when the following conditions obtain:

• *Damage is traced to legitimate action.*   Far from reflecting pathology and deviance, environmental damage often results from normal, routinized, legitimate behavior that may be condoned, if not lauded, worldwide.

- *Force cannot work.* In such situations, the deployment of troops, the conventional instrument of force, is likely to be ineffective, even useless in that a military response is irrelevant to the nature of the challenge.
- *Compliance is imperative.* The pervasiveness of environmental dislocation leaves no one immune from "attack," and everyone's security is contingent on global cooperation.
- *Doing nothing contributes to the damage done.* By choosing not to take a stand—by doing nothing—nations can accentuate prevailing environmental problems. Thus, the effect of not participating in evolving environmental accords will be equivalent to that of overt opposition.

The turning point came with the United Nations Conference on Environment and Development (UNCED), also known as the Earth Summit. UNCED was a landmark event. For the first time there was a near worldwide recognition of pervasive threats to human societies at all levels created by the growth and expansion of human activities. UNCED was particularly important in consolidating a negotiated agenda and utilizing the convening power of the lead institutions to endow the stated outcomes and proposed intents with a degree of authoritativeness. It also marked the starting point for a process that shaped the intersection of two very different and unrelated trajectories—the construction of cyberspace and the quest for sustainability—and their convergence on the global agenda.

The most comprehensive and far-reaching UNCED document is *Agenda 21: Programme of Action for Sustainable Development* (UNCED 1992b), a statement of goals and objectives to be met on the path toward sustainability. The role of information and communication is defined in this document largely as an enabling mechanism to support decision making; however, it provides an important baseline for tracking the salience of cyberspace in the trajectory toward sustainable development.

At UNCED, sustainable development was taken to mean the process of meeting the needs of present and future generations without damaging the natural environment. The conference sought to engage stakeholders with diverse perspectives and from different parts of the world at each stage in the process.[40] In the initial stage, working groups were appointed to draft the agenda, establish the emphasis, identify the obstacles, and forge an international consensus around the text to be presented at Rio for official intergovernmental endorsement.[41] The drafting process included inputs from a wide range of stakeholders, and the final product represented a negotiated outcome in which the most diverse and diffuse segments of the international community participated.

Agenda 21, the final product of UNCED, presented a program of action along four major issue areas: social and economic goals, resources for development, the role of major group, and mechanisms for implementation of UNCED goals.[42] Establishing goals, however, does not mean they can or will be achieved. But the goals that were defined represent authoritative views of the international community as legitimized by its member states, with inputs from NGOs, the business community, and the politicized segments of civil society, all of which have emerged as decision entities in the global system.

At the UNCED summit, a set of practices was articulated and legitimized. Among these was the concept of public-private partnerships, whose objective was to encourage private foreign investment projects that would, over time, become self-sustaining while also contributing to the sustainability of society. For the most part, the financial plan was to be underwritten by public funds, generally in the form of grants or preferential loans. Various other collaborative measures to support the overall trajectory were discussed, including prospects for monitoring performance, codes of conduct, and promoting voluntary agreements. None of these measures is particularly novel, but their conjunction at UNCED showed a degree of pragmatism in designing an overarching strategy whose implementation is based on voluntary commitment rather than legal obligations.

While the international community is committed, in theory, to the pursuit of trajectories toward sustainability, the concept itself is intensely political in the most conventional view of the term. The UNCED recommendations provide only the broadest guidelines for research, policy, and action.[43] They focus on economy, environment, and society—a useful but limited way to draw attention to the issues at hand. While this perspective continues to dominate policy and academic circles,[44] a more complex and differentiated approach has been adopted by the scientific community, notably with reference to the problems of governance and their solutions at the very early stages.[45]

The Millennium Development Goals, promulgated ten years after UNCED, represent a pragmatic follow-up statement designed specifically to improve the conditions of the poorer segments of the world's population (e.g., Glenn and Gordon 2007). The development of these goals was an important initiative on the overall path toward convergence for cyberspace and sustainability. In the next chapter we explore the logic and reality of this convergence and the increased relevance of cyberspace and sustainability to the overall development process. Especially relevant is the expansion of the use of cyber venues—transcending its relevance to decision making to empower individuals, groups, and societies at all levels of organization.

Perhaps it should come as no surprise that international institutions are increasingly framing their mission and practices in a broader context of human rights and sustainable development, buttressed by supporting global public goods and enhancing security. By definition, the Rio+20 event (or UNCSD 2012, twenty years after the United Nations Conference on Sustainable Development) is anchored in such considerations. Interestingly, the ITU's posture in relation to WCIT-12 also signals such framing. The ITU's collaborative activities with UNESCO, the International Meteorological Organization (WMO), and other international institutions on environmental issues are underscored as part of its activities leading up to Rio+20.

Such trends may be seen as evidence of increasing collaboration among international instructions. Conversely, they could also be interpreted as institution expansion and completion over spheres of influence. In many ways, preparations for Rio+20 induced convergence rather than divergence by assigning different international institutions the lead responsibility for reporting on a sector or issue area. The pervasive and cross-cutting nature of information and communication technologies—cyberspace matters included—provides the ITU with an equally pervasive and cross-cutting position as manager of major issues on the global agenda. These matters are all contextual as we consider the convergence of cyberspace and sustainability.

9

Cyberspace and Sustainability: Convergence on the Global Agenda

Extending the logic of the previous analysis, this chapter explores the emerging synergy between cyberspace (a new arena of interaction) and sustainability (a new initiative for the global system), and their convergence on the global policy agenda. This convergence reflects the conjunction of two processes, the growing pressures for transitions toward sustainability in the real context of human interactions and the expanded, cyber-enabled opportunities for the pursuit of goals and objectives.

We highlight the processes that are effectively integrating traditional and cyber international relations, and the dynamics that support this integration. The empirical basis of the sustainability dilemma is the global burden of growth. The politics—and the cyberpolitics—of sustainability have to do with moving from ambiguity toward greater clarity and, in the process, rewriting the conventional parameters shaping who gets what, when, how, and why. The quest for sustainability—a new policy trajectory—departs from the traditional theories, models, and practices of economic growth that dominated the twentieth century.

The separate processes shaping cyberspace and the imperatives of sustainable development all converged early in the twenty-first century. This convergence, unexpected as it is, results mainly from the properties of cyberspace as we know it and those of sustainability as we seek to frame it, and has been reinforced by the role of knowledge in international forums. Interestingly, both cyberspace and sustainability are relative newcomers to international relations theory, policy, and practice. They are also the target of contention and the subject of debates over uncertainties. Above all, they are powerful manifestations of the sources and consequences of growth, expansion, and globalization.

The foundations for exploring the synergy between cyberspace and sustainability can be traced to major threads running through several chapters of this book. For example, in chapter 3 we identified some of the most significant patterns of cyber access worldwide and differentiated among the various patterns of such participation. In chapter 4 we focused on knowledge and the networking multipliers, which yielded an important perspective on the individual and aggregations. We noted that the articulation of new knowledge objectives is the result of competition in the market for loyalties to alternative global goals. In chapters 5, 6, and 7 we explored politics and cyberpolitics at different levels of analysis, and in chapter 8 we described the characteristic features of the overall global system, with special reference to the sources and consequences of its transformation and change, all of which contributed to the global quest for sustainable development.

In this chapter we first present the basis for the synergy between cyberspace and sustainability, then consider the role of knowledge as a powerful agent creating and reinforcing this synergy in theoretical as well as operational terms. Next we trace the coevolution of cyberspace and sustainability on the global agenda and demonstrate how trajectories of global accord are converging on both sustainability-centered and cyber-focused objectives. We also show that the international community has reached— at least in theory—a consensus that could expand cyber access worldwide and at the same time support transitions toward sustainability.

9.1   The Logic for Synergy

The logic for exploring the synergy between cyberspace and sustainability can be described in the terms of inquiry in *The Social Life of Information* (2000), by John Seely Brown and Paul Duguid. In this book, Brown and Duguid identify six forces unleashed by advances in information technology (IT)—demassification, decentralization, denationalization, despatialization, disintermediation, and disaggregation—which they consider to be fundamental correlates of cyber venues that altered the social fabric in new and powerful ways. Brown and Duguid argue that these forces—we call here the "6 D's"—are critical and distinct properties of the cyber context. Although they do not address growth, development, or sustainability, it is not too much of a stretch to assign these same forces central roles in the nascent domain of sustainable development. At the very least, massification, materialization, spatialization, and centralization reinforce the ways in which human beings continue to stress and damage the natural environment. Clearly, none of the stresses or impacts is intentional; rather, they are largely the by-products of routine human activities.

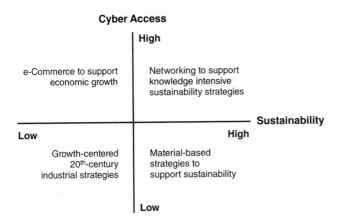

Cyber Access

High

e-Commerce to support economic growth

Networking to support knowledge intensive sustainability strategies

Sustainability

Low   High

Growth-centered 20ᵗʰ-century industrial strategies

Material-based strategies to support sustainability

Low

Figure 9.1
Illustrative strategies for cyberspace and sustainability.

Of course, neither cyberspace nor sustainability can be reduced to the 6 D's; nonetheless, these forces may harbor both mutually reinforcing dynamics and hidden complexities. For example, while any alternative to continued growth will involve a great deal of dematerialization, we cannot yet argue that an expansion of cyberspace will also have the same effect. As a practical matter, the 6 D's, individually and jointly, are currently located at the periphery of contemporary theory in terms of social relations, political behavior, power politics, and economic growth.

To illustrate the synergy argument more specifically, we identify in figure 9.1 four cases across two issues, cyber access and sustainability. The entries in the quadrants show different types of situations in policy and practice and different modalities of the synergy at hand. In principle, we anticipate that development strategies in the twenty-first century will increasingly shift away from the bottom left quadrant and toward the top right quadrant. Such an outcome would be contingent on reducing barriers to cyber access and on the acceptance of sustainable development as the dominant paradigm shaping the authoritative allocation of value in terms of who gets what, when, and how. It would also be contingent on a continued convergence of cyberspace and sustainability, which are two independent processes with no obvious common origins.

To increase the likelihood of the anticipated shift toward knowledge-intensive sustainability solutions, and in a situation of relatively underdeveloped scientific and technological foundations for sustainable development, it is imperative that existing knowledge of all types be readily accessible to interested communities everywhere. Over time, we expect access to cyber venues to reinforce the synergy and to improve performance along the cyber and the sustainability trajectories.

9.2 Convergence on the Global Agenda

With the convening of the World Summit on the Information Society (WSIS), a clear connection was forged between sustainability issues and the pursuit of information-related objectives. This connection reinforces and is reinforced by the Millennium Development Goals promulgated by the United Nations introduced in chapter 8.

World Summit on the Information Society
The World Summit on the Information Society is especially relevant for our purposes as it was convened to bring information technologies and cyber functionalities to bear on the challenges of development, specifically strategies to reduce poverty. The conference became a major landmark in the establishment of global accord, and with its explicit mandate for facilitating developmental strategies, the synergy between cyberspace and sustainability took on an institutional form. If, as posited in chapter 1, cyberspace constitutes an emerging dimension of international relations, then international institutional responses should exhibit an observable cyber presence. And if, as also posited in chapter 1, the increased knowledge intensity of economic activities is enhancing the policy relevance of knowledge in the international arena, particularly in the domain of sustainable development, we would expect knowledge content to be a critical element in the articulation of policy responses to sustainability challenges. Currently, several agencies of the United Nations, notably UNESCO, are adopting the goal (or idiom) of pursuing knowledge and evidence-based policy.

The WSIS will be remembered more for its introduction of a new issue on the evolving agenda for international collaboration than for its immediate effects. That the virtual is now formally recognized as a domain for institutionalized international collaboration is itself evidence of the salience of the critical nexus at this point in time. At the same time, the WSIS exemplifies cyberpolitics in international relations par excellence.

The WSIS focused on information technology (IT) and assumed that greater use of available technologies would enable increased access to content worldwide. In practical terms, it established a direct connection between advances in information and communication technologies, especially the forging of cyberspace, and the new global priorities focusing on transitions toward sustainable development. An important WSIS target is to render half the world's population cyber accessible by the year 2015.

The summit was organized in two phases. The first, held in Geneva, Switzerland, on December 10–12, 2003, sought to identify the necessary steps to bring technologies to smaller, more isolated countries. Phase 1 concluded with a Declaration of Principles and a Plan of Action. The Declaration of Principles defined the countries' commitment to using information and communications technology to benefit citizens of all countries by helping to stop pandemics, allowing freedom of speech, eradicating poverty, promoting education, and working toward similar social goals. The document stated the signatories would work toward "digital opportunity for all," develop many more public access spots in Third World countries, and increase opportunities for e-training for those unfamiliar with recent advances in technology.

The Plan of Action focused on actions to achieve an "inclusive Information Society" and required governments to allow cyber access at many public places, such as libraries, schools, government departments, hospitals, and research centers. It encouraged governments of all countries to begin taking action by 2005, by establishing partnerships, discussing e-strategies with stakeholders, exploring the creation of technological portals for poor citizens, investing in software development and research for their countries, and publishing information about their conclusions and successes with technological advances. The Plan of Action also encouraged governments to form partnerships with private organizations, explore connectivity systems, promote satellite services for less densely populated areas, and assist in the production of communications equipment. Governments were required to report their actions in this regard for presentation in phase 2 of the summit.

The Declaration of Principles formally tied the WSIS initiative to the UN's Millennium Development Goals. What appeared initially as a technologically oriented summit rapidly took on many features of cyberpolitics. For example, the summit contributed to the mobilization of civil rights groups that did not feel the digital divide was of particular salience and argued that by bringing the Internet and technological advances to less-developed countries, the UN would be denying the rights of citizens to live as they always had, without that technology. Similarly, participants could not agree on the role of Internet technology in governance within states (i.e., e-Government). Overall, relevant to the WSIS agenda were matters related to the governance of cyberspace that pertained to the formation of authoritative allocation of values, and a working group was established to examine the progression of Internet governance.

As noted in chapter 7, the second phase of the WSIS took place in Tunis, Tunisia, on November 16–18, 2005. The official goals were to create an ongoing strategy for resolving the critical differences in cyber access worldwide and to develop a plan to provide affordable Internet access to 50 percent of the world's population by 2015. This segment of the WSIS undertaking, too, was not devoid of political contentions. For example, several reporting sources noted that the Association for Progressive Communications had earlier claimed that Internet governance deprives people of their basic human rights. They sought to ensure that the Internet would be fully accessible to citizens in developing countries before world leaders began to implement technologically advanced methods of e-government. Phase 2 concluded with the Tunis Commitment and the Tunis Agenda for the Information Society. The international community agreed that the progress of each country should be evaluated periodically to ensure that each country was reaching its goals as agreed upon at the summit.

The Tunis Commitment affirmed the representatives' support for the two documents formulated in Geneva during phase 1, as well as their commitment to building an information society enabled by technological advancements. The representatives promised an enabling environment for their citizens to use technology, and agreed to strive to bridge the digital divide by allowing increased access to new technologies and creating new opportunities for access by everyone—adults of both sexes, children, disabled persons, and others traditionally lacking full access.

The Tunis Agenda for the Information Society focused on specific actions rather than on identifying problems and goals. It called on the international community to promote the spread of technology in developing countries and to assist in financing technologies in these countries. Its goals included urging low-income countries to provide radio and television programs to citizens and endorsing increasing multilingualism online to enable people everywhere to engage in the retrieval of information and knowledge.

Jointly, the two segments of the WSIS contributed to endogenizing its objectives in the overall global agenda such that formal strategies for sustainability, framed in a different venue and in an earlier period, were taken into account. In this way, information technologies and cyber venues were embedded in the institutional fabric and international processes shaping the future of the global agenda. In an effort to build continuity in policy, planning, and performance, the UN Secretary-General was asked to hold another meeting of the Internet Governance Forum in 2006 to discuss the progress as a result of this plan and to update the plan within five years based on its success. Governments were also asked to identify any aspects of the plan that would require additional outside resources.

Both the WSIS preparatory phase and the eventual follow-up events were designed to address the Millennium Development Goals, thus reinforcing the connection between development challenges and cyber access plus capabilities.

Millennium Development Goals

The Millennium Development Goals (MDGs), introduced in chapter 8, an important and overarching initiative during the second part of the twentieth century, provide institutional connection between the vision in *Agenda 21* and the goals of the WSIS initiative. As such, the MDGs serve as critical linkage mechanisms in the evolution of global accord on sustainability goals.

The MDG initiative was organized to focus on reducing poverty and marginalization and demonstrates a shift toward collective responsibility for the least advantaged individuals and societies on a worldwide basis. As with the UN's *Agenda 21*, the MDGs are statements of general principles, intents, and directions of action. They illustrate a gradual shift away from problem definition to shared responsibility. But they are not legally binding. Rather, they express specific goals, with reference to targets for attainment by 2015. Interestingly, the MDGs reflect the view of the global *problematique* from the perspective of the disadvantaged populations. Attainment of the goals expressed would result in the eradication of extreme poverty, universal private education, increased gender equality for women, reduced child mortality, better maternal health, arrested trends in major diseases, greater environmental sustainability, and collaborative partnering strategies for development and other key benefits. The proposed strategy is global in scale and scope, but its implementation efforts target individuals and groups in local contexts.

This round of global accords points to the learning process as the international community seeks to reach agreement on the policy implications of the evolving cyberspace-sustainability synergy:

• Since the MDG goals are the outcome of negotiation among diverse states and non-state actors, the result demonstrates broadening participation in global discourse.

• Since states are required to report on their performance toward attainment of the MDG targets, the result is to create roots of accountability.

• Since non-state agencies, the business community, the IT industry, and other interests involved in the framing, formulation, and conduct of the WSIS all participated under the auspices of a UN task force, the result is to legitimize the process as well as the expected products.

• Since both the preparatory phase for the WSIS and the eventual follow-up were designed to buttress the MDGs, the result is an emerging institutional connection between the nature of the development challenges and the empowering potentials of cyber access for facilitating responses to recognized challenges.

Institutional Alignments for Cyber Management

Joint action among nations has increasingly assumed greater scope and greater breadth. The international community's responses are often seen as a set of moving targets in conjunction with equally shifting trajectories, and a better understanding of development and sustainability may generate improved response modalities. Such improvements would be expected to involve political adjustments, both in defining newer understandings and organizing state-based responses, and in taking into account the views of and pressures from a wide range of governmental and nongovernmental entities.

Theoretical explanations of how and why abound, along with questions about intents and impacts and matters of methods and models related to types of international responses. Underlying the differences in orientations and approaches is the presumption of a shared responsibility among states in the international system, and this commonality necessitates a degree of jointness in responses. Although the process of coordinated international action has largely been piecemeal, the overall effects are cumulative.

In practice, the development of international management modes accompanies the evolution of shared understandings, a common formulation of the nature of the problem (not necessarily of its origins), and a joint quest for modes of coordinated action. International accords themselves are the end product of one type of process, that of reaching an agreement—on goals, substance, management, policy, or institutional requirements.

This process, ambiguous and uncertain as it often seems, is predicated on the recognition that the state is not able to exert effective jurisdiction over cross-border processes. Non-state actors are increasingly important, and at a minimum their participation in and compliance with emerging accords are necessary. Moreover, the hierarchical networks of influence (local to global and global to local) create added complexities that cannot be ignored. Once some form of consensus is reached, collaboration is pursued as a goal.

Consistent with the central theme of this chapter, the convergence of cyberspace and sustainability, we turn to a three-step rough mapping of international institutional responsibilities for the management of information and communications technologies relevant to cyberspace and its intersection with the development agenda. Based on a report of the G8 Digital Opportunity task force and summarized by David Souter (2008), the alignment of responsibilities cross two axes. One pertains to the scope of international decision making on information and communications technologies, ranging from narrow to broad. The other is about the results of such decision making, ranging from hard to soft results.

Given the complexity of the management structure to date—a result of the greater number of decision entities worldwide, the salience of the private sector in cyber management, the emergence of a global agenda on sustainable development, and the increased focus on the deployment of knowledge for improving the human condition—we begin with the institutional responsibilities central to the very operations of the Internet itself and associated functionalities, and then turn to other agencies and institutions.

Figure 9.2 shows the responsibilities of three international institutions, two public and one private. Of relevance here is not only the distinct spheres of responsibility but the overlapping scope and results of decision making. For example, the responsibilities of the World Trade Organization (WTO) have to do with trade among sovereign states. The WTO is also concerned with standards, policy coordination, and development assistance, over and above matters of law and regulation. Its responsibilities overlap with those of the International Telecommunication Union, whose mandate provides it with a claim on all matters related to telecommunications. Then there is the Internet Corporation for Assigned Names and Numbers (ICANN), a private corporation created by the United States for the management of common resources, notably the Internet and its operations, discussed in chapter 8.

Figure 9.3 extends the view of institutional management by listing the responsibilities of international organizations and the Internet Engineering Task Force (IETF), a private sector entity. This figure shows the

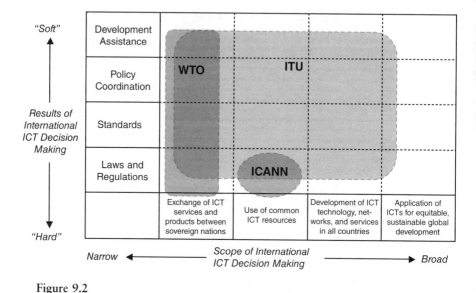

Figure 9.2
WTO, ITU, and ICANN.
Source: Drake and Wilson 2008, 434. By permission of the MIT Press.

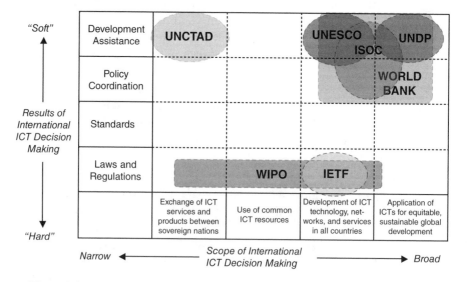

Figure 9.3
International agencies and private sector organizations.
Source: Drake and Wilson 2008, 435. By permission of the MIT Press.

concentration on development assistance, with different agencies focused on their respective mandates and constituencies. The figure also highlights the role of the World Intellectual Property Organization (WIPO) and the IETF. Overall, the focus of management has shifted from core Internet-related functionalities to broader management and developmental considerations. In this connection, note should be made of the intersecting responsibilities of UNESCO, the UN Development Programme, the Internet Society (ISOC), and the World Bank, all of which have adjusted their policies and programs to respond to sustainability challenges.

Figure 9.4, the last in this display of a complex international institutional ecosystem, shows the involvement of private sector actors and entities, for-profit and not-for-profit. The scope of interests and their concentration should be noted as they illustrate a wide range of constituencies and hence of priorities, as should the designation of "civil society," a relatively new addition to the conventional displays of relevant actors in international relations.

If the institutional responsibilities noted above were to be displayed in one figure, it would be nearly impossible to understand their respective foci of activities. At the same time, this three-figure representation underscores the high degree of intersection in spheres of responsibility and

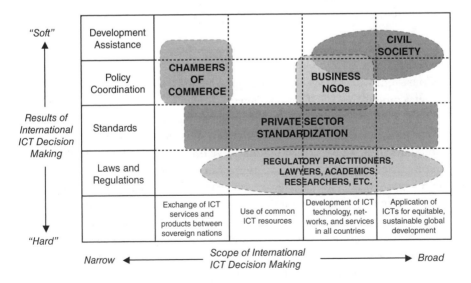

Figure 9.4
Nonstate institutions and private entities.
Source: Drake and Wilson 2008, 435. By permission of the MIT Press.

influence. It is not difficult to expect potential institutional competition and contentions. In the previous chapter we noted the increased density of decision-making entities worldwide. Here we point to the enhanced intersection and overlapping domains of activity and responsibility. If there is one lesson we have learned from institutionalist theories in international relations, it is that organizations generally seek to expand rather than reduce their scope of influence.

In sum, if cyberspace is increasingly being colonized, then the domain of sustainable development is being colonized even more intensively. Sustainability is understood to be of relevance to all societies everywhere, and the global accords surrounding transitions toward sustainability are being supported by efforts to expand cyber access. As an arena of interaction, cyberspace has created potentials for a "weightless world," a term coined by Diane Coyle (1997). This is a world of reduced material use, greater efficiencies in all activities, and improved environmental conditions. International institutions have taken the lead in arguing for the deployment of cyberspace in support of sustainability strategies. Concurrently, the growing demand for new knowledge to help manage transitions toward a sustainable future further reinforces the relevance of cyberspace in the process. To increase the likelihood of the anticipated shift toward knowledge-informed solution strategies to the sustainability dilemma, it is imperative that existing knowledge of all types be readily accessible to all interested communities everywhere.

9.3   Knowledge Imperatives for Cyberpolitics

Consistent with the synergy between cyberspace and sustainability—and their convergence on the global agenda—we propose to draw on lessons in the sustainability domain that are highly relevant to cyberpolitics in international relations. The lessons are derived from experience with the Global System for Sustainable Development (GSSD), a multilingual knowledge system focusing on the uses of cyber venues for knowledge provision, access, and retrieval, with particular emphasis on all aspects of sustainable development. The system was designed at a time when sustainable development was a new issue in both the scholarly and the policy communities, with little foundational knowledge or empirical grounding.[1]

The same situation holds today in the domain of cyberpolitics. Despite a growing literature on cyber-related issues in the study of international relations, a body of knowledge on this general domain has yet to be developed. There is no consensual view on these issues or on what constitutes data, analysis, cases, comparisons, or any of the usual tools of inquiry in the social sciences. Since people in many countries, notably the developing states, may experience difficulty obtaining access to knowledge, even when cyber access is already assured, and reducing barriers to knowledge development, retrieval, and distribution is a growing concern worldwide.

Accordingly, we point to three knowledge-building imperatives essential to the development of cyberpolitics as a knowledge domain. These are formulating the *domain ontology*, leveraging *knowledge networking*, and creating the *multilingual capability*. All three are foundational to cyberpolitics in international relations.

Domain Ontology

The first imperative is about establishing knowledge coherence and organization by developing an internally consistent method for determining, identifying, and connecting different facets of the issue in question in an empirically verifiable way. In the cyber domain, the operational constraint is less the dearth of knowledge, data, information, published materials, raw observations, and so on than it is the absence of internally consistent logics to help organize and make best use of existing materials. Codification, that is, establishing some common "coordinates," is essential to building the stock of new knowledge (Foray 2006).

The GSSD ontology of sustainability is anchored in the master variables—population, resources, and technology—and their constituent elements and rooted in an integrated theoretical framework, and rests on empirically based core organizing principles.[2] This case demonstrates not only the fundamental role of ontology but also its foundational function, that is, to enable and support knowledge development, sharing, use, and reuse.

An initial or base-line ontology of cyberpolitics would greatly enhance existing knowledge, facilitate knowledge development, and, given the rapid rate of change in the structure and functions of cyber access and cyber features, help to take into account and incorporate key features of new knowledge into the base-line ontology.

Ontology itself carries several specific benefits. The first is conceptual: in light of the increasing importance of cyberpolitics, a holistic and integrative view buttressed by constituent elements and their linkages would be a major step in constructing knowledge about the different features of cyberspace and cyberpolitics, and about the interlinkages.[3] The second is strategic: ontology facilitates navigating through the growing volume of materials in cyberspace and enables access to cutting-edge analysis, innovative technologies, and multidisciplinary knowledge. The third benefit is cohesion: defining the dimensions of cyberpolitics provides varieties of perspectives and signals situations in which the solution to one problem becomes the source of another. The fourth is functional: it helps guide the use and reuse of knowledge as needed.[4] The fifth benefit is operational: ontology is central to the design of web-based systems for the management, e-distribution, and sharing of knowledge devoted to the issues in question. All of these features are important in the development of new knowledge.

Knowledge Networking

Leveraging the power of networking is the second major imperative for cyberpolitics in international relations. Many countries, especially the developing states, may experience difficulty locating knowledge of relevance even when cyber access is assured. Networking practices help reduce barriers to knowledge access by drawing on the power of collaboration. Barriers to knowledge invariably constrain economic activity and may also impede involvement in political discourse and participation in policy debates.[5] It is important to recognize the value of supporting top-to-bottom as well as bottom-to-top knowledge provision, communication, innovation, and diffusion as well as the use and reuse of knowledge. This dual path enables both the globalization and the localization of knowledge.

Among the potential benefits of networking in the domain of cyberpolitics is extending reach via the networking multiplier. Earlier we posited the basic multiplier and proposed that networking activities can help different types of functions diffuse throughout society and the economy. Another benefit of networking relates to managing new demands for knowledge—or demands for new knowledge. An increase in knowledge provision via networking can even lead to changes in the basic ontology and help to update knowledge. And, as noted in earlier chapters, the added, and politically important, benefit is that networking contributes to the consolidation and empowerment of constituency.[6]

Multilingual Capability

The third imperative for cyberpolitics in international relations is created by the remarkable growth in cyber access and participation and an expansion in the use of languages other than English. With powerful linguistic barriers still existing worldwide, multilingual functionalities are needed to reduce impediments to understanding in cyber interactions. Such functionalities should allow people to express themselves in their own language and idioms and likewise for others to understand and to engage in their own language and idioms.[7]

Whether these factors constitute essential elements of a viable solution strategy for understanding and tracking cyberpolitics in the longer run, and whether the strategy is scalable and portable, remain to be seen. Based on the GSSD initiative, we believe that this approach can be generalized and applied to many other issues and aspects of cyberpolitics in international relations.

Karl W. Deutsch observed that relevant knowledge depends on four things: the interests of the knower, the characteristics of situation to be known, the methods by which situation features can be determined, and the "system of symbols and physical facilities by which the data selected are recorded and used for later application" (Deutsch et al. 1957, 5–6). Furthermore, understanding any issue or problem involves more than just producing a good representation of it; it also requires taking into account relevant situational features. The lessons of the Global System for Sustainable Development are especially relevant in light of the coevolution of cyberspace and sustainability on the global agenda. In these areas as in others, broadening the discourse about any issue area—the problems, the issues at stake, the questions to be addressed, and the designing of solution strategies—will enhance its understanding and the wisdom that comes with it.

10
Conclusion: Lateral Realignment and the Future of Cyberpolitics

The properties of cyberspace are difficult to reconcile and address effectively by traditional theory or modes of inquiry in the analysis of world politics. This chapter pulls together the diverse threads of this book to highlight the new imperatives for twenty-first-century international relations theory created by various forms of cyberpolitics. Cyberspace has shaped new, fluid, and ever changing spaces—as well as structures and processes—for the conduct of international relations. Many of the cyber issues addressed in this book have already contributed to political realignments that are affecting international politics today. It is not too soon to consider alternative visions for the future of cyberspace and the attendant implications for international implications broadly defined.

10.1   Lateral Realignment

Lateral pressure theory addresses the roots and the dynamics of transformation and change, but we must render our theoretical and policy perspectives congruent with constructed cyber domain and the realities it is creating.[1] The addition of the cybersphere to the social and environmental spheres as a new context for individual, social, economic, and political behavior has transformed twenty-first-century international relations by introducing notable shifts in demands and capabilities, actors and interests, influences and leverages, as well as globalization and localization, at all levels of analysis and in all parts of the world.

The Old and the New
For the first time in human history, global processes are transcending the traditional borders of the state system in pervasive and transformative ways. As a result, the traditional response strategies and rules of conduct appear inconsistent with the emerging—and rapidly changing—empirical

parameters. This disjunction is a powerful aspect of contemporary reality. Central among the international legacies of the twentieth century are the end of the Cold War and the rise of the United States as the only great power. Another is the unprecedented increase in the number of sovereign states (most notably as a result of the decolonization process, the breakup of the Soviet Union, or the outcome of civil war), all with claims on the international community. There are new regional centers of power with new political aspirations, competing for resources and influence on a global scale. In addition, the proliferation of international institutions with mandates to facilitate development and sustainability has created a legitimate mechanism to extend influence deep into the structure of the state system, most often in developing regions. On a worldwide basis, international institutions also seek to draw on the power and influence of the private sector in ways that appear consistent with their legal status and formal mandates.

We have seen the expansion of private and public interests, coupled with the creation of new markets and innovative practices, shape overlapping spheres of influences and ever fluid playing fields—each governed by distinct rules and regulations—making it increasingly difficult to understand and track the various systems of interaction. This process reinforces the power of the private sector in many parts of the world and on almost all issues. In some cases we observe something akin to competing sovereignties and overlapping jurisdictions within the same territorial boundaries as the private sector seeks to meet its interests or the international institutions work to meet particular objectives.

Various types of non-state actors, notably those focusing on development assistance and humanitarian needs, religious groups, or those with a distinctive ideological or political agenda, seem to be growing faster than our ability to track and assess their roles and responsibilities, constraints and contributions, threats and vulnerabilities. Non-state actors of various types are anchored deeply in the global landscape.

During the last decades of the twentieth century changes in the nature of conflict and violence were evident across the globe.[2] Wars of liberation from colonial rule have been superseded by conflicts waged by non-state actors, expanded civil conflicts, and a wide range of terrorist initiatives. Conflicts between major powers over spheres of influence have been replaced by contentions over control of these spheres by various local entities. (Afghanistan is a good example.) More important, however, is the notable decline in armed conflict during the last decade of the twentieth century, as discussed in chapter 8.

An additional legacy of importance is the introduction of the environmental domain into political and social discourse at all levels of decision making. Though still anchored more in low politics than might otherwise be the case, environmental factors are not marginal to twenty-first-century realities.[3] A related concern, sustainability, is now central to the international agenda.

Each of these factors individually contributes to lateral realignment, and together they create pressures on the "normal" mechanisms of assessments, analysis, and responses. All of these issues are significant in their own right. Especially important, however, is that they are also contextual in nature. They constitute the landscape on which patterns of cyber access continue to shape distinctive and unique modes of lateral realignment.

The well-known international systems of the twentieth century, which are generally characterized by hierarchical power relations, such as those with bipolar, multipolar, or unipolar structures, are being replaced by new structural configurations characterized by the diffusion of power, different types of asymmetries and a relatively weak hierarchy, if any. New asymmetries and their complexities are already taking shape, replacing the seemingly entrenched vertical structures of power and influence. When we factor in the effects of cyberspace—especially the dramatic expansion of cyber access in all parts of the world, the growth in "voicing" and cyber participation, global civil society, and the new opportunities afforded by access to cyberspace—it becomes apparent that cyber venues are more than enablers of power and influence. They have become the critical drivers of the ongoing realignments, the means by which all actors at all levels of analysis pursue their goals and objectives. Furthermore, they have assumed constitutive features of their own.[4]

Signals of Realignment

We now turn to some significant "new" features of the international system, and the conduct of international relations. While state-based and still anchored in the twentieth-century conceptions of purpose, politics and power, the operational context is defined by twenty-first-century realities. Here we note only some of the most dominant factors.

First are the unmistakable new challenges to *national security,* with new sources of vulnerability (cyber threats), new dimensions of national security (cyber security), and new drivers of fear and uncertainty.

Second are new types of *asymmetries,* such as the unprecedented potential for weaker actors to influence or even threaten stronger actors (e.g., by penetrating the U.S. government's computer systems). Conversely, we observe the emergence of new symmetries (e.g., the ability of states to penetrate the computers of other states). In either case, we are witnessing a potentially powerful shift in the nature of the game.

Third is the empowerment of *new actors,* some with formal identities and others without. These include cyber-centered national actors (e.g., those that exercise access control or denial),[5] new sets of non-state actors (e.g., new commercial entities, agents, creators of new products, processes and markets, or proxies for state actors), and new criminals (too varied to list and too anonymous to identify). All things considered, the proliferation of actors with international scope is creating unprecedented types of uncertainties and ambiguities in the international system.

Fourth are the *institutions for cyber management* and the contentions they engender. These are largely private sector institutions created specifically to enable cyber interactions, such as ICANN and IETF, or to support cyber security, such as CERTS). International contentions arise surrounding the membership, mandates, and management of these institutions as developed countries perceive excessive U.S. control and developing countries seek access to the management structures already in place.

Fifth are the increasingly *interconnected politics* in the kinetic and the cyber domains. In the United States, for example, the Patriot Act, adopted by Congress in response to the tragic events of September 11, 2001, included provisions enabling the government to monitor Internet communications without obtaining prior permission from the Justice Department. The presumption was that cyberspace provided potential terrorists with a clear venue for undermining the security of the United States. President Obama's Sixty Day Review of the cyber situation in early 2009 also recognized critical vulnerabilities and was designed to bring cyberspace into the policy domain. The Wikileaks episodes of 2010 and the tight coupling of the kinetic and virtual domains—regarded by the United States as a major security crisis—showed in unambiguous ways the politicization and disruptiveness of cyberspace. Responses to the cable leaks varied across the international landscape, but in general, most countries viewed this episode as a threat to their sovereignty and security—even if they were not the target of the leaks—and recognized the importance of developing preventative measures.

Sixth are the various types of *cyber conflicts and contentions* that create new challenges to the stability and security of the state system. We have focused on major types of conflicts and contentions, and broad manifestations of each, rather than on specific incidents or events. For example, when we explored the contentions over internet architecture and the management of cyberspace we pointed to notable cases, such as the end-to-end argument, the view that code is law, network neutrality, and others. Cyber threats to national security include the militarization of cyberspace, the conduct of cyber warfare, threats to critical infrastructures, and cyber espionage. Concurrently, however, we are aware of the emergence of politically and socially disruptive groups whose objectives are to undermine the security of the state, to engage in industrial espionage, or to threaten other states. The viability of such entities remains relatively unknown, and investigations into their resilience are in early stages, although their presence is already quite evident in cyber venues, as are manifestations of their cyberpolitics.

Seventh are the commensurate initiatives in *cyber cooperation and collaboration,* partly in response to newly evident cyber conflicts, but also driven by the consolidation of interests in the international system around particular clusters of goals. Insofar as cyberspace is managed by private sector agencies, many of the management details and related contentions are not always apparent. But we identify some important initiatives, such as the institutions created to track and measure cyber threats around the world. There is some degree of international collaboration in the search for global norms and search for agreement on supporting cyber-related public goods, such as knowledge provision via cyber venues, the recognition of cyber rights (analogous to human rights), or the creation of new norms for cyber behavior. Perhaps the most pervasive type of collaboration centers on the formation of a twenty-first-century global agenda, broadly defined.

Eighth is the increased expansion of cyber access and attendant activities and interactions, supported by a highly complex and growing *institutional landscape* of private sector entities defined more by areas of responsibilities and less by principles of accountability. Issues of governance are increasingly being raised, with the implication that the current arrangement must be reviewed and revised.

Ninth is the contestation of influence and control over the structures, processes, and uses of cyber venues by the *traditional international institutions,* whose roles intersect with the cyber managers' mission. One of these institutions, namely, the International Telecommunication Union, defines its mandate to cover all facets of cyberspace. Others, such as UN's development agencies, consider cyber venues to be central to the realization of their visions, and therefore extend their claims accordingly.

Tenth—and especially important—is the enhanced visibility, leverage, and potential power and influence of the *individual*—singly or in groups— which are manifested at all other levels of analysis—the state, the international system, and the global system.

These are all important "new" features of the international system. They are hybrids created by the reality of mutual and pervasive interconnections of the kinetic and the cyber domains. Hybrid challenges are likely to shape hybrid response strategies. This coupling is more by necessity than by design.

Jointly, all of these features reinforce the ongoing lateral realignments of power and influence, leverage and decision making, throughout the international system. It is highly unlikely that the international system will regain its characteristic features as defined by the traditional Westphalian system and its derivatives. From the evidence to date, we can expect more lateral realignment and more conflicts among contending principles of order. We can also expect greater countervailing efforts by sovereign states, international institutions, and the business community to resist and contain, if not eliminate entirely, any realignments that might seriously impede their pursuit of power and influence or leverage and wealth.

10.2   Lateral Realignments and Levels of Analysis

Earlier in this book we outlined our expectations about the potential impacts of cyberspace for the various levels of analysis in international relations. We now summarize some fundamentals of the lateral pressure theory that shape new realities for the twenty-first century worldwide. First is the recognition of the fourth level of analysis, the overarching global system. Second is the extension of contexts or spheres of activity to include the natural environment and the cyber domain. Third are the multiple influences and feedback effects within and across the three spheres of human activity as well as the four levels of analysis. Turning next to each level, we highlight some of the notable realignments as well as their implications for cyberpolitics.

The Individual: New Power and Influence
In principle, access to cyberspace and participation in cyberpolitics facilitate demands and enhance capability. As long as all individuals are potentially able to engage in cyber interaction, it is difficult to separate the personal from the social, the political expression from the statement

of threat, and so forth. By participating in cyber venues, individuals escape the constraints of territoriality and even of formal identity. More important is the possibility that the individual—and not necessarily in the aggregate—can threaten the state in unforeseen ways.

As noted earlier, cyberspace enables and empowers the individual in new and diverse ways. It provides different parameters for permissible action that cannot always be ignored by the state. It is usually difficult to identify the specific individual who is responsible for a particular cyber message. This means that the individual level in international relations theory is at least as privileged as other levels of analysis – a major departure from traditional theory.

Enabled by infrastructure developments, buttressed by institutional supports, and steered by policy directives, the individual is now endowed with access to cyber arenas and powered in ways that were not possible, or even fathomed, earlier. The range of state efforts to control cyber uses, differential access to cyberspace, and differences in the enabling functions of knowledge and skills mitigate the practical value of individual access in some nations. But on balance, few would dispute that the individual has gained power.[6]

Cyber interaction allows self-definition as well as the individual framing of political stances. We cannot assume that cyberspace provides a venue for voicing that replaces traditional interest articulation and aggregation within an established political process. It does, however, serve as an effective venue of expression outside the traditional channels, even in ways that challenge the established order, as amply demonstrated by the ongoing Wikileaks episodes.[7] Individuals and groups have found many ways to bypass the power of the state and pursue their own policies, thus drawing attention to units of decision other than the state itself and to the emergence of new organizational principles in world politics. In several parts of the world political blogs have become mechanisms for the expression of interests and for organization of individuals into a critical mass. All of this is facilitated in situations where the political rights of individuals are articulated, understood, and protected by the political system itself.[8] At the same time, however, we have seen that when individual views threaten the established order, the state is not likely to accommodate.

Overall, access to cyberspace provides and shapes the parameters of the potential or possible action. While each person is always bounded by the realities of the natural system and the social system, to some extent strong demands (high motivation) may compensate for low capabilities, just as high capabilities may compensate for low demands (or low motivation).[9] Access to cyber venues facilitates this compensation. It offers a new means for expressing views and interests in world politics. Under these conditions, lateral pressure theory would suggest that *Homo individualis* introduced in chapter 2 could also potentially become *Homo sustainabilis*.[10]

The State System: New Security Dilemmas

The state remains the basic unit of organization for the international system—the major actor and the dominant level of analysis in international relations theory. With the acceptance that the state is embedded in some configuration of the natural environment and its life-supporting properties, the challenge now is to take account of the emergent cyber context, as well as interactions with the social and the natural systems.

At this time, the security of the state is a hostage to a range of disparate factors, many of which are not addressed by the traditional security calculus.[11] Different countries are vulnerable in different ways. Early on we argued for and presented an integrated vision of national security, one that spans external, internal, environmental, and cyber domains and thus provides an overarching view of threats to security. This view transcends the traditional approaches to national security by expanding the scale and scope of state responsibility for protecting sovereignty, security, and society.

The creation of cyberspace places the state in an unprecedented situation. It provides new and potentially uncomfortable conditions, and the state may feel threatened.[12] In the early years of cyber access there was much in this new context that states could not readily control. But they adapted by developing and deploying new instruments of control, and many clearly aspire to be the major players as regulators and managers of this arena. With few exceptions, these predicaments are shared by all states to varying degrees. This adds one more item to a growing list of common concerns that may well call for international agreements on global norms and operational goals.[13]

As noted earlier, international relations theory has little to say about sustainability and the state. The extensive literature on state failure is not matched by commensurate studies on the conditions of and propensities for state sustainability, despite the reasonable expectation that a decline in indicators of sustainability must surely be a precursor to state failure.[14] Lateral pressure theory would suggest that in the absence of external threat, a sustainable state is also a secure state. We have traced the emerging synergy between cyberspace and sustainability. And we have examined how the international community, through the World Summit on the Information Society (WSIS), is pursuing two objectives: to enhance cyber participation and to support transitions toward sustainability. By pushing for uses of cyberspace for sustainability purposes, the WSIS effectively coupled two issues that were separate in their origin and development.

Many states have begun to routinize the delivery of social services by means of cyber venues, with varying success. The degree of effectiveness depends on the reliability of cyber access, the clarity of purpose, and the specificity of instructions. While we would expect industrial states to excel in the use of cyber venues, we already observe leapfrogging initiatives by the other states. For example, in chapter 5 we examined key features of the traditional or kinetic international system in order to understand its recent configuration and, more important, to compare it with the cyber-based view of the international system. To begin with, the entire state system is increasingly engaged in cyber venues. But we can discern some general patterns, for example, as in figure 5.5b: the shared clustering of less-developed states, the developmental propensities illustrated by a semi-arc, some common linear patterns, and the proverbial S-shaped curve of growth followed by leveling off.

On balance, we find greater convergence among countries when we examine their cyber features than we do when we observe their, basic attributes or or characteristic features. We have also noted a general trend toward greater use of e-government, irrespective of level of development. In addition, the relatively strong positive relationship between the performance of e-government and the perceptions of government effectiveness signals that something is indeed happening on the ground.

But there are many puzzles. Most notable is the rather weak relationship between ratings on the UN's e-Government Readiness Index and indicators of perceived political stability. One would expect political stability to facilitate government performance and thus to shape perceptions of government effectiveness. Alternatively, it might be that there is more information about political stability than about its relationship to e-government. All of this is based on observations of the state system that, almost by definition, obscure important changes at the individual level of analysis.

States have not been slow to control access to cyber venues and, when possible, to prosecute presumed offenders. Some go to great lengths to limit the exposure of their citizens to messages deemed undesirable.

Many governments have used cyber venues to exert their power and influence and extend their reach as well as their instruments of sanction and leverage—and to pursue their own security by increasing the insecurity of their critics or detractors.[15]

All of this becomes increasingly important given that who gets what, when, and how is influenced not only by cyber access but also by the growth and diversity of actors with different levels of power and capability. They all participate in one way or another in the international forums, and all seek venues for shaping the evolving agenda.

The International System: Density of Decision Entities

The challenge cannot be underestimated. Today's international system includes actors and entities enfranchised by the state, notably those commonly thought of as transnational. We have witnessed the increasing density of decision entities as well as the remarkable expansion of governance structures for the management of information and communications technologies and the support of development goals. With the growth of international institutional initiatives and new trends in forming a global agenda, organizational linkages with the state and its bureaucracies and agencies are increasing. States are formal voters in international institutions. Various non-state groups have been accorded observer status or otherwise allowed to participate in international forums, though they lack decision-making power.

All of these can be readily understood in a world where the state continues to provide the rules of the game, even if it is no longer the only relevant player. What is a challenge for international relations theory, policy, and practice is that, despite its ubiquity, pervasiveness, and global reach, much of cyberspace is managed by private sector. This seeming disconnect can only be understood in its historical moment. It was the dominant power, the United States, that delegated to the private sector the operational management of cyberspace. This was a decision of the sovereign that constructed cyberspace. It was not an international decision. We are now observing some push-back from different state actors and their agents around the world. This, however, can be anticipated by traditional theory. But the outcome is not a foregone conclusion. Issues of cyberspace management may not remain entirely within the purview of the private sector. Powerful ambiguities remain. Despite lateral realignments and shifts in the geostrategic landscape, the United States remains the world's technology leader. U.S. institutions, scientists, and engineers invented and constructed the Internet and much of the computing infrastructure the Internet connects. But with rapid growth in other parts of the world, the expansion of information communications and technology created new uses and users, as well as a range of previously unforeseen stakeholders.

What does international relations theory have to say about this? U.S. dominance in the Internet's creation and management is entirely consistent with a power-based realist theory, concerned with state capability and national security. The push-back from various actors and entities is an entirely predictable reaction from the liberalism perspective, and its manifestations and consequences are consistent with institutional theory, which concentrates on coordinated and formally organized international behavior.[16] Time will tell how constructivist theory will address these issues.

These developments are consistent with the proposition we put forth earlier to help frame the dynamics of change. The proposition argues that, in the short run, uneven patterns of cyber access and activity likely reflect the distribution of power in the international system. Over time, the diffusion of capabilities worldwide is expected to lead to the expansion of cyber access and participation. In the long run, these changes will result in new ways of exerting power and leverage, and create new demands for norms and structures that reflect the influence and goals of the ascending states.[17]

Given the built-in dominance of the private sector early on, cyberspace has further reinforced the formation and organization of private interests, which become influential international entities in their own right, with goals and purposes, priorities and problems. Some private entities are embedded in purposeful networks that change over time—some expand, some retract, and some alter in shape.[18] We have chosen to highlight knowledge networks because of the centrality of knowledge to power, technology, and overall capability. Moreover, the evolving attention to potentials for the knowledge economy, which has reinforced the expansion of civil society actors and new knowledge-based businesses, has also expanded knowledge-related entrepreneurships—with tangible as well as intangible products and services.

Concurrently, the international community is in the midst of a grand experiment: developing viable modes of international governance in a state-centered world in the absence of central authority over the entire system of sovereign states. What is novel for international relations theory as well as policy is focused attention to the provision of public goods at the global level.[19] How the issue is addressed will be defined by the distribution of expectations regarding who gets what, when, and how. An immediate follow-up challenge pertains to the rules and institutional mechanisms for such provision.[20] The outcome will be shaped by type and extent of the cyber-based participation as national positions are crystallized in global forums. Alternatively, the extent of cyber participation could undermine the established processes and lead to a transformation of state-centric exclusivity in international decision making. All of this is still "under development." All of this will become increasingly important for international relations theory and policy as the twenty-first century unfolds.

The Global System: All-Encompassing Commons

In principle, the fourth image refers to the Earth, and all life-supporting properties, as well as to cyberspace, created by human ingenuity. We have already seen the politicization of both the natural and the man-made features of the fourth image. And we expect a continued trend in that direction. In addition, when cyber venues are used to pursue global objectives via international institutions, a whole new set of challenges emerges. We now anticipate at least three clusters of challenges or critical tasks, and there are surely many more.[21]

The first pertains to appropriate uses of cyber-based facilities and mechanisms for the performance of international organizations. Although states are the stockholders as well as the voters in international governance, non-state actors increasingly resort to cyber venues for interest articulation and aggregation, as well as influence on international decision forums. Among the challenges at hand is to converge on norms and practices in the uses of cyber-based instruments for this purpose.[22]

The second challenge, central to the mission of almost all international institutions, pertains to the use of cyber venues for the provision of services in one form or another. Almost all institutions have extended their reach and performance in the primary domains of responsibility, as well as in the educational supports, by using cyber capabilities. The trend is unsurprising, except perhaps the speed at which the use of cyber access is taking shape. What remains to be seen is the extent to which this bears on who gets what, when, and how—as well as who decides on each of these issues.

The third notable challenge involves the characteristic features of vertical linkages—connecting global and local—for information, communication, and knowledge building to and from the grass roots. At the same time, however, we recognize that if stakeholders are organized, then access to cyberspace becomes a major asset. Some of these linkages are converging around the notions of a global civil society and the companion concept of civic global responsibility—both of which enhance the potential consolidation of a global social order.

In many ways, cyberspace can be seen to assume properties that are characteristic of the global commons. At issue here is less the matter of equivalence than the query as to the potential for a cyber tragedy of the commons, at this time or at any point in the future.[23] Some countervailing trends persist. On the one hand, cyber access and use can legitimately be characterized as chaotic, reinforcing global anarchy (as understood in international relations theory). No one is in control. On the other hand, the expansion of cyberspace and cyber participation may generate a demand for governance structures and processes that transcend territorial sovereignty and rein in the potential chaos of interaction.

We cannot anticipate how the contentions surrounding who governs the future of cyberspace will evolve. Nor can we predict the extent of future disruptive uses of cyberspace for gains on the ground. At a minimum, we are confronted with two political puzzles. One is how to resolve the difficulties that may emerge when decisions and policies pertaining to the fourth image are made at the other levels of analysis—if and when the various constituencies recognize the need to make decisions.[24] The other is how to navigate through the various forms of cyberpolitics surrounding existing as well as new policy spaces as they begin to consolidate. These puzzles are especially relevant as we see struggles on the horizon over the management of cyberspace.

10.3 The Future of Cyberpolitics

In this book we have considered different modes and manifestations of cyberpolitics in international relations, some entirely collaborative but many reflecting struggles over influence and control. For the most part, a common expectation is that the eventual outcomes will be both legitimate and authoritative. Given the rapid growth of Internet users, the increased complexity of managing cyberspace, and the record of governments' control or denial of access, it is reasonable to consider potential trajectories of international relations and their cyberpolitics.

Our efforts to differentiate among alternative cyber futures are based on one key assumption: that the traditional real systems of interactions, power, and influence will shape the contours of cyberspace in the future. Technological decisions, alternative Internet architectures, and different modes of governance of cyberspace and management system will follow accordingly.

For conceptual purposes, we draw on two trajectories or dimensions to provide an internally consistent frame of reference. One pertains to the dominant principle underlying authority and decision, namely, state sovereignty versus private authority. The other relates to modes of international behavior, that is, conflict and violence versus cooperation and collaboration. Jointly they provide the criteria and dimensions to identify alternative futures. On this basis we present four generic but very different models of the future of cyberpolitics, with the understanding that these are modal at best and are not intended to be specific predictions. Our purpose is to signal the possibilities and potentials, given the many facets of cyberpolitics we have considered.

The first model is a future anchored in high sovereign control over cyber venues in the context of a high level of international conflict and violence. We call this model future the *garrison cyber system*, in respectful memory of Harold Lasswell, who first coined the term "garrison state" and outlined its critical features more than sixty years ago. Countries like Saudi Arabia, Myanmar, North Korea, and China may become candidates.

The second model of cyber futures proposes a world of high conflict and violence worldwide in the absence of sovereign control or any centralized authority. We refer to this future as one of *cyber anarchy*. This is a world where private order dominates, with no overarching authority or forms of governance and no constraints on the activities of actors or agents. In many ways, this future approximates the proverbial Hobbesian state of nature, the war of all against all.

The third cyber future issues from international cooperation and coordination in a world dominated by non-state actors, agents, and entities. This is a "hands-off" future in which only the minimum coordination necessary for core Internet and other cyber operations is put in place. We call this model the *global cyber commons*. Civil society, local and global, would be the main supporters and constituencies of this model.

The fourth model of cyber futures is a world managed by sovereign states and characterized by a high degree of international cooperation and collaboration. We term this future the *cyber grand bargain* to highlight collaborative management, bargaining, and negotiations. This future is an extension—with refinements and alterations—of the original vision of the Internet, as well as the current cyber system and its manage-

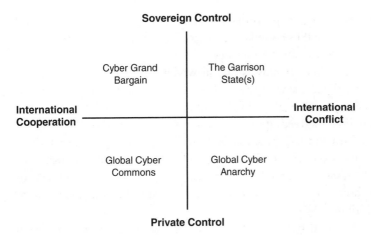

Figure 10.1
Potential futures of cyberpolitics in international relations.

ment. The United States, the European Union, and other political democracies may potentially be supportive of such a future and help realize it.

Figure 10.1 locates each of these modal cyber futures in a common framework. Each model is based on different normative underpinnings, different assumptions about international relations, and different expectations about interactions among decision entities. We do not expect the future of cyberpolitics to conform to any model in its pure form, but we suggest that each model highlights different contingencies and thus helps inform our overall expectations.

The garrison cyber system is a major departure from the vision of the Internet as a free and open network. Based on the power of the rules and framework of the state system, it expands current practices of control or denial of access adopted by many states to prevent citizens accessing politically undesirable content. Logistics aside, this model endogenizes cyber security within the overall purview of national security, law and order, and allows the public sector to impose norms and restrictions when the private sector is responsible for Internet and related cyber operations. It exercises increased control over points of access, such as total control over Internet Service Providers (ISPs), and reviews and monitoring of all content transmitted. By definition, this future requires more reliance on organizational capability for implementation, routinization, and oversight. The lead constituency is the state and its government, and the driving principle is containing voices deemed disruptive or even threatening. We have witnessed the garrison cyber system in action when the government of Egypt ordered total denial of cyber access and demanded that the ISPs comply forthwith. For a brief period the country was totally cut off from the Internet.

A future of cyber anarchy is one in which international conflict and violence prevail, the state system is weak, and the private sector (for profit, not-for-profit, legal, and illegal) dominates; the model is characterized by few if any agreed-upon rules and regulations and no overarching authority of any kind. Cyberspace is devoid of governance systems, there are no regulatory norms or practices, and there are no mechanisms for tracking "damages"—and little incentives to do so. It is difficult to anticipate how cyber access as currently understood could persist under such conditions.

The cyber grand bargain future assumes the enhanced routinization and reinforcement of the current system such that it operates entirely on the basis of consensus without resort to unilateral action at any time. Its distinctive feature is improvement of management rather than control of access or content. It also recognizes the role of nongovernmental institutions and the legitimacy of the civil society worldwide. The bargain also includes greater coordination among the various international and other agencies concerned with deploying cyber tools for improving the human condition, especially in developing countries. Framed broadly, this vision is responsive as well to the sustainability agenda that, in principle, spans industrial as well as developing countries. As such, it supports the convergence of cyberspace and sustainability and reinforces the synergy.

Among the improvements to the current system anticipated in the cyber grand bargain model are a reduction in cyber threats and the growth of norms that support a viable cyberspace. The lead constituency for the bargain is the network of organizations enfranchised to manage different aspects of the global Internet system and their constituencies. The guiding principle is equity and efficiency in interaction and communication. (Parenthetically, if there were a return to business as usual and an erosion of the core features, then, in extreme cases, the resulting future would eventually begin to approximate the garrison cyber system.)

The global cyber commons model represents a future that elevates access to cyberspace to the status of a human right and reduces barriers to access to the minimum levels required for effective operation. It assumes that the state system and international agencies, private and public, continue to expand the facilities for cyber access across the world. The lead constituency for this model is civil society, and enabling the expression of its voice is the driving principle. This model also assumes the establishment of self-governance mechanisms and the self-management of conflicts and contentions.

The global cyber commons is predicated on the design and implementation of protections against the potential for tragedy in the cyber commons. In this model of cyberpolitics, everyone has a stake in the system and in preserving its underlying norms. How much flexibility can be managed without insurmountable segmentation and partial degradation? How resilient can such a system be? Will the spheres of influence so prevalent in traditional international relations be replicated in the cyber domain?

These alternative modal cyber futures are characterized by different design principles, buttressed by attendant norms and operational mechanisms. Each of these futures is contingent on different dynamics of cyberpolitics in international relations. It is not difficult to differentiate the characteristics. They also harken back to some well-known questions. For example, do advances in technology lead to demands for governance? Or do governance practices and principles shape technology trajectories? Alternatively, are both of these trajectories shaped by the driving principles defining legitimate forms of actions and interaction?

Whatever answers one might favor, the fact remains that each of these modal future will inevitably encounter and must address, even resolve, foundational issues pertaining to their very existence. These involve *jurisdiction* (the boundary of governance), *legitimacy* (the basis for acceptance and recognition), *authority* (the source of and principles of legitimacy), and *accountability* (responsibility for behavior). Each of these models will manage these issues in very different ways.

Such visions of cyber futures must be understood only as modal types, that is, representing central tendencies, anchored in fundamentally different parameters of politics in any context. While we do not argue for or discuss particular architectural underpinnings or conditions, we do assume that each model is a representation predicated on some feature of the world we know. The development of any one of these cyber futures will necessarily involve alterations, additions, or extensions of the current infrastructure and managerial systems. We recognize the transformative functions of social demands and technological innovation. At the same time, the close connection of technology and society requires that we also recognize the growing politicization of cyberspace, reinforced by continued lateral realignments among actors, and agents, interests and influences, worldwide.

The construction of cyberspace and the expansion of access and participation have led to new ambiguities and uncertainties and created new challenges to theory, policy, and practice for both the traditional kinetic and the cyber domains. We have come to the end of an era for tradition and convention in international relations. The salience of cyberspace is recognized worldwide. It is now an integral feature of the world we live in and of the interactions within and across sovereign states. With growing access to cyberspace, objective factors may assume their own subjectivities. With little consensus over the nature of prevailing "truths," we can expect more rather than less international contentions over matters of jurisdiction, legitimacy, authority, and accountability.

If twenty-first-century international relations theory is to address cyberpolitics as an important aspect of the field, it cannot avoid the fundamentals of this new domain—defined by distinctive properties related to temporality, physicality, permeation, fluidity, participation, attribution, and accountability. The immediate challenge for theory broadly defined is to consider, clarify, and converge on matters of concepts and metrics—or at least on some rules of thumb—to address the objective and subjective for cyberpolitics in international relations.

Notes

Chapter 1

1. Around two billion people are connected to the Internet, roughly one-third of the global population.

2. For example, competition between political parties and debates over budgetary allocations, changes to the military budget, the deployment of troops overseas, and so on are in the nature of high politics. In politics, these elements are all close to the proverbial tip of the iceberg of conflict, competition, and contention.

3. In this connection, see the theory and evidence in Choucri, North, and Yamakage (1992), an analysis of Japan over the span of the twentieth century.

4. Consistent with Deutsch (1963), we take the view that power is "neither the center nor the essence of politics. It is one of the currencies of politics," and that "force is another and narrower currency" (124).

5. As a result of Lasswell's (1958) work, this view of politics remains central to political science and international relations.

6. The single most influential study providing important foundations for what we now consider cyberpolitics may well be Karl W. Deutsch's *The Nerves of Government: Models of Political Communication and Control* (1963). Deutsch focused on communication, feedback, equilibrium, and related concepts in an effort to articulate the body politic "with its nerves—its challenge of communication and decision" (ix).

7. Notable exceptions include Litfin (1998), Haas (1990), and Choucri and North (1995), and earlier Pirages (1977, 1978).

8. Aside from well-known renderings, such as Sprout and Sprout (1971), Aron (1966), and Renouvin and Duroselle (1967), notable exceptions to this generalization include Ruggie (1986, 1999), Kratochwil and Mansfield (1994), and North (1990).

9. The *Blackwell Dictionary of Political Science* notes that power is the central concept in political science but has remained relatively ambiguous and undefined (Bealey 1999, 255). Conceptually, power usually denotes the ability of one entity to make others conform to its wishes. A distinction is commonly made among

the scale, scope, and domain of power. In addition, power as an attribute is considered different from power as a relationship.

10. The social science vocabulary for this new arena is at an early stage of development. The technical terminology is being created as technological parameters are expanded. But there is no agreed-upon ontology for all facets of cyberspace.

11. For a list of definitions of cyberspace, see Kramer, Starr, and Wentz (2009, 26–27).

12. Spinello (2002, 28), citing Barrett (1997).

13. I am grateful to an anonymous reviewer for framing the issues as quoted.

14. Karl W. Deustch has observed that through the "interplay of habitual compliance and probable enforcement, societies protect their institutions, the allocation and reallocation of their resources, the distribution of the values, incentives and rewards among their population" (Deutsch 1968, 19).

15. Influence in this context refers to conditions shaped by hierarchy, forms of social stratification, both formal and informal, and uneven access to centers of decision and power.

16. Many of the issues we address at this point are encapsulated in the title of David Warsh's *Knowledge and the Wealth of Nations* (2006), which focuses on the power of knowledge.

17. Our purpose here is not to review the theoretical issues associated with matters of might and right, since these are the subject of extensive literatures in the realist tradition of international relations and the various literatures that critique realist perspectives. We seek only to highlight the matter of capabilities.

18. Thanks to the insights of Harold D. Lasswell (1950), this definition is standard in political science. The term "authoritative" refers to a decision considered legitimate by those participating in the decision-making process.

19. The concept and the reality of "advantage" may be defined differently by different actors and for different purposes. If the issues are not fully articulated, if the contours of the interaction domain are fraught with uncertainty, and if the past is not the best instructor for present predicaments, then the politics will first be concerned with defining the terms of the authoritative allocation of value and the configuration of the nature of value. Once these tasks are accomplished, distributive conflicts and contentions concentrate on who gets what, when, and how.

20. The major journals of international relations have paid little attention to cyber venues since then. Our review of articles in the *International Political Science Review*, the *American Political Science Review*, the *Journal of Conflict Resolutions*, *World Politics*, and *International Studies Quarterly* from 2000 to 2008 uncovered only two articles, other than those in the *International Political Science Review* from 2000 cited above. Such evidence is illustrative, not definitive.

21. In practice, however, states are seldom able to exercise their authority over external factors as effectively as they desire. They are generally unable to control

the flow of people, goods, and services across their boundaries entirely, if at all; their boundaries cannot insulate them or protect them from the physical actions of other states; and boundaries cannot regulate flows of environmental effluence from other states (Choucri 1993a, 24–26). In short, while the foundations of sovereignty are located in international law, the realities on the ground impose limits on the state's autonomy and control.

22. A related but broader argument, with a wider historical sweep, is put forth by Ronald J. Deibert (1997), who examines the impacts of advances in information and communications technologies and highlights their fundamental distributive effects. Deibert refers to the "information revolution," while others have addressed related processes as "the knowledge revolution" (Chichilnisky 1996), focusing primarily on the effects of the increased knowledge intensity of economic activity. The relevance of this difference is discussed in chapter 4. The term "global information society" is generally used to emphasize the scope and scale of the communications in question.

23. There are many variants of realism and its derivatives, but they all generally share basic assumptions. These include the following: (1) the international system is anarchical in nature and states are the primary actors; (2) states are unitary actors; (3) the individual is conflict-oriented; and (4) decisions follow a rational calculus.

24. In this connection, Clarke and Knake (2010) address these issues from a realist perspective, as we discuss in chapter 6.

25. Institutionalism is based on many liberal assumptions, such as (1) the international system is potentially harmonious, (2) individuals are relatively benign, (3) collaboration is necessary and feasible, and (4) international institutions have autonomous impacts on outcomes. See Shepsle (1989) for an account of endogenous institutional change and the role of institutional interests.

26. See Campbell and Pedersen (2001) for a comparison of four types of institutional perspectives. See Mahoney and Thelen (2010) for institutional evolution as an alternative to equilibrium as the stability-ensuring assumption.

27. This is somewhat ironic, insofar as many cyberspace technologies grew from U.S. government research and were originally intended for government use, as we discuss in a later chapter.

28. Constructivism views international relations as social relations shaped by social interactions. See Kubalkova, Onuf, and Kowert (1998) for the underlying logic; for intellectual evolution in a historical context, see pp. 42–43. Related are the investigations that focus on the core principles on which international relations are shaped. At issue is the legitimacy of contending principles of world order.

29. See Choucri and Reardon (2010) for a distribution of the cyber-centered studies in international relations to illustrate their central tendencies.

30. Common understandings of globalization are bracketed by two different perspectives. At one end is the traditional view, which defines globalization in terms of the movement of factors of production across territorial boundaries. At the other end is the broader view argued, for example, by lateral pressure theory,

which defines globalization in terms of the transformation in states and societies resulting from the movement of people, resources, and technology, as well as ideas and influences, across state boundaries.

31. An important exception is Robert Gilpin (1987), who defines international politics and economics in dynamic terms according to specific "rules" held to the dynamics of transformations and change in ways more pervasive and detailed than the power transition adjustment. Drawing on the logic of realism focused on the major powers, Gilpin argues that in the short run, the distribution of power and influence in the international system shapes the rules of interaction and the framework for conduct in politics and economics. In the long run, changes in efficiency and economic performance alter the prevailing distribution of power and change the structure of the international system. These changes are shaped by the power and preferences of the ascending state, whose new position of power enables it to make claims on the international system and influence the rules and regulations that govern relations among states. This approach works in the real-world domain of major powers in the international system; the overall logic has some degree of portability to relations in the cybersphere.

32. This is true for Gilpin (1987), who begins with change and then focuses on its consequences.

33. This logic is central to the theory of lateral pressure and consistent with the processes of change outlined in Gilpin (1987). Clearly, it is difficult to anticipate the actual forms of agreement. Nonetheless, growing convergence rather than divergence in the management of cyber and real behavior by all actors and at all levels of development would be expected to shape the emergence of a new world.

34. Conversely, greater divergence than convergence would create cleavage in the cyber domain that would invariably spill over into the real domain. We might then imagine a reemergence of the systems of conflict described by leading scholars of twentieth-century international relations, such as Kaplan (1957) and Rosecrance (1963).

35. As we discuss in chapter 6, this neutrality itself is the subject of cyberpolitics.

36. Different actors operate in different segments of cyberspace with different degrees of influence on and proximity to the Internet (Clark 2010).

37. It goes without saying that conflict and cooperation are not "pure" types of behaviors. Conflict, however intense, usually involves some degree of cooperation, however minor. By the same token, all forms of cooperation usually involve some degree of disagreement, even conflict. Accordingly, these chapters focus on situations where conflict or cooperation dominates the nature of the interaction.

38. This is to be distinguished from e-governance, or the use of cyber venues for conducting the functions of government in states and societies.

39. Despite the large number of definitions of sustainable development rotating in scholarly as well as policy circles, there is as yet no formally understood set of factors over which this function is defined.

Chapter 2

1. This view of politics, enunciated by Harold Lasswell (1950), remains central to political science and international relations.

2. See, for example, Barraclough (1999).

3. For specific examples, case studies, comparative analyses, and longitudinal inquiries, see Choucri and North (1975, 1989), Ashley (1980), Lofdahl (2002), and Wickboldt and Choucri (2006).

4. Interestingly, lateral pressure theory shares with Jared Diamond (*Collapse*, 2005) the importance given to environment, but there are major differences in assumptions, the logic of the argument, and the inferences drawn. Diamond concludes that "societies developed differently on different continents because of differences in continental environments" (426). Lateral pressure theory does not support this conclusion.

5. Lateral pressure theory sees this restrictive system boundary as fundamentally distorting, and sees "externalities" more as a conceptual liability than a facilitating element.

6. In this connection, lateral pressure theory is also at variance with other dominant views in the social sciences.

7. This issue is examined in chapter 6 with reference to cyberspace control policies in a large number of countries.

8. In the most general terms, individuals take action to close the gap between the actual and the desired situation and possibly approach or establish a preferred condition, and their actions inevitably leave traces on the natural and the social environments. To close the gap between actual and desired conditions, individuals may prefer to use cyber venues. The impacts depend on the nature of the gap and the kind of cyberspace action employed.

9. As North (1990) reminds us, individuals (and social actor–systems) act across the boundaries between their internal and external environments. Not only are the boundaries themselves important constructs but how they are managed often becomes intensely political.

10. Among the most pressing cyberspace issues at the individual level is the protection of privacy. Protecting privacy is an important feature of a public policy in democratic societies, and deploying cyber tools for privacy protection is considered a corollary of cyberspace access. But many countries, notably the nondemocratic societies, have deployed e-tools to invade users' privacy (we recognize that the term "privacy" may not hold in this context).

11. Viewed thus, population can be differentiated into a number of subfactors or variables, depending on the issues at hand or the interests of the analyst. The same can be said of resources and technology, as we show later in this chapter.

12. This extended concept of technology encompasses both "soft" and "hard" dimensions, and often the former are as important as the latter. Underlying this formulation is the understanding that more advanced technologies are expected to, but do not always, result in more efficient socioeconomic processes.

13. While applications often create unintended impacts, at the same time, their deployment usually generates knowledge about these impacts. By the same token, technological change enables the creation of alternatives and choices while improving tools for analyzing complex situations and systems. As the application of stored knowledge, technology also contributes to the generation of new knowledge (Simon 1983, 39).

14. The operationalization of the state profile is done for the traditional international relations domain. The initial quantitative analysis provided the first empirical application in world politics (Choucri and North 1993).We are currently developing the cyberspace counterpart, an important element of the research agenda for the twenty-first century.

15. The selection of technology for the diagonal is simply because it is more readily manipulable by public policy than are the other two variables. A reorganization of each profile location in this table would yield either a population-driven display or a resource-driven display (with the population or the resource variable on the diagonal).

16. The table is a set of hypotheses that are only partially tested and validated to date.

17. See Lofdahl (2002) for a detailed analysis of the environmental features of states in each profile.

18. If demands and loads exceed the capacities to respond effectively, then the sustainability of the system is called into question (Choucri, Goldsmith, et al. 2007). In a more practical vein, governance and institutions are organized venues through which societies seek to manage, modify, or drastically alter the configuration of one or more of the master variables in their raw form (such as increased or decreased population growth). In many cases the instruments of governance are used to influence the interaction among the master variables and to manage their consequences. If demands and loads exceed the capacities to respond effectively, then the sustainability of the system is called into question.

19. *Extraction* refers to taxation and other forms of public levy. This capability is fundamental for all polities except rentier states, such as the oil-rich countries of the Gulf region in the Middle East, where the abundance of capital reduces if not eliminates entirely the need for the extractive capability. These are countries where the distributive capability is far more important. *Distribution* refers to the mechanisms and institutions for distributing state revenues and granting entitlements, benefits, and other forms of distributive value. *Regulation* denotes the organized practices and institutions for establishing and maintaining law and order. *Responsiveness* refers to forms of accountability and institutional mechanisms whereby the impacts of decisions are taken into account in subsequent decision making. *Symbolic identity* encompasses overt forms of identity expression, reinforcement of affinity with the state, and formal recognition of and respect for national symbols such as the flag and the national anthem.

20. Citing Kaufmann, Kraay, and Zoido-Lobaton (1999), the World Bank's *World Development Report* (2003, 43) draws attention to the positive effects of this close association, specified as the rule of law and GDP per capita.

21. A recent cross-national study of this relationship over time (and its attendant implications) shows the relation of property rights to the environmental performance of countries (Wickboldt 2007). When rights are not identified or enforced, a wide range of negative effects can follow. Contentions between private stakeholders and public interests often come to a head in the language and intent of national legislation.

22. Some of our most cherished (and effective) institutions are mechanisms for creating social burdens and transmitting effects that can be problematic, nationally and internationally. For example, the market, both its competitive form and in its distorted modes, serves to exchange goods among buyers and sellers. It is designed to undertake that task in the most effective manner, generally without concern for potential social or environmental dislocations. In countries where participation is central to both the conduct and the discourse of politics, voters are increasingly expressing their concerns about the quality of the environment through the ballot box.

23. This is central to realism as a theory of international relations, and it is generally accepted in liberalism.

24. At the same time, however, threats to the security of borders can come from a wide variety of non-state actors, and military threats do not necessarily involve invading the homeland.

25. At this point we refer to each of the master variables, and to the environmental arena, in aggregate terms. This means we do not differentiate among different facets, aspects, or aggregations of individual terms. For example, when we refer to the population master variable, we are referring to aggregate demographic characteristics rather than to any specific manifestations (e.g., urbanization, migration, or any other population facet).

26. Insofar as the prevailing ecological balances provide the basic parameters and constraints on the viability of the population, resource, and technology variables in any natural environment, few states find the balances entirely satisfying. In many cases, ensuring environmental security is akin to a juggling act if (or when) population growth leads to commensurate resource needs whose accessibility is contingent on prevailing levels of technology. Indeed, changes in any (or all) of the master variables could undermine the overall security balances in ways that may not have been fully anticipated.

27. We refer here to matters of security. We have not yet addressed the related issues of sustainability. Moreover, if we consider sustainability itself a defining feature of security, then each of the elements in the integrated security calculus must either remain within some bounds of sustainability or, alternatively, some commensurate mechanisms must be employed to counter any deficits in any of the four elements. In the last analysis, such issues may best be resolved on empirical grounds.

28. Cory Lofdahl (2002) took the important step of drawing attention, both theoretically and empirically, to the environmental behaviors associated with human activities and by this logic developed the contours of environmental lateral pressure theory. This is the concept that nature is far from being inert

or constant in human affairs but rather is an active variable in social activities.

29. For an application of lateral pressure theory to multinational corporations, see chapter 6 in Choucri (1993).

30. Organizational fields, defined as the policy spaces within which decisions are made about the actions of firms, are in practice determined by the characteristic features of product lines, industry, and the size of firms. Certainly, managers (and analysts) appreciate that corporate activities cannot be seen independently of the state. See chapter 6 in Choucri (1993) for a more developed argument of state-firm relationships.

31. Parenthetically, while the institutional status and mechanisms of international organizations are fairly well formalized, there is greater ambiguity as well as more variety in the types, forms, modes, and methods of NGOs.

32. Indeed, we cannot point to one map of the international system or one mode of accounting for its various actors that can be considered inclusive of most major arrangements recognized as currently constituting the entirety of the international system. By convention, official interactions between states are differentiated from private interactions (e.g., trade, banking, tourism) between individuals and organizations located in different states. Since crossing boundaries takes many different shapes and forms, the management of cross-border transactions and exchanges is also increasingly varied in form and content. Considerable challenges to theory and practice are raised by the changing configurations of multinational corporations.

33. Multilateralism, as a form of coordinated behavior among states, is generally considered to be an important feature of international relations. (Even less attention has been accorded multilateralism for the management of environmental degradation resulting from human activities.) If we consider the traditional literature in the study of international relations as articulated by Kenneth E. Boulding (1956) and Kenneth Waltz (1959) and synthesized and extended by North (1990), multilateralism emerged as a means of accommodating state-level actions to the requirements and conditions of the anarchy of the international system. Posed as coordinated action among sovereign states, multilateralism originated as a means of protecting the interests and activities of states in the international system in their pursuit of wealth and power (Gilpin 1987). But in a systematic analysis of its conceptual foundations and historical roots, John Ruggie notes how little attention has been paid to a "core feature of current international institutional arrangements," namely, their "multilateral form" (Ruggie 1982, 565).

34. For the purposes of this discussion, we use the terms "international organization" and "international institution" interchangeably, while fully recognizing the subtle theoretical and empirical distinctions that are often made in the literature.

35. A related argument, put forth in an edited volume titled *Global Environmental Accord,* defines a distinct set of principles, namely, *legitimacy, equity, efficiency, volition,* and *universality* (Choucri and North 1993, 506–507).

36. Recognizing the dilemmas facing international institutions, Ernst B. Haas (1980) argued for international governance enabled by "networks of networks" with state as well as non-state actors. He reminded us that such governance must be anchored in the performance of critical institutional functions in a decentralized (or loosely coupled) framework, conceptually as well as operationally.

37. Except for matters of military importance, multilateralism as a form of coordinated behavior among states has received relatively little attention from international realist theorists.

38. Related efforts in international relations theory that contribute to the articulation of the fourth image are Modelski (1996), Alker and Haas (1993), Ostrom (1990), Starr (1997), Vitousek et al. (1977), Holling (1995), and, of course, Hardin, *The Tragedy of the Commons* (1968), in the context of sustainability. The implications of the fourth image for the properties of the second image can be derived from Litfin (1998) while at the same time taking into account select imperatives of the third image.

39. In this connection, Peter M. Haas's (1989) argument about the role of epistemic communities in shaping the "fourth image reversed" is a clear acknowledgment of the direction of influence, so to speak, and, more important, of the formal recognition of a fourth image. It can be compared only indirectly to Peter Gourevitch's (1978) "second image reversed" since the latter focuses entirely on social interactions (political, economic, strategic), with no recognition of or reference to the natural system.

40. This logic draws attention to the fundamental differences between economists and political scientists in their conceptions of demand. For economists, demand means willingness to purchase, and this willingness is contingent on the dollar in hand; that is, in practice demand must include the *ability* to purchase. Making claims on the political system (rather than the willingness to purchase) is the essence of the political scientists' view. The former generates loads that need to be accommodated. The latter highlights the capacities available to accommodate the loads.

41. All of this is well illustrated by the follow-up initiatives associated with the Earth Summit (1990) and its aftermath, and is further reinforced by preparations for the World Summit on the Information Society (2003 and 2005) and its outcomes. Such trends illustrate the increased penetration of cyber venues in the conduct of international relations.

Chapter 3

1. It is illustrative of trends and timing that *Time* magazine's 1999 Person of the Year was the chief of Amazon.com. The magazine bore the cover page note, "E-commerce is changing the way the world shops." *Time*, December 27, 1999.

2. This chapter considers patterns of participation in cyberspace, drawing on Internet access data. The latter are indicators of usage only; they do not reflect participation in the infrastructural, institutional, and related functions and features that enable and support Internet access.

3. This view reflects a common belief at the time. Nonetheless, contentions suggest that both anonymity and free access may well be transient rather than fundamental features of the Internet.

4. An important common element in many different countries in developing regions and significant in almost all known "push" cases is the development of community-based organization for access. What would be called cybercafés in industrial countries have a wide range of counterparts in the developing world.

5. While sustainability considerations were not part of the investigation, this analysis and the results provide important insights into potentials for deploying IT in transitions to sustainable development.

6. First, investments in IT increase the capital stock available to workers, thereby increasing labor productivity. Second, the IT-producing segment of the IT sector is small but not negligible, and it propels strong demand. And third, through the value chain, IT contributes to improved performance in individual firms. Most interesting of all is the implied feedback relations shaping the political economy of IT, in the sense that the impact of IT is influenced by the nature of the business environment and the business environment in turn affects the viability of the IT sector. Focusing on the concept of the value chain, in the following chapter we distinguish between the supply chain and the knowledge chain, and highlight the increasing importance of the latter.

7. One important conclusion of this report is that considerable effort should be made to improve the quality of IT-related statistics, which stresses again that the nature of the results is shaped largely by the availability of data.

8. At the microlevel, the evidence does indicate that the use of IT is "positively linked to firm performance" (OECD 2003, 59). Among the specifics: IT technologies are more conducive to firm performance than others and, in this context, networking technologies are singled out since these are more often than not associated with spillover, diffusion, or network effects. On balance, one of the most significant findings of the OECD study is that the use of IT at the firm level has a positive impact on performance "primarily, or only, when accompanied by other changes and investments" (ibid., 66).

9. Asia also dominates in the semiconductor industry. See Hachigian and Wu (2003) for details.

10. In 2008 the OECD estimated that only one-fifth of the global population was able to gain access to the cybernet (OECD 2008c, 15). But it also pointed to the growing use of mobile devices that enable users in remote areas to connect in ways that were not possible earlier.

11. Parenthetically, a back-of-the-envelope view of other non-OECD countries reveals that some of the wealthiest countries, such as Saudi Arabia and Libya, have low rates of cyberspace access and that their telecommunications policy reinforces restriction rather than encouraging connectivity.

12. See, for example, *Time* magazine for December 27, 2010—January 3, 2011, specifically the evolutionary time line (p. 58) and the annotated graphics (pp. 58–59).

13. See Mahoney (2011).

Chapter 4

1. This phrase was offered by Anne Keatley (1983) in an article in *Science*, "Knowledge as Real Estate."

2. This phrase was coined by Charles Osgood, George Suci, and Percy Tannenbaum (1957) and aptly reflects the challenges at hand.

3. As noted in chapter 3, Facebook, the social networking site, has close to 600 million users, with roughly one billion new items of content posted each day. If Facebook were a country, its user population would make it the third largest in the world (*Time*, December 27, 2010–January 3, 2011, 43). The mixtures of representational metaphors, namely, "social" and "country," are noteworthy.

4. This approach was applied to environmental politics in the Mediterranean region by Peter M. Haas (1990), who argued that new ideas become institutionalized within international bureaucracies and organizations when social learning has taken place.

5. It is difficult to overlook the relevance of Wikipedia in this context. As an evolving, open-use, dynamic knowledge system based on voluntary participation and user updates and corrections, it has seen dramatic growth, matched by skepticism from the scholarly community. In recent years Wikipedia has made an effort to introduce quality control measures. These may have contributed to a softened stance, even a reluctant recognition of its potential utility and contributions.

6. An important theoretical, empirical, and policy issue relates to *whose* sustainability is most relevant in international relations.

7. Interestingly, the idea of sustainable growth appears as a new element in the evolving political discourse surrounding sustainability.

8. It is to Herbert Simon that we owe both the insights as well as the intellectual foundations for making the transition from a knowledge economy to a sustainable economy more than forty years ago—well before the creation of the knowledge economy in theory and in practice (Simon 1972, 1983).

Chapter 5

1. This means that no state is likely to retain a fixed position in the international system, unless we make the unrealistic assumption that all master variables in all states change at the same rates over time. Each of the master variables for each country is taken as a percentage of the total global value. The countries are aligned in terms of the relative dominance of their individual master variables. See figure 2.1 for the definition of the master variables.

2. This is closely connected to the notion of the parameters of permissible behavior, first introduced in Choucri (1969).

3. In this connection, it is reasonable to assume that if "the economy changes drastically and grows in scale, then the relationship of this growth to the earth's carrying capacity, the issue of scale, becomes more important than efficiency,

even if one accepts a wealth creation goal" (Driesen 2003, 5). Efficiency always matters. Conventionally, it is seen as allocating fixed resources; to the extent that it becomes a resource enhancer, its allocative functions become more important.

4. Note the differences in the values signaled by the distribution of states in profiles 1 and 2 compared to profiles 3–6.

5. Since we are not involved in statistical estimation of any type, only descriptive displays, we do not have to worry about exploring the congruence of a component variable in the overall indicator of interest.

6. For reasons of parsimony, we show in figures 5.18 and 5.19 the results for two variables, government effectiveness and political stability, with the understanding that the others are located in between.

Chapter 6

1. Among the most insightful reviews of international relations theories of conflict, violence, and war is that put forth by Jack S. Levy (1989).

2. The list in table 6.1 reflects key views at this time. There are others, to be sure, some already far advanced in legal or legislative battles.

3. See chapter 1 for a brief discussion of cyberspace features.

4. The layers are organized vertically (to be also understood as hierarchical and sequential).

5. Solum and Chung provide several examples to demonstrate why a clear understanding of Internet architecture is necessary to avoid misplaced interventions that create unintended consequences. They point to cases in which states attempted to regulate content and adopted measures that were ineffective and counterproductive. Solum and Chung's arguments and underlying logic are substantially more developed and robust than portrayed here. Our only purpose now is to draw attention to the specific cases of government violation they describe.

6. I am grateful to David D. Clark for a discussion helping to clarify the underlying challenges.

7. This is not simply a case of putting the cart before the horse but rather of recognizing the need for a cart, inventing the artifact, putting it in the correct alignment in relation to the horse, utilizing and enabling functionality, and then convening a committee to reach a consensus about the name that is to be assigned to this new artifact.

8. There are important similarities and differences in the formation and conduct of cyberpolitics between the broadband issue, on the one hand, and the framing and pursuance of sustainable development on the other. The most notable differences are in the clear currency of gain associated with the former and the great ambiguities thereof inherent in the latter. The similarities pertain to the politics of definition: some of the critical and determining contentions surrounding cyberpolitics are about defining the domain itself.

9. Denial of service is a blunt instrument, as governments came to realize.

10. The terms are as defined in *Access Denied* (Deibert et al. 2008). Political controls are usually the best implemented.

11. Each country is given a score on a five-point scale that reflects the observed level of control over four types of conflict: political, social, conflict and security, and Internet tools. The numbers in parentheses refer to the state profile (defined in chapter 2), and the appendix in chapter 5 lists the countries in each state profile group.

12. As reported in the *New York Times*, July 18, 2006. More specifically, "the government has directed local Internet service providers to block access to web-sites that are hosts to blogs." On July 23 the *New York Times* reported that, confronted with this situation, the government of India stated it was actually due to technical errors.

13. We may well be observing a game or a "race" of evasion and control.

14. Historians point to Howard Dean's 2004 campaign as a critical milestone in national cyberpolitics. Through his websites, Dean raised more money than any of his Democratic rivals in the primary race, which positioned him as an early leader. His most used website was meetup.com, which organized group meetings. He used the web to organize supporters to go door-to-door, distribute flyers, and organize meetings. The money and enthusiastic supporters translated into media attention for Dean, which further helped his campaign.

15. For a comparative and multifaceted analysis of privacy issues, see Agre and Rotenberg (2001).

16. In this connection, "net-centric" refers to interconnections among people, communication devices, and information systems designed to enhance efficiency in the pursuit of particular objectives.

17. The differences between matters of security and matters of warfare cannot be ignored, nor is it our intent to blur distinctions or meanings. Rather, we seek only to take note—point to—various forms of emerging conflicts and contentions.

18. "Cyber terrorism," a new addition to the semantics of cyberspace and attendant referents, is increasingly recognized as salient, in both academic and policy circles. It is also penetrating the popular press. See, for example, the op-ed essay in the *New York Times*, November 20, 2005, A31.

19. In this connection, realist theory posits a set of propositions about the immediate causes of war, almost all based on power differentials, challenges to the existing order by emerging powers, the dynamics of power transitions, arms competition, the type of political system, motives of the leaders, the dominance of offensive versus defensive strategies, and misperceptions and miscalculations, to name only a few.

Chapter 7

1. There are various institutional perspectives. Among the perspectives most relevant to the challenges at hand are those of Elinor Ostrom (1990), who views

"governing the commons as the major task for contemporary international institutions; Karen T. Litfin (1998), who examines the joint implications of technology and knowledge for the management of the global environment; and Friedrich Kratochwil and Edward D. Mansfield (1994), whose selection of issue areas central to the analysis of international institutions reflects the field's current understanding. Especially insightful in terms of emerging challenges in international relations is Thom Kuehls (1998), who draws attention to the "discourse of government" in the context of sovereignty and environment. We have seen the growth of literatures on regimes, international institutions, collective international actions, and so forth, with important insights into particular arrangements but with relatively few robust generalizations across cases, issues, contexts, or time frames. For an important reminder of the evolving nature of attention to environmental issues, see Hayward R. Alker and Peter M. Haas's (1993) review of ecopolitics in international relations.

2. The term *world government* refers to the structures and functions of government (as well as institutional and organizational mechanisms) endowed with authority and legitimacy that transcend the sovereignty of states and thus subsume the authority of each state under theoverarching umbrella of a world institution. The term *governance*, by contrast, refers to the functions of governance with no prior provision for or presumption of overriding state sovereignty, and no prior specification of structures or institutional mechanisms to be utilized.

3. We would expect all these objectives to be contingent on a minimum degree of common understanding of the challenges at issue, in combination with the dual principles of participation and representation in a world based on the principle of national sovereignty.

4. Framed thus, the referent is the actor whose behavior is designed to shape who gets what, when, and how; all other factors are derivative.

5. We use the term "global" in the inclusive overarching sense, namely, to cover individual, group, state, interstate, and all other levels of analysis and forms of aggregation.

6. It is to Gabriel A. Almond and H. Bingham Powell, Jr. (1966) that we owe the clearest perspective on national capabilities and institutional performance. We consider their contributions to be relevant to all domains and levels of analysis.

7. This section is based on the research, analysis, and discussion reported in Ferwerda, Choucri, and Madnick (2011).

8. Given this complex ecosystem, we consider only those institutions concerned with cyber threats and cyber crime, and discuss only those institutions with coordinating responsibilities at the international level.

9. These organizations are also referred to as Computer Security Incident Response Teams (CSIRTs).

10. As a result, CERTs tend to differ from each other mainly in their area of focus (academic, private, national, regional) or area of expertise (phishing, viruses, information security). These roles are largely self-defined

according to each team's level of funding (which can vary widely), technical expertise, and the presence of perceived gaps within the CERT collaborative network.

11. These features are formally called nonrival consumption and nonexcludable benefits.

12. See, for example, the United Nations Development Programme analysis of this complex set of issues in Kaul et al. (2003).

13. The issue of protecting human rights has a long and rich history, in theory and in practice. Here we consider only immediate issues related to cyberpolitics. Interestingly, the scale and scope of rights have changed over time, and with access to cyberspace, we can expect a consolidation of current rights as well as a further expansion. In 1986, for example, the UN General Assembly adopted the "right to development," which has remained controversial since then (Greenstein and Esterhuysen 2006, 281).

14. Of relevance here is Chichilnisky's (1998) report to the United Nations Development Programme, *Knowledge and the Internet as Global Public Goods.* The Internet is seen in terms of its contribution to global public service, including facilitating markets and the emergence of future markets. Chichilnisky then argues for a property rights regime to enable equity as well as efficiency in markets for knowledge. The reference here is solely with respect to the matter of global public goods. In chapter 4 we addressed the matter of property rights.

15. An additional goal was to ensure that countries violating human rights would be denied representation on the Human Rights Council of the UN.

Chapter 8

1. In chapter 4 we discussed the power of knowledge and the multiplier effects of networking. In some cases the knowledge-related role was part of the mission as initially framed. The point, however, pertains to the increased importance of this role in theory as well as practice.

2. This burgeoning literature on international collaboration is anchored in several core concepts in the study of international relations, such as coordination, collaboration, regimes, international institutions, international organizations, and the like. Some serious scholarly efforts have been made to provide some clarity and consistency in the usage of each term. While as yet there are no agreed-upon definitions for terms such as these, there is gradual convergence on the basic understandings. Finally, we note again that whenever there are prospects for accord, discord is the usual companion.

3. For example, the expansion of ISO 14000/EMAS certification/registration in the world is appreciated as an important development. Less well recognized is the wide range of differences among countries in their response to ISO measures to date.

4. The separation of church and state, a feature shared by many Western countries, is often an alien concept in other regions.

5. Clearly, the indicators are not directly comparable: GDP is a "value-added" concept; "sales" is not. Greater congruence can be achieved, as noted in the United Nations Conference on Trade and Development report (2002, 90, citing De Grauwe and Camerman 2002), by estimating value added for firms as a function of total salaries and benefits, depreciation, amortization, and pretax income.

6. In chapter 3 we signaled that the construction of cyberspace was an activity of the private sector—with incentives from and supports by the U.S. government—and the structure of its management also rested in private sector hands. In chapter 6 we singled out the management of cyberspace as a source of significant and unresolved contention. In chapter 7 we cited initiatives in the management of cyberspace as an indicator of evolving collaboration.

7. In chapter 4 we noted the demand for new knowledge focusing on this issue area.

8. In chapter 6 we noted the growth of "illegals" in the cyber domain and the problems that they create.

9. There remains considerable skepticism as to the meaning of the term "global civil society" and its empirical referent.

10. Worldwide, life expectancy at birth has increased by approximately twenty years over the past five decades. Today, roughly one million people reach sixty years of age every month (and 80 percent of these individuals are in developing countries). Concurrently, however, we also see reports of the termination of life as a result of the use of prebirth gender identification technologies (in India) and postbirth terminations (China), in each case because of an aversion to female children. These examples illustrate interactions between population and technology variables.

11. At the beginning of 2005 it was estimated that young people between the ages of fifteen and twenty-four years accounted for 18 percent of the world's population, and of these, 85 percent were in developing countries; children under fifteen years accounted for an added 30 percent of the world population; and jointly, these two age groups constituted almost half the population alive today (United Nations 2005b, 3). These people are candidates for participation in the labor force, either now or at some point in the near future.

12. The number of people aged one hundred years or older is expected to increase fifteen times between 1999 and 2050. The older age group itself is aging, and forms the fastest-growing segment of the world's population.

13. We saw in chapter 3 some of the unevenness mirrored in access to cyberspace and the digital divide—often described as the real divide.

14. Aside from the obvious differences in definition, urbanization and migration share common features that are often best understood by comparing before and after conditions for people as well as for territory affected by the crossing of legal jurisdictions.

15. Lateral pressure theory highlights the dynamics of change and transformation triggered by cross-border movement (voluntary or otherwise) and reminds us that population factors that have an impact on international relations are not

restricted to matters of fertility, mortality, aging, or urbanization. For an insightful analysis of the domestic policy implications of international migration focusing specifically on national security, see Rudolph (2003). For an aggregate larger-scale review of processes and patterns, see Weiner (1993), and see Zolberg and Brenda (2001) for specific illustrations.

16. As is to be expected, these cities suffer from most if not all of the usual problems found in urban areas. At the same time, they usually host a high degree of political and economic power, sometimes competing with the power concentrated in the capital city. Given present trends, it is difficult to envisage a future other than one with a growing number of megacities worldwide.

17. The term "diaspora" is often used interchangeably to refer to the dispersion of populations outside their territorial boundaries. In this chapter, we subsume this term under the general rubric of international migration, while at the same time recognizing the normative implications associated with diaspora.

18. Migration is an increasingly prominent issue on the national agenda in the United States.

19. Interestingly, we are beginning to discern some arguments linking migration to the natural environment—for example, the view that immigration "could ease climate-change impact" and thus "allow the big gas-emitters to take their share of responsibility" (Byravan and Rajan 2005).

20. Figures such as these do not include internally displaced people. These are migrations due to conflict and violence that do not (theoretically) cross territorial boundaries. While the figures are highly imprecise, the various estimates of internally displaced people range between eight and ten million or more.

21. This means that a lot of money is in private hands, and thus an important target for public policies designed to capture remittances.

22. The flight of people from conflict and violence is such a common feature of international relations that the status of refugee has been formally introduced in international law to articulate the attendant rights and responsibilities—of states, individuals, and the international community. It is not unusual for conflict and violence to influence and even alter the characteristics of the master variables for one or more of the contending parties. Depending on the scale and scope of disturbances, the profile of states may change, as may the nature of the related sustainability challenges.

23. These effects are manifested in added demand on the recipient community to help meet the demands generated by those that have crossed territorial boundaries, irrespective of the cause or source. Multipliers are also manifested as added claims on resources at the destination. Depending on the skill level of migrants as well as those in the recipient communities, the prevailing technological capabilities embedded in people will also be affected. In light of the highly interactive nature of the master variables, human migration across borders provides new parameters for politics and pressures for governance and institutional performance.

24. The knowledge representation of agriculture as a domain of human activity incorporates activities on both the supply side (production) and the demand side

(consumption), including various forms of management thereof. John L. Gittleman and Matthew E. Gompper capture these ecological issues appropriately in the title of their 2001 *Science* article, "The Risk of Extinction: What You Don't Know Will Hurt You."

25. These responses include (1) improved market mechanisms, (2) better government oversight, (3) reducing socioeconomic inequalities and improving health and related conditions, (4) improved policy responses, in both formal and informal networks, and (5) new policy principles, such as polluter pays and the precautionary principle, both important innovations in the domain of collaborative responses.

26. These include new techniques for forest uses and reforestation, better logging practices, and, most important, applications of tools and methods for monitoring change. In the sociopolitical domain, an emphasis on improved legislation, coupled with "responsible" agroforestry and forest management programs, are among the most conventional strategies.

27. See Gaston (2000) for a systematic survey of global patterns in biodiversity, and McCann (2000) for the set of contentions that have been referred to as the "diversity-stability debate" (228) referring to the issue of how we expect ecosystems, which are life supporting systems, to adjust or respond to the loss of diversity.

28. For recent political contentions, see Stone (1992), and for future scenarios for global biodiversity, see Sala et al. (2000). Central to the latter are matters of uncertainty.

29. See Chapin et al. (2000) for a discussion of the consequences of changing biological diversity.

30. The research communities supporting various alternatives—notably solar, wind, geothermal, hydro, tidal, fuel cell, and hydrogen—appear vibrant in their quest for viable options. The differences in priorities and preferences may well prevent distortions associated with "picking a winner" independent of performance.

31. It is often tempting to overlook yet another critical feature of the energy domain, namely the provision system. As Herman Scheer (2002) aptly reminds us, all effective utilization of all sources of energy requires a supply chain in place. The nature, length, security, and flexibility of the supply chain go a long way in contributing to the more practical dimensions of social choices of energy sources. Scheer also points to what he calls the "distorting" effects associated with conventional sources, specifically fossil fuels, and most notably those associated with the added hazards of nuclear energy (ibid., 121–127, 154–157).

32. This is a good example of potential gains from the transfer of U.S. knowledge to other parts of the world, notably China.

33. To date, there seems to be no consistent patterns indicating what or where that "elsewhere" is likely to be, other than away from densely populated centers in industrialized countries. In essence, some form of global zoning may be taking shape, driven more by the policies of industrialized countries and those of developing countries but not necessarily on environmental issues.

34. We return to these and related issues in chapter 9 when we consider the implications of cyberspace.

35. See Vincent (1992, 1651) for the argument that the "tropical timber trade appears to have promoted neither sustained forest management nor sustained forest-based industrialization," an observation that reflects prevailing concerns surrounding the trade-sustainability issue in this domain.

36. In chapter 6 we considered a wider range of cyber conflicts; here we consider only the physical conflicts, specifically (1) wars and armed conflicts (2) violent and nonviolent conflicts, and (3) inter- and intrastate armed conflicts, for different and partially overlapping time frames (e.g., Collier et al. 2003). It is not easy to reconcile the various quantitative bases in the field or the different ways in which conflict is defined and measured.

37. Scholars and analysts alike have their preferred sources. In some cases, there is a common source that serves as the "default option," such as the Correlates of War Project.

38. See *Statistics of Deadly Quarrels* (Richardson 1960) as a major statistical account of war. The first econometric simulation and forecasting study of the dynamics leading to violence, *Nations in Conflict* (Choucri and North 1975), motivated by this earlier work, is also the first formal specification of the theory of lateral pressure. Comparative reviews of contending theories of international conflict, such as Midlarsky (1989) and Levy (1989), highlight some of the differences in assumptions and analysis. For the most part, studies of international conflict focus on the state as a unit of analysis (individually, in dyads, or in groups, but always with the state as the focus).

39. When countries commit to formal responses, they do so without necessarily implying commonality of type or form of response. They are only expressing their commitment to the principle of joint response. What is shared is a form of collective responsibility, however defined, not necessarily the agreement on the "causes" of the problem but a commitment to jointness of the solution. Again, there are major differences in the content, extent, and seriousness with which jointness is viewed and acted upon. Even when responsibility for environmental degradation is accorded to one country or another, there still is an underlying presumption of shared concern and of a need for a common response.

40. Stakeholder engagement is an important new mechanism in institutional development.

41. As a member of the Working Group on Technology Transfer and Cooperation, the author was able to observe the drafting and formulating process at close quarters.

42. See United Nations Conference on Environment and Development's *Agenda 21: Programme of Action for Sustainable Development* (1992).

43. Debates abound, however, about the precise definition of sustainable development, the dimensions of sustainability, and the ways in which societies can or should endeavor to meet sustainability conditions. The issues are complex, as are the interconnections within, among, and between causes and consequences. More recently, the term "sustainable growth" may have amended the initial concept, or

perhaps reintroduced the very concept that sustainability was designed to avoid, namely, growth per se. Later we provide a more comprehensive—and possibly less diplomatic and less political—definition of sustainability.

44. This threefold perspective on society, economy, and environment is framed largely for diplomatic if not political purposes. It is as neutral a specification as one could possibly imagine.

45. For example, Choucri (1999b) developed a generalized "causal logic" of the relationship between institutional capabilities, as defined by Almond and Powell (1966) and aspects of national security. Christie and Warbuton (2001) presented an overview of current thinking pertaining to good governance for sustainability. International institutions themselves can provide powerful motivations for the development of new institutional systems and new mechanisms of governance (Haas, Keohane, and Levy 1993).

Chapter 9

1. When we examined ten major self-defined sustainable development knowledge systems, taking into account mission, management, and material, and compared them in terms of structure and content, the GSSD stood out in important ways. Of the original set of knowledge systems examined, only four survived for the second round of comparisons. In the second round, undertaken two years later, only one system, the GSSD, was found to have a formal ontology to enable knowledge organization for provision and retrieval and also operated in two major non-Western languages. Reports on the analysis and supporting materials are available from the author upon request.

2. These are (1) types of human activities, (2) known problems associated with human activities, (3) scientific and technological solutions to known problems, (4) socioeconomic and national policy responses, and (5) international accords and coordinated action. Each principle provides the basis for a system of nested subcategories.

3. More important, there is as yet no comprehensive view of the ways in which major forms of human activities generate problems, nor is there a coherent understanding of various solutions, social or technical. Providing a systematic and internally consistent conceptual map is a step in the direction of intellectual order and coherence, one that serves as an important means of unbundling the knowledge content of sustainable development. Google provides excellent search functions but does not provide content organization services, nor does it seek to do so.

4. The tendency to focus on the uses of knowledge underestimates the power inherent in its reuses. Exploiting two characteristics of knowledge, complementarity and leakage, contributes to our understanding of "the potential for virtuous and vicious circles" (Easterly 2002, 153).

5. As Suzanne C. Iacono and Peter A. Freeman note (2006, 467), such joint activity is made easier "when a shared language exists and the countries' policies encourage and enable working across geographic areas." If these conditions hold,

then the power of synergy embedded in networking can be greatly enhanced. If they do not, then the cleavages and the fault lines remain.

6. This consolidation can be done through knowledge provision by customizing the routing of e-materials from the point of origin (anywhere in the world) and through knowledge retrieval by enhancing user capacities for identification and selection.

7. The GSSD operates in two non-Western languages, Arabic and Chinese. Most of the world is non-English speaking, but despite the great variety of languages used in cyber venues, English is still the major language but, as shown in chapter 3, its dominance is on the decline. It is increasingly important that knowledge users as well as knowledge providers from various parts of the world express themselves in appropriate languages and idioms, using appropriate concepts and terms.

Chapter 10

1. Chapter 2 presents the highlights of lateral pressure theory and some extensions of the theory to cyberspace.

2. See chapter 8 for an illustrative discussion of trends in war and in other key features of the global system.

3. Few self-respecting national leaders would declare publicly that "the priority is unrestricted growth at any cost—environment is not relevant." Anything along those lines would now be considered poor public relations and potentially damaging to the international image of the leader and the nation.

4. Chapters 6, 7, 8, and 9 illustrate different types of constitutive features.

5. In chapter 6 we examined the different ways in which countries make it difficult for citizens to participate in cyber venues, as well as more recent efforts to control access to particular content.

6. The specific uses of this power are not at issue here. This type of power can be constructive—in support of peace, for example—or destructive, fueling hatred and inciting extremist activities.

7. This episode was triggered by the decisions and actions of individuals at two locations, the source of materials and the dissemination point.

8. Even in highly controlled political systems, we see signs of aggregation efforts—at least as inferred from the patterns of state cyber controls.

9. As Robert C. North (1990) reminds us, individuals (and systems of social actors) are situated and interact across the boundaries of their internal and external environments. Not only are the boundaries themselves important constructs, but how they are managed often becomes intensely political.

10. This observation must be placed in the context of the theoretical discussion in chapter 2.

11. For example, the United States has traditionally focused on external military threats and more recently has become more aware of cyber threats, but

environmental concerns are not central to its overall security calculus, nor is the nature of the regime or the support of its constituencies. The breakup of the Soviet Union was largely a function of the failure of internal security, in all senses of the term, and unrelated to external or military security. For the most part, authoritarian regimes are generally more concerned about internal threats to their survival than about external factors or threats to the life-supporting properties of the natural environment. At this point almost every state is on alert with respect to cyber sources of insecurity, but to different degrees and for different reasons.

12. In chapter 6 we discussed states' uses of different forms of filtering to control access to content via cyber venues by their citizens. The filtering strategy is more discriminating than the earlier strategy of denying access entirely and perhaps is expected to be considered less intrusive.

13. The constitutive potentials of cyberspace can be powerful enough to alter the nature of interactions among actors—cooperation or conflict, as the case may be—and possibly alter the stakes themselves.

14. Elsewhere we have argued that the sustainability of a state is contingent on (1) the resilience of its natural environment; (2) the efficiency of its economic activities; (3) the performance of its political system; and (4) the effectiveness of its institutions and organizations (Choucri, Goldsmith, et al. 2007). We have also outlined the derivative conditions and contingencies such that more specific criteria can be articulated to reflect each of these requisites.

15. All evidence indicates that the state will not hesitate to intervene in cyber-related processes if its national interests are impinged upon, as shown in chapter 6.

16. Chapter 6 shows how dynamics of conflict and warfare that have traditionally been articulated in the context of state interactions must now be reframed to take into account non-state groups and their activity.

17. This feature, drawn from the theory of lateral pressure, is related to Gilpin (1987), who articulated the cogent logic of change in international power relations.

18. For the most part, social scientists have approached networks mainly in comparative and cross-sectional terms rather than in intertemporal and longitudinal terms. For an insightful set of essays, see Kahler (2009).

19. Introduced earlier in chapter 7, the provision of global public goods may well become one of the most important features of twenty-first century politics, national and international. As noted, among the thorny questions associated with global public good is an agreement among the providers (defined as states, most notably) regarding each of the terms, *global, public,* and *good.*

20. As Nives Dolsak and Elinor Ostrom (2003) demonstrate in *The Commons in the New Millennium,* there are multiple ways of addressing such issues rooted in current understandings of the commons, and none of these is particularly easy.

21. These emergent institutional modes can be viewed as collaborative in form, consistent with and extending the analysis in chapter 7. Alternatively, they might

be candidates for conflictual cyberpolitics, consistent with the investigations in chapter 6. Given the situational interconnections between conflict and cooperation, it can be difficult to extract the pure form.

22. The comparisons of cyber access in chapter 3 are only the tip of the a proverbial iceberg, one that is increasingly complex and changing.

23. Earlier we noted that one of the distinctive modalities of cyberpolitics involves contentions over the management of cyberspace. Indeed, recently formulated notions surrounding the "command of the commons," as framed in military and security circles, may be more readily applicable to the management or governance of cyberspace than as a reflection of an emergent cyber commons.

24. Sustainability at the global level is contingent on the viability and resilience of all living elements, including humans as well as other entities, species, and domains. This observation will not find immediate resonance in traditional international relations theory, even though human-induced climate change is now well recognized as one of the most important legacies of the twentieth century. On normative grounds, clearly, everyone's sustainability matters. But politics, real or virtual, creates powerful complexities.

References

Abramson, Bram Dov. 2000. Internet Globalization Indicators. *Telecommunications Policy* 24:69–74.

Agnew, John A., and Stuart Corbridge. 1995. *Mastering Space: Hegemony, Territory and International Political Economy*. New York: Routledge.

Agre, Philip E., and Marc Rotenberg. 2001. *Technology and Privacy: The New Landscape*. Cambridge, MA: MIT Press.

Alker, Hayward R., Jr. 1996. *Rediscoveries and Reformulations: Humanistic Methodologies for International Studies*. Cambridge: Cambridge University Press.

Alker, Hayward R., Jr., and Thomas J. Biersteker. 1984. The Dialectics of World Order: Notes for a Future Archeologist of International Savoir Faire. *International Studies Quarterly* 28:121–142.

Alker, Hayward R., Jr., and Peter M. Haas. 1993. The Rise of Global Ecopolitics. In *Global Accord: Environmental Challenges and International Responses*, ed. Nazli Choucri, 133–71. Cambridge, MA: MIT Press.

Almond, Gabriel A., and H. Bingham Powell, Jr. 1966. *Comparative Politics: A Developmental Approach*. Boston: Little, Brown.

Analysis Ltd. 2000. *The Network Revolution and the Developing World Report: A Literature Review*. Washington, DC: World Bank.

Alt, James E., and Kenneth A. Shepsle, eds. 1990. *Perspectives on Positive Political Economy*. New York: Cambridge University Press.

Anderson, Philip W., Kenneth J. Arrow, and David Pines, eds. 1988. *The Economy as an Evolving Complex System*. Reading, MA: Addison-Wesley Publishing Co.

Anderson, Sarah, John Cavanaugh, and Thea Lee. 2000. *Field Guide to the Global Economy*. New York: New Press.

Anderson, Ross, and Tyler Moore. 2006. The Economics of Information Security. *Science* 314 (October): 610–613.

Arbetman, Marina, and Jacek Kugler, eds. 1997. *Political Capacity and Economic Behavior*. Boulder, CO: Westview Press.

Arens, V., C. Y. Chee, C.-N. Hsu, and C. A. Knoblock. 1993. Retrieving and Integrating Data from Multiple Information Sources. *International Journal of Intelligent and Cooperative Information Systems* 2 (2): 127–158.

Arnold, Fred. 1990. International Migration: Who Goes Where? *Finance and Development* 27 (June): 46–47.

Aron, Raymond. 1966. *Peace & War: A Theory of International Relations.* New York: Doubleday.

Aronson, Jonathan. 2002. Global Networks and Their Impact. In *Information Technologies and Global Politics: The Changing Scope of Power and Governance,* ed. James Rosenau and J. P. Singh. Albany: State University of New York Press.

Arthur, W. Brian. 1995. Complexity in Economic and Financial Markets. *Complexity* 1 (1): 20–26.

Arzberger, Peter, Peter Schroeder, Anne Beaulieu, Geof Bowker, Kathleen Casey, Leif Laaksonen, David Moorman, Paul Uhlir, and Paul Wouters. 2004. An International Framework to Promote Access to Data. *Science* 303 (March): 1777–1778.

Ásgeirsdóttir, Berglind. 2006. OECD Work on Knowledge and the Knowledge Economy. In *Advancing Knowledge and the Knowledge Economy,* ed. Brian Kahin and Dominique Foray. Cambridge, MA: MIT Press.

Ashley, Richard A. 1980. *The Political Economy of War and Peace: The Sino-Soviet-American Triangle and the Modern Security Problematique.* New York: Nichols Publishing.

A. T. Kearney. Foreign Policy Magazine Globalization Index. 2001. Measuring Globalization. *Foreign Policy* 122 (January/February): 56–65.

Ausubel, Jesse H., and H. Dale Langford, eds. 1997. *Technological Trajectories and the Human Environment.* Washington, DC: National Academy Press.

Axelrod, Robert, and Michael D. Cohen. 1999. *Harnessing Complexity: Organizational Implications of a Scientific Frontier.* New York: Free Press.

Baker, Wallace R. 1994. Law, Chaos, and Complexity. Lecture delivered at the Workshop on Crude Look at the Whole (CLAW), Santa Fe Institute, Santa Fe, NM, April 9–11.

Balkin, Jack M., James Grimmelmann, Eddan Katz, Nimrod Kozlovski, Shlomit Wagman, and Tal Zarsky, eds. 2007. *Cybercrime: Digital Cops in a Networked Environment.* New York: New York University Press.

Barabási, Albert-László. 2002. *Linked.* New York: Plume Books.

Barraclough, Geoffrey, ed. 1999. *HarperCollins Atlas of World History.* Ann Arbor, MI: Borders Press.

Barrett, Neil. 1997. *The State of the Cybernation: Cultural, Political and Economic Implications of the Internet.* London: Kogan Page.

Barzel, Yoram. 1997. *Economic Analysis of Property Rights: Political Economy of Institutions and Decisions.* 2nd ed. New York: Cambridge University Press.

Baskaran, Angathevar, and Mammo Muchie. 2006. *Bridging the Digital Divide: Innovation Systems for ICT in Brazil, China, Thailand, and Southern Africa.* London: Andonis & Abbey Publishers Ltd.

Bates, Robert H. 2001. *Prosperity and Violence: The Political Economy of Development.* New York: W. W. Norton.

Baylis, John, Steve Smith, and Patricia Owens, eds. 2011. *The Globalization of World Politics*. 5th ed. New York: Oxford University Press.

Beagle, Donald. 1999. Conceptualizing an Information Commons. *Journal of Academic Librarianship* 25 (2): 82–89.

Bealy, Frank. 1999. *Blackwell Dictionary of Political Science: A User's Guide to Its Terms*. Oxford: Blackwell.

Becker, Theodore, and Christa Daryl Slaton. 2000. *The Future of Teledemocracy*. Westport, CT: Praeger.

Becker, Egon, and Thomas Jahn, eds. 1999. *Sustainability and the Social Sciences*. London: Zed Books.

Benedikt, Michael, ed. 1994a. *Cyberspace: First Steps*. Cambridge, MA: MIT Press.

Benedikt, Michael. 1994b. Cyberspace: Some Proposals. In *Cyberspace: First Steps*, ed. Michael Benedikt, 119–224. Cambridge, MA: MIT Press.

Benkler, Yochai. 2006. *The Wealth of Networks: How Social Production Transforms Markets and Freedom*. New Haven, CT: Yale University Press.

Berners-Lee, Tim, and James Hendler. 2001. Publishing on the Semantic Web. *Nature* 410 (April): 1023–1024.

Best, Samuel J., and Brian S. Krueger. 2008. Political Conflict and Public Perceptions of Government Surveillance on the Internet: An Experiment of Online Search Terms. *Journal of Information Technology & Politics* 5 (2): 191–212.

Bhagwati, Jagdish. 1993. The Case for Free Trade. *Scientific American* 269 (November): 42–49.

Bisby, Frank A. 2000. The Quiet Revolution: Biodiversity Informatics and the Internet. *Science* 289 (September): 2309–2312.

Black, Richard, and Howard White. 2004. *Targeting Development: Critical Perspectives on the Millennium Development Goals*. Oxford: Routledge.

Bloom, David E., and David Canning. 2000. The Health and Wealth of Nations. *Science* 287 (February): 1207–1209.

Bloomfield, Lincoln P., and Allan Moulton. 1997. *Managing International Conflict: From Theory to Policy*. New York: St. Martin's Press (supplemented by CASCON web site http://mit.edu/cascon).

Blumenthal, Margory, and David D. Clark. 2001. Rethinking the Design of the Internet: The End-to-End Arguments vs. the Brave New World. *ACM Transactions on Internet Technology* 1 (1): 70–109.

Borgatti, Stephen P., Ajay Mehra, Daniel J. Brass, and Giuseppe Labianca. 2009. Network Analysis in the Social Sciences. *Science* 323 (February 13): 892–895.

Borgman, Christine L. 2000. *From Gutenberg to the Global Information Infrastructure: Access to Information in the Networked World*. Cambridge, MA: MIT Press.

Boulding, Kenneth E. 1956. *The Image: Knowledge and Life in Society*. Ann Arbor: University of Michigan Press.

Braman, Sandra. 2006. *Change of State: Information, Policy, and Power*. Cambridge, MA: MIT Press.

Brecher, Michael. 1996. Introduction: Crisis, Conflict, War—State of the Discipline. *International Political Science Review* 17 (2): 127–139.

Brecher, Michael, and Frank Harvey, eds. 2005. *Millennial Reflections on International Studies*. Ann Arbor: University of Michigan Press.

Bremmer, Ian. 2010. Democracy in Cyberspace: What Information Technology Can and Cannot Do. *Foreign Affairs (Council on Foreign Relations)* 89 (6): 86–92.

Bridges.org. 2001. *Comparison of e-Readiness Assessment Models*. Durbanville, SA: Bridges.org.

British Petroleum. 2007. *BP Statistical Review of World Energy 2007*. London: British Petroleum.

British Petroleum. 2010. *BP Statistical Review of World Energy 2010*. London: British Petroleum.

Brodhag, Christian. 2000. Information, gouvernance et développement durable. *International Political Science Review* 21 (3): 311–327.

Brown, John Seely, and Paul Duguid. 2000. *The Social Life of Information*. Cambridge, MA: Harvard Business Press.

Brown, Karen. 2002. Environmental Data. Water Scarcity: Forecasting the Future with Spotty Data. *Science* 297 (August): 926–927.

Brynjolfsson, Erik, and Brian Kahin. 2000. *Understanding the Digital Economy*. Cambridge, MA: MIT Press.

Butler, Alison. 2000. Environmental, Protection and Free Trade: Are They Mutually Exclusive? In *International Political Economy: Perspectives on Global Power and Wealth*. 4th ed., ed. Jeffrey A. Frieden and David A. Lake, 446–461. New York: St. Martin's Press.

Byravan, Sujatha, and Sudhir Chella Rajan. 2005. Immigration Could Ease Climate-Change Impact. *Nature* 434 (March): 435.

Calvet, A. L. 1981. A Synthesis of Foreign Direct Investment Theories and Theories of the Multinational Firm. *Journal of International Business Studies* 12 (1): 43–47.

Camp, L. Jean. 2000. *Trust and Risk in Internet Commerce*. Cambridge, MA: MIT Press.

Campbell, John, and Ove Pedersen. 2001. *The Rise of Neoliberalism and Institutional Analysis*. Princeton, NJ: Princeton University Press.

Capra, Fritjof. 2002. *The Hidden Connections: Integrating the Biological, Cognitive, and Social Dimensions of Life into a Science of Sustainability*. New York: Doubleday.

Castells, Manuel. 2000. *The Rise of Network Society*. 2nd ed. New York: Wiley-Blackwell.

Castells, Manuel. 2001. *The Internet Galaxy: Reflections on the Internet, Business, and Society*. New York: Oxford University Press.

Castells, Manuel. 2005. Global Governance and Global Politics. *PS: Political Science and Politics* 38 (5): 9–16.

Castells, Manuel, Mireia Fernandez-Ardevol, Jack Linchuan Qiu, and Araba Sey. 2004. *Mobile Communication and Society: A Global Perspective.* Cambridge, MA: MIT Press.

Cengage Learning. 2003. *Modern Distribution of World Religions.* Florence, KY: Cengage Learning. http://www.wadsworth.com/religion_d/special_features/popups/maps/matthews_world/content/map_01.html.

Cerny, Philip G. 1995. Globalization and the Changing Logic of Collective Action. *International Organization* 49 (4): 595–625.

Chapin, F. Stuart III, Erika S. Zavaleta, Valerie T. Eviner, Rosamond L. Naylor, Peter M. Vitousek, Heather L. Reynolds, et al. 2000. Consequences of Changing Biodiversity. *Nature* 405:234–242.

Chen, John-ren, Richard Hule, and Herbert Stocker. 2000. Introduction. In *Foreign Direct Investment*, ed. John-ren Chen, 1–5. New York: St. Martin's Press.

Chichilnisky, Graciela. 1996. *Development and Global Finance: The Case for an International Bank for Environmental Settlements.* United Nations Development Programme. New York: United Nations.

Chichilnisky, Graciela. 1998. The Knowledge Revolution. *The Journal of International Trade and Economic Development* (71): 39–54.

Chichilnisky, Graciela, Geoffrey Heal, and A. Vercelli. 1998. *Sustainability: Dynamics and Uncertainty.* New York: Singer Publishing Co.

Christie, Ian, and Mark Hepworth. 2001. Towards the Sustainable e-Region. In *Digital Futures: Living in a Dot-Com World*, ed. John Wilson, 140–162. Sterling, VA: Earthscan.

Choucri, Nazli. 1969. The Perceptual Base of Nonalignment. *Journal of Conflict Resolution* 13:57–74.

Choucri, Nazli. 1974. *Population Dynamics and International Violence: Propositions, Insights, and Evidence.* Lanham, MD: Lexington Books.

Choucri, Nazli. 1981. *International Energy Futures: Petroleum Prices, Power, and Payments.* Cambridge, MA: MIT Press.

Choucri, Nazli, ed. 1984. *Multidisciplinary Perspectives on Population and Conflict.* Syracuse, NY: Syracuse University Press.

Choucri, Nazli. 1992. Environment and Conflict: New Principles for Environmental Conduct. *Disarmament* 15 (1): 67–78.

Choucri, Nazli, ed. 1993a. *Global Accord: Environmental Challenges and International Responses.* Cambridge, MA: MIT Press.

Choucri, Nazli. 1993b. Multinational Corporations and the Global Environment. In *Global Accord: Environmental Challenges and International Responses*, ed. Nazli Choucri, 205–254. Cambridge, MA: MIT Press.

Choucri, Nazli. 1993c. Political Economy of the Global Environment. *International Political Science Review* 14 (1) (January): 103–116.

Choucri, Nazli. 1994a. Corporate Strategies toward Sustainability. In *Sustainable Development and International Law*, ed. Winfried Lang, 189–201. Boston: Graham & Trotman/Martinus Nijhoff Publishers.

Choucri, Nazli. 1994b. Innovative Strategies in Technology and Finance for Sustainable Development. Prepared for the Environment and Natural Resources Group of the United Nations Development Programme.

Choucri, Nazli. 1995. Globalization of Eco-Efficiency: GSSD on the WWW. *UNEP Industry and Environment,* October–December, 45–49.

Choucri, Nazli. 1999a. Innovations in Use of Cyberspace. In *Sustainability and the Social Sciences*, ed. Egon Becker and Thomas Jahn, 274–283. New York: Zed Books.

Choucri, Nazli. 1999b. The Political Logic of Sustainability. In *Sustainability and the Social Sciences*, ed. Egon Becker and Thomas Jahn, 143–161. New York: Zed Books.

Choucri, Nazli. 1999c. Strategic Partnerships with Multilingual Functionality for Globalisation and Localisation. Prepared for the European Commission Directorate-General Information Society Workshop on Sustainability and Environment, IST99, Helsinki, Finland.

Choucri, Nazli. 2000. CyberPolitics in International Relations. *International Political Science Review* 21 (3): 243–263.

Choucri, Nazli. 2001. Environmentalism. In *Oxford Companion to Politics of the World*. 2nd ed., ed. J. Krieger, 253–255. New York: Oxford University Press.

Choucri, Nazli, Vincent Maugis, Stuart Madnick, and Michael Siegel. 2003. *Global e-Readiness – for WHAT? Paper 177.* Center for eBusiness at MIT. http://ebusiness.mit.edu/research/papers/177_choucri_global_ereadiness.pdf.

Choucri, Nazli. 2004. Value of Knowledge Project. Alliance for Global Sustainability, MIT, Cambridge, MA.

Choucri, Nazli, Daniel Goldsmith, Stuart Madnick, Dinsha Mistree, J. Bradley Morrison, and Michael D. Siegel. 2007. Using System Dynamics to Model and Better Understand State Stability. CISL Working Paper No. 2007–03. Composite Information Systems Laboratory, Sloan School of Management, MIT, Cambridge, MA. http://web.mit.edu/smadnick/www/wp/2007-03.pdf

Choucri, Nazli, Gerard McHugh, and Steven M.L. Millman. 1998. Innovations in Cyberpartnering for Sustainability. In *Care Innovation '98: Proceedings, Second International Symposium.* Brokerage Event and Environmental Exhibition, Vienna, Austria.

Choucri, Nazli, Dinsha Mistree, Farnaz Haghseta, Toufic Mezher, Wallace R. Baker, and Carlos I. Ortiz, eds. 2007. *Mapping Sustainability: Knowledge e-Networking and the Value Chain.* New York: Springer.

Choucri, Nazli, and Robert C. North. 1972. Dynamics of International Conflict: Some Policy Implications of Population, Resources, and Technology. *World Politics* 24:80–122.

Choucri, Nazli, and Robert C. North. 1975. *Nations in Conflict: National Growth and International Violence.* San Francisco: W. H. Freeman.

Choucri, Nazli, and Robert C. North. 1989. Lateral Pressure in International Relations: Concept and Theory. In *Handbook of War Studies*, ed. Manus I. Midlarsky, 289–326. Ann Arbor: University of Michigan Press.

Choucri, Nazli, and Robert C. North.1993a. Global Accord: Imperatives for the Twenty-First Century. In *Global Accord: Environmental Challenges and International Responses*, ed. Nazli Choucri, 477-507. Cambridge, MA: MIT Press.

Choucri, Nazli, and Robert C. North. 1993b. Population and Security: National Perspectives and Global Imperatives. In *Emerging Trends in International Security*, ed. David B. Dewitt, David Haglund, and John Kirton. New York: Oxford University Press.

Choucri, Nazli, and Robert C. North. 1993c. Growth, Development, and Environmental Sustainability: Profile and Paradox. In *Global Accord: Environmental Challenges and International Responses*, ed. Nazli Choucri, 67–132. Cambridge, MA: MIT Press.

Choucri, Nazli, Robert C. North, and Suzumu Yamakage. 1992. *The Challenge of Japan before World War II and After: A Study of National Growth and Expansion.* London: Routledge.

Choucri, Nazli, Robert C. North. 1987. Roots of War: The Master Variables. In *The Quest for Peace: Transcending Collective Violence and War Among Societies, Cultures and States*, ed. Raimo Väyrynen in collaboration with Dieter Senghaas, and Christian Schmidt, 204–216. London, England: Sage Publications Ltd.

Choucri, Nazli and Robert Reardon. 2010. CyberPolitics and International Relations Theory. Working Paper, MIT: Explorations in Cyber International Relations Project.

Choucri, Nazli, and Thomas W. Robinson, eds. 1978. *Forecasting in International Relations.* San Francisco: W. H. Freeman.

Cincotta, Richard P., Robert Engelman, and Daniele Anastasion. 2003. *The Security Demographic: Population and Civil Conflict after the Cold War.* Washington, DC: Population Action International.

Cioffi-Revilla, Claudio. 1998. *Politics and Uncertainty: Theory, Models and Applications.* Cambridge: Cambridge University Press.

Clark, David D. 2010. Characterizing Cyberspace: Past, Present and Future. MIT Working Paper Series, Version 1.2, March 12.

Clark, William C. 1991. Energy and Environment: Strategic Perspectives on Policy Design. In *Energy and the Environment in the 21st Century*, ed. Jefferson W. Tester, David O. Wood, and Nancy A. Ferrari, 63–78. Cambridge, MA: MIT Press.

Clarke, Richard A., and Robert Knake. 2010. *Cyber War: The Next Threat to National Security and What To Do About It.* New York: HarperCollins.

Coase, R. H. 1992. The Institutional Structure of Production. Occasional Papers from the Law School, the University of Chicago, No. 28. Noble Prize Lecture. Chicago: Hein & Co.

Collier, Paul. V. L. Elliott, Håvard Hegre, Anke Hoeffler, Marta Reynal-Querol, and Nicholas Sambanis. 2003. *Breaking the Conflict Trap: Civil War and Development Policy.* World Bank Policy Research Reports. Washington, DC: World Bank.

Conca, Ken. 2006. *Governing Water.* Correlates of War (COW) Project. Cambridge, MA: MIT Press. http://www.correlatesofwar.org.

Costanza, R., Andrade, F., Antunes, P., van den Belt, M., Boersma, D., Boesch, D.F., Catarino, F., Hanna, S., Limburg, K., Low, B., Molitor, M., Pereia, J.C., Rayner, S., Santos, R., Wilson, J., Young, M. 1988. Principles for Sustainable Governance of the Oceans. *Science* 281 (July): 198–199.

Costanza, Robert, Ralph d'Arge, Rudolf de Groot, Stephen Farber, Monica Grasso, Bruce Hannon, Karin Limburge, et al. 1997. The Value of the World's Ecosystem Services and Natural Capital. *Nature* 387 (May): 253–260.

Coyle, Diane. 1997. *The Weightless World: Strategies for Managing the Digital Economy.* Cambridge, MA: MIT Press.

Crandall, Robert W., and James H. Alleman. 2002. *Broadband.* Washington, DC: Brookings Institution Press.

Culotta, Elizabeth, Andrew Sugden, Brooks Hanson, Michael Balter, Ann Gibbons, and Eliot Marshall. 2001. Human Evolution: Migrations. *Science* 291 (March): 1721–1732.

Cyert, Richard M., and James G. March. 1963. *A Behavioral Theory of the Firm.* Englewood Cliffs, NJ: Prentice-Hall.

Daly, Herman E. 1991. *Steady-State Economics.* 2nd ed. Washington, DC: Island Press.

David, Paul A. 2000. Understanding Digital Technology's Evolution and the Path of Measured Productivity Growth: Present and Future in the Mirror of the Past. In *Understanding the Digital Economy*, ed. Erik Brynjolfsson and Brian Kahin, 49–95. Cambridge, MA: MIT Press.

David, Paul A. 2006. Towards a Cyberinfrastructure for Enhanced Scientific Collaboration: Providing Its "Soft" Foundation May Be the Hardest Part. In *Advancing Knowledge and the Knowledge Economy*, ed. Brian Kahin and Dominque Foray, 431–453. Cambridge, MA: MIT Press.

Day, Richard H. 2004. *The Divergent Dynamics of Economic Growth: Studies in Adaptive Economizing, Technological Change, and Economic Development.* Cambridge: Cambridge University Press.

de Borchgrave, Arnaud, Frank J. Cilluffo, Sharon L. Cardash, and Michele M. Ledgerwood. 2001. *Cyber Threats and Information Security: Meeting the 21st Century Challenge.* Center for Strategic and International Studies. Washington DC: CSIS Press.

De Grauwe, P., and F. Camerman. 2002. How Big Are the Big Multinational Companies? *Review of Business Economics* 47 (3): 311–326.

Deibert, Ronald J. 1997. *Parchment, Printing, and Hypermedia.* New York: Columbia University Press.

Deibert, Ronald J. and Janet Gross Stein. 2003. Social and Electronic Networks in the War on Terror. In *Bombs and Bandwidth: The Emerging Relationship Between Information Technology and Security,* ed. Robert Latham, 157–174. New York, NY: New Press.

Deibert, Ronald, John Palfrey, Rafal Rohozinski, and Jonathan Zittrain, eds. 2008. *Access Denied: The Practice and Policy of Global Internet Filtering.* Cambridge, MA: MIT Press.

Diebert, Ronald, John Palfrey, Rafal Rohozinski, and Jonathan Zittrain, eds. *Accessed Controlled: The Shaping of Power, Rights, and Rule in Cyberspace.* 2010. Cambridge, MA: MIT Press.

de Sola Pool, Ithiel, and Manfred Kochen. 1978–1979. Contacts and Influence. *Social Networks* 1 (1): 5–51.

Deutsch, Karl W. 1963. *The Nerves of Government: Models of Political Communication and Control.* New York: Free Press.

Deutsch, Karl W. 1968. *The Analysis of International Relations.* Englewood Cliffs, NJ: Prentice-Hall.

Deutsch, Karl W. 1980. *Politics and Government: How People Decide Their Fate.* 3rd ed. Boston: Houghton Mifflin.

Deutsch, Karl. W., S. A. Burrell, R. A. Kann, M. Lee, Jr., M. Lichterman, R. E. Lindgren, F. L. Loewenheim, and R. W. van Wagenen. 1957. *Political Community and the North Atlantic Area: International Organization in the Light of Historical Experience.* Princeton, NJ: Princeton University Press.

Diamond, Jared. 1999. *Guns, Germs, & Steel.* New York: W. W. Norton.

Diamond, Jared. 2001. Unwritten Knowledge. *Nature* 410 (March): 521.

Diamond, Jared. 2002. Life with the Artificial Anasazi. *Nature* 419 (October): 567–569.

Diamond, Jared. 2005. *Collapse.* New York: Penguin Group.

Dickson, David. 2001. Weaving a Social Web. *Nature* 414 (December): 587.

Dodge, Martin, and Rob Kitchin. 2001. *Mapping Cyberspace.* New York: Routledge.

Dolsak, Nives, and Elinor Ostrom. 2003. *The Commons in the New Millennium Challenges and Adaptation.* Cambridge, MA: MIT Press.

Dowty, Alan, and Gil Loescher. 1996. Refugee Flows as Grounds for International Action. *International Security* 21 (1): 61.

Drake, William J., and Ernest J. Wilson III eds. 2008. *Governing Global Electronic Networks: International Perspectives on Policy and Power.* Cambridge, MA: MIT Press.

Driesen, David. 2003. *The Economic Dynamics of Environmental Law.* Cambridge, MA: MIT Press.

Dryzek, John S. 1997. *The Politics of the Earth: Environmental Discourses.* Oxford: Oxford University Press.

Dunning, J. H. 1999. *Governments, Globalization, and International Business.* New York: Oxford University Press.

Easterly, William. 2002. *The Elusive Quest for Growth: Economists' Adventures and Misadventures in the Tropics.* Cambridge, MA: MIT Press.

Easton, David. 1953. *The Political System: An Inquiry into the State of Political Science.* New York: Alfred A. Knopf.

Easton, David. 1965. *A Systems Analysis of Political Life.* New York: Wiley.

Economic Commission for Latin America and the Caribbean. 2003. Road Maps towards an Information Society in Latin America and the Caribbean. Regional Preparatory Ministerial Conference of Latin America and the Caribbean for the World Summit on the Information Society, Bávaro, Punta Cana, Dominican Republic, January 29–31. http://www.eclac.org/cgi-bin/getProd.asp?xml=/noticias/noticias/8/11548/P11548.xml&xsl=/tpl-i/p1f.xsl&base=/tpl-i/top-bottom.xsl.

Ehrlich, Paul, John P. Holdren, and Anne H. Erhlich. 1978. *Ecoscience: Population, Resources, Environment.* San Francisco: W. H. Freeman.

Ehrlich, Paul R., and Edward O. Wilson. 1971. Biodiversity Studies: Science and Policy. *Science* 253 (August): 758–762.

Elkins, D. J. 1997. Globalization, Telecommunication, and Virtual Ethnic Communities. *International Political Science Association* 18 (2): 139–152.

Ellickson, Robert C. 1991. *Order Without Law: How Neighbors Settle Disputes.* Cambridge, MA: Harvard University Press.

Eriksson, Johan, and Giampiero Giacomello. 2004. International Relations Theory and Security in the Digital Age. Paper Presented at the Annual International Studies Association Convention, Montreal, March 17–20.

Eriksson, Johan, and Giampiero Giacomello. 2006. The Information Revolution, Security, and International Relations: (IR)relevant Theory? *International Political Science Review* 27 (3): 221–244.

Etheredge, Lloyd S. 2006. Grand Challenges: Mapping the Brain-Mind Connection of Emotion and Politics. Prepared for the National Science Foundation Grand Challenges of Mind and Brain project. Faculty paper, MIT, Cambridge, MA.

Evans, James A., and Jacob Reimer. 2009. Open Access and Global Participation in Science. *Science* 323:1025.

Feller, Joseph, Brian Fitzgerald, Scott A. Hissam, and Karim R. Lakhani, eds. 2005. *Perspectives on Free and Open Source Software.* Cambridge, MA: MIT Press.

Fensel, Dieter Andreas. 2001. *Ontologies: A Silver Bullet for Knowledge Management and Electronic Commerce.* Berlin: Springer.

Ferguson, Niall. 2000. A Powerful Leap from Chaos. *Nature* 408 (November): 21–22.

Ferguson, Yale H., and Richard W. Mansbach. 2008. *A World of Polities: Essays on Global Politics.* New York: Routledge.

Ferwerda, Jeremy, Nazli Choucri, and Stuart Madnick. 2010. Institutional Foundations for Cyber Security: Current Responses and New Challenges. CISL Working Paper No. 2009-03. Composite Information Systems Laboratory, Sloan School of Management, MIT, Cambridge, MA, September. http://web.mit.edu/ecir/pdf/madnick-2010-03.pdf.

Fligstein, Neil. 1990. *The Transformation of Corporate Control.* Cambridge, MA: Harvard University Press.

Food and Agriculture Organization. 1995. *Forest Resources Assessment 1990: Global Synthesis.* FAO Forestry Paper No. 124. Rome: Food and Agriculture Organization of the United Nations.

Foray, Dominique. 2004. *The Economics of Knowledge.* Cambridge, MA: MIT Press.

Foray, Dominique. 2006. Optimizing the Use of Knowledge. In *Advancing Knowledge and the Knowledge Economy,* ed. Brian Kahin and Dominique Foray, 9–15, Cambridge, MA: The MIT Press.

Foray, Dominique, and Brian Kahin, eds. 2006. *Advancing Knowledge and the Knowledge Economy.* Cambridge, MA: MIT Press.

Forrester, J. W. 1971. Counterintuitive Behavior of Social Systems. *Technology Review* 73 (January): 52–68.

Foster, Kenneth R., Paolo Vecchia, and H. Michael Repacholi. 2000. Risk Management: Science and the Precautionary Principle. *Science* 288 (May): 979–981.

Franklin, Jason, Adrian Perrig, Vern Paxson, and Stefan Savage. 2007. *An Inquiry into the Nature and Causes of the Wealth of Internet Miscreants.*Abstract from CCS: Proceedings of the 14th ACM Conference on Computer and Communications Security.

Frauenfelder, Mark. 2004. Domain Master. *Technology Review* 107 (March): 74–75.

French, Hilary. 2000. *Vanishing Borders: Protecting the Planet in the Age of Globalization.* New York: W. W. Norton.

French, Hilary. 2002. Reshaping Global Governance. In *State of the World 2002.* Worldwatch Institute, 174–198. New York: W. W. Norton.

Gaston, Kevin J. 2000. Global Patterns in Biodiversity. *Nature* 405 (May): 220–227.

Gewin, Virginia. 2002. All Living Things, Online. *Nature* 418 (July): 362–363.

Gell-Mann, Murray. 1994. *The Quark and the Jaguar: Adventures in the Simple and the Complex.* New York: W. H. Freeman.

Gell-Mann, Murray. 1995. What Is Complexity? *Complexity* 1:16–19.

Geller, Daniel S., and J. David Singer. 1997. *Nations at War: A Scientific Study of International Conflict.* New York: Cambridge University Press.

Georgescu-Roegen, N. 1978. *The Entropy Law and the Economic Process.* Cambridge, MA: Harvard University Press.

Getz, Wayne M., Louise Fortmann, David Cumming, Johan du Toit, Jodi Hilty, Rowan Martin, Michael Murphee, et al. 1999. Sustaining Natural and Human Capital: Villagers and Scientists. *Science* 283 (March): 1855–1857.

Ghosh, B. N. 2001. *Contemporary Issues in Development Economics.* London: Routledge.

Gibbons, Michael. 1999. Science's New Social Contract with Society. *Nature* 402 (supp.): C81–C84.

Gibson, William. 1984. *Neuromancer.* New York: Berkeley Publishing Group.

Giles, Jim. 2002. When Doubt Is a Sure Thing. *Nature* 418 (August): 476–478.

Gills, Barry, and William Thompson, eds. 2006. *Globalization and Global History.* London: Routledge.

Gilpin, Robert. 1987. *The Political Economy of International Relations.* Princeton, NJ: Princeton University Press.

Gilpin, Robert. 2001. *Global Political Economy: Understanding the International Economic Order.* Princeton, NJ: Princeton University Press.

Gittleman, John L., and Matthew E. Gompper. 2001. The Risk of Extinction: What You Don't Know Will Hurt You. *Science* 291:997–999.

Gleick, James. 1987. *Chaos: Making a New Science.* New York: Viking.

Gleick, Peter H. 2002. Soft Water Paths. *Nature* 418 (July): 373.

Glenn, Jerome C., and Theodore J. Gordon. 2007. *State of the Future.* World Federation of United Nations Associations: The Millennium Project. New York: United Nations.

Goldemberg, Jose. 1995. Energy Needs in Developing Countries and Sustainability. *Science* 269 (5227): 1058–1059.

Goldsmith, Jack, and Tim Wu. 2006. *Who Controls the Internet? Illusions of a Borderless World.* New York: Oxford University Press.

Goldstein, Joshua. 2003. *International Relations.* 5th ed. New York: Longman.

Goldstein, Joshua. 2011. *Winning the War on War: The Decline of Armed Conflict Worldwide.* New York: Dutton.

Goodman, Seymore E. and Herbert S. Lin, ed. 2007. Toward a Safer and More Secure Cyberspace. *National Research Council,* Washington, DC: National Academies Press.

Gosler, James R. 2005. The Digital Dimension. In *Transforming US Intelligence,* ed. Jennifer E. Simms and Burton Gerber, 96–114. Washington, DC: Georgetown University Press.

Goulder, Lawrence H., and Robert N. Stavins. 2002. An Eye on the Future. *Nature* 419 (October): 637–638.

Gourevitch, Peter. 1978. The Second Image Reversed: The International Sources of Domestic Politics. *International Organization* 32 (4): 881–912.

Gowdy, John. 1999. Economic concepts of Sustainability: Relocating Economic Activity within Society and Environment. In *Sustainability and the Social Sciences: A Cross-Disciplinary Approach to Integrating Environmental Considerations into Theoretical Reorientation,* ed. Egon Becker and Thomas Jahn, 162–181. London: Zed Books.

Graedel, Thomas E., and Braden R. Allenby. 1995. *Industrial Ecology.* Englewood Cliffs, NJ: Prentice Hall.

Graham, Stephen. 2002. FlowCity: Networked Mobilities and the Contemporary Metropolis. *Journal of Urban Technology* 9 (1): 1–20.

Gray, Paul E., Jefferson W. Tester, and David O. Wood. 1991. Energy Technology: Problems and Solutions. In *Energy and the Environment in the 21st Century,* ed. Jefferson W. Tester, David O. Wood, and Nancy A. Ferrari, 121–137. Cambridge, MA: MIT Press.

Greenstein, Ran, and Anriette Esterhuysen. 2006. The Right to Development in the Information Society. In *Human Rights in the Global Information Society,* ed. Rikke Frank Jørgensen. Cambridge, MA: MIT Press.

Greenstein, Shane. 2000. The Evolving Structure of Commercial Internet Markets. In *Understanding the Digital Economy,* ed. Eerik Brynjolfsson and Brian Kahin, 151–184. Cambridge, MA: MIT Press.

Gregory, Richard L. 2001. Perceptions of Knowledge. *Nature* 410:21.

Grieco, Joseph M. 1988. Anarchy and the Limits of Cooperation: A Realist Critique of the Newest Liberal Institutionalism. *International Organization* 42 (3): 485–507.

Guidelines Agreed for New Social Contract. 1999. *Nature* 400 (July): 100.

Haas, Ernst B. 1980. Why Collaborate? Issue-Linkage and International Regimes. *World Politics* 32 (3): 357–405.

Haas, Ernst B. 1990. *When Knowledge Is Power: Three Models of Change in International Organizations.* Berkeley: University of California Press.

Haas, Ernst B., Mary Pat Williams, and Don Babai. 1977. *Scientists and World Order: The Uses of Technical Knowledge in International Organizations.* Berkeley: University of California Press.

Haas, Peter M. 1989. The Fourth Image Reversed: Epistemic Communities and Knowledge Based Bargaining as a Response to Uncertainty. Paper presented at the 1989 Annual Meeting of the American Political Science Association, Atlanta, GA.

Haas, Peter M. 1990. *Saving the Mediterranean.* New York: Columbia University Press.

Haas, Peter M., and Jan Sundgren. 1993. Evolving International Environmental Law: Changing Practices of International Sovereignty. In *Global Accord: Environmental Challenges and International Responses,* ed. Nazli Choucri, 401–429. Cambridge, MA: MIT Press.

Haas, Peter M. 2003. Addressing the Global Governance Deficit. *Global Environmental Politics* 4 (4), 1–15.

Hachigian, Nina, and Lily Wu. 2003. *The Information Revolution in Asia*. Santa Monica, CA: RAND.

Haghseta, Farnaz Saboori. 2003. Information Technology and Sustainable Development: Understanding Linkages in Theory and Practice. M.S. thesis, MIT.

Halpern, S. L. 1992. *United Nations Conference on Environment and Development: Process and Documentation*. Providence, RI: Academic Council for the United Nations System.

Hardin, Garrett. 1968. The Tragedy of the Commons. *Science* 162 (December): 1243–1248.

Hargittai, Eszter. 1999. Weaving the Western Web Explaining Differences in Internet Connectivity among OECD Countries. *Telecommunications Policy* 23 (10): 1–32.

Harris, Shane. 2008. China's Cyber-Military. *National Journal Magazine*. May 31.

Hauben, Michael, and Ronda Hauben. 1997. *Netizens: On the History and Impact of UseNet and the Internet*. IEEE Computer Society Press.

Harvey, Jeff. 2001. The Natural Economy. *Nature* 413 (October): 463.

Hatton, Timothy J., and Jeffrey G. Williamson. 2005. *Global Migration and the World Economy*. Cambridge, MA: MIT Press.

Held, David, and Anthony McGrew. 2001. Globalization. In *The Oxford Companion to Politics of the World*. 2nd ed., ed. Joel Krieger, 324–327. New York: Oxford University Press.

Helfin, J., and J. Hendler. Dynamic Ontologies on the Web. In *Proceedings of the 11th National Conference on Artificial Intelligence*, 443–449. Menlo Park, CA.

Herz, John H. 1950. Idealist Internationalism and the Security Dilemma. *World Politics* 2 (2): 157–180.

Hess, Charlotte, and Elinor Ostrom, eds. 2007. *Understanding Knowledge as a Commons: From Theory to Practice*. Cambridge, MA: MIT Press.

Hoffman, Donna P., and Thomas P. Novak. 2000. The Growing Digital Divide: Implications for an Open Research Agenda. In *Understanding the Digital Economy*, ed. Erik Brynjolfsson and Brian Kahin, 245–260. Cambridge, MA: MIT Press.

Hollifield, Ann C., Joseph F. Donnermeyer, Gwen H. Wolford, and Robert Agunga. 2000. The Effects of rural Telecommunications Self-Development Projects on Local Adoption of New Technologies. *Telecommunications Policy* 24:761–779.

Holling, C. S. 1995. Sustainability: The Cross-Scale Dimension. In *Defining and Measuring Sustainability: The Biogeophysical Foundations*, ed. Mohan Munasinghe and Walter Shearer, 65–75. Washington, DC: World Bank.

Holm, Soren, and John Harris. 1999. Precautionary Principle Stifles Discovery. *Nature* 400 (July): 398.

Holsti, Ole R. 1972. *Crisis, Escalation, War*. Montreal: McGill-Queens University Press.

Holsti, Ole R., Randolph M. Siverson, and Alexander L. George, eds. 1980. *Change in the International System.* Boulder, CO: Westview Press.

Homer-Dixon, T. E. 1993. Physical Dimensions of Global Change. In *Global Accord: Environmental Challenges and International Responses,* ed. Nazli Choucri, 43–66. Cambridge, MA: MIT Press.

Huberman, Bernardo A. 2001. *The Laws of the Web: Patterns in the Ecology of Information.* Cambridge, MA: MIT Press.

Huberman, Bernardo A., and M. Lukose Rajan. 1997. Social Dilemmas and Internet Congestion. *Science* 277 (July): 535–537.

Iacono, Suzanne C., and Peter A. Freeman. 2006. Cyberinfrastructure-in-the-Making: Can We Get There from Here? In *Advancing Knowledge and the Knowledge Economy,* ed. Brian Kahin and Dominque Foray, 455–478. Cambridge, MA: MIT Press.

International Political Science Review 21 (3) (July 2000).

International Telecommunication Union. 2003. ITU Internet Reports 2003: Birth of Broadband. 5th ed. Geneva: International Telecommunication Union. http://www.itu.int/wsis/tunis/newsroom/stats/BirthofBroadband_2003.pdf

International Telecommunication Union. 2005. A Comparative Analysis of Cybersecurity Initiatives Worldwide. *WSIS Thematic Meeting on Cybersecurity.*

Internetworldstats.com. 2001–2011. http://www.internetworldstats.com. Miniwatts Marketing Group.

James, Peter, and Peter Hopkinson. 2001. Virtual Traffic: E-commerce, Transport and Distribution. In *Digital Futures: Living in a dot.com World,* ed. J. Wilsdon, 165–196. London: Earthscan.

Jervis, Robert. 1997. *System Effects: Complexity in Political and Social Life.* Princeton, NJ: Princeton University Press.

Johnson, Loch K., and James J. Wirtz. 2004. *Strategic Intelligence: Windows into a Secret World.* Los Angeles, CA: Roxbury Publishing Co.

Johnson, David R., and David G. Post. 1997. The Rise of Law on the Global Network. In *Borders in Cyberspace: Information Policy and the Global Information Infrastructure,* ed. Brian Kahin and Charles Nesson. Cambridge, MA: MIT Press.

Kahler, Miles, ed. 2009. *Networked Politics: Agency, Power, and Governance.* Ithaca, NY: Cornell University Press.

Kahin, Brian, and Charles Nesson, eds. 1997. *Borders in Cyberspace.* Cambridge, MA: MIT Press.

Kaplan, Morton A. 1957. *System and Process in International Politics.* New York: Wiley, Chapman and Hall.

Karatzogianni, Athina, ed. 2009. *Cyber Conflict and Global Politics.* London: Routledge.

Katzenstein, Peter, Robert O. Keohane, and Stephen N. Krasner, eds. 1999. *Exploration and Contestation in the Study of World Politics: A Special Issue of International Organization.* Cambridge, MA: MIT Press.

Kaufmann, Daniel, Aart Kraay, and Massimo Mastruzzi. 2010. The World Governance Indicators: Methodology and Analytical Issues. World Bank Development Research Group, Macroeconomics and Growth Team, Policy Research Paper 5430. September. Washington, DC: World Bank. http://papers.ssrn.com/sol3/papers.cfm?abstract_id=1682130.

Kaufmann, Daniel, Aart Kraay, and Pablo Zoido-Lobaton. 1999. Governance Matters. World Bank Policy Research Working Paper 2196. Washington, DC: World Bank.

Kaul, Inge, Pedro Conceicao, Katell Le Goulven, and Ronald U. Mendoza, eds. 2003. *Providing Global Public Goods: Managing Globalization.* New York: Oxford University Press.

Keatley, Anne. 1983. Knowledge as Real Estate. *Science* 222 (November): 717.

Keohane, Robert O., and Elinor Ostrom, eds. 1995. *Local Commons and Global Interdependence: Heterogeneity and Cooperation in Two Domains.* Thousand Oaks, CA: Sage.

Kennedy, Donald, and the Editors of *Science*, eds. 2006. *Science Magazine's State of the Planet 2006–2007.* Washington, DC: Island Press.

Killcrece, Georgia. 2004. *Steps for creating national CERTs.* Carnegie Mellon Software Engineering Institute. http://www.cert.org/archive/pdf/NationalCSIRTs.pdf.

Klesius, Michael. 2002. The State of the Planet. *National Geographic* 202 (September): 102–115.

Kohl, Uta. 2007. *Jurisdiction and the Internet: Regulatory Competence over Online Activity.* Cambridge: Cambridge University Press.

Korten, David. 1996. *When Corporations Rule the World.* Bloomfield, CT: Kumarian.

Koutsoukis, Nikitas-Spiros, and Gautam Mitra. 2003. *Decision Modelling and Information Systems: The Information Value Chain.* Norwell, MA: Kluwer Academic Publishers.

Kramer, Franklin D., Stuart H. Starr, and Larry K. Wentz, eds. 2009. *Cyberpower and National Security.* Washington, DC: NDU Press and Potomac Books.

Krasner, Stephen D. 1881. Global Communications and National Power: Life on the Pareto Frontier. *World Politics* 43 (April): 336–366.

Kratochwil, Friedrich, and Edward D. Mansfield, eds. 1994. *International Organization.* New York: HarperCollins College Publishers.

Kratochwil, Friedrich, and John Gerard Ruggie. 1986. International Organization: A State of the Art on an Art of the State. *International Organization* 40 (4): 753–775.

Krugman, Paul. 1991. *Geography and trade.* Cambridge, MA: MIT Press.

Kruzel, Joseph, and James N. Roseanau, eds. 1989. *Journeys through World Politics: Autobiographical Reflections of Thirty-Four Academic Travelers. Issues in World Politics.* Lanham, MD: Lexington Books.

Kubalkova, Vendulka, Nicholas Onuf, and Paul Kowert, eds. 1998. *International Relations in a Constructed World*. New York: M. E. Sharpe.

Kuehls, Thom. 1998. Between Sovereignty and Environment: An Exploration of the Discourse of Government. In *The Greening of Sovereignty in World Politics*, ed. Karen T. Litfin, 31–54. Cambridge, MA: MIT Press.

Kuhn, Thomas S. 1970. *The Scientific Structure of Revolutions*. 2nd ed. Chicago: University of Chicago Press.

Kuznets, Simon. 1996. *Modern Economic Growth: Rate, Structure and Spread*. New Haven, CT: Yale University Press.

Lasswell, Harold D. 1941. The Garrison State. *American Journal of Sociology* 46 (4): 455–468.

Lasswell, Harold D. 1958. *Politics: Who Gets What, When and How*. New York: McGraw-Hill.

Latham, Robert, ed. 2003. *Bombs and Bandwidth: The Emerging Relationship between Information Technology and Security*. New York: Social Science Research Council.

Lawrence, Steve, and Lee C. Giles. 1999. Accessibility of Information on the Web. *Nature* 400 (July): 107–109.

Lawson, Chappell. 2007. New Media Undermining Elite Control of Public Diplomacy. Internal memorandum, Department of Political Science, MIT, Cambridge, MA, April 2.

Lazer, David, Alex Pentland, Leda Adamic, Sinan Aral, Albert-Laszlo Barabasi, Devon Brewer, Nicholas Christakis, et al. 2009. Computational Social Science. *Science* 323 (February): 721–723.

Lehaney, Brian, Steve Clarke, Elayne Coakes, and Gillian Jack, eds. 2004. *Beyond Knowledge Management*. Hershey, PA: Idea Group Publishing.

Lessard, Donald, and Cristiano Antonelli, eds. 1990. *Managing the Globalization of Business*. Naples: Editoriale Scientifica.

Lessig, Lawrence. 1997. The Constitution of Code: Limitations on Choice-based Critiques of Cyberspace Regulation. *CommLaw Conspectus* 5:181–191.

Lessig, Lawrence. 1999. *Code and Other Laws of Cyberspace*. New York: Basic Books.

Lessig, Lawrence. 2001. *The Future of Ideas: The Fate of the Commons in a Connected World*. New York: Vintage Books.

Levy, Jack S. 1989. The Causes of War: A Review of Theories and Evidence. In *Behavior, Society, and Nuclear War*, vol. 1, ed. Philip E. Tetlock, Jo L. Husbands, Robert Jervis, Paul C. Stern, and Charles Tilly, 209–333. New York: Oxford University Press.

Lewin, Roger. 1992. *Complexity: Life at the Edge of Chaos*. New York: Macmillan.

Libicki, Martin C. 2007. *Conquest in Cyberspace: National Security and Information Warfare*. New York: Cambridge University Press.

Litfin, Karen T. 1998. The Greening of Sovereignty: An Introduction. In *The Greening of Sovereignty in World Politics*, ed. Karen T. Litfin, 10–27. Cambridge, MA: MIT Press.

Livnat, Adi, and Marcus W. Feldman. 2001. The Evolution of Cooperation on the Internet. *Complexity* 6 (July/August): 19–23.

Lofdahl, Corey L. 2002. *Environmental Impacts of Globalization and Trade: A Systems Study*. Cambridge, MA: MIT Press.

Lofdahl, Corey. 2010. Governance and Society. In *Estimating Impact: A Handbook of Computational Methods and Models for Anticipating Economic, Social, Political, and Security Effects in International Interventions*, ed. Alexander Kott and Gary Citrenbaum, 179–200. New York: Springer-Verlag.

Lowi, Miriam R. 1995. *Water and Power: The Politics of a Scarce Resource in the Jordan River Basin*. Cambridge: Cambridge University Press.

Lynn, William F. III. 2010. Defending a New Domain: The Pentagon's Cyberstrategy. *Foreign Affairs* 89 (5): 97–108.

Madnick, Stuart. 2000. The MIT Context Interchange Project. In *Data Quality*, ed. R. Y. Wang, M. Ziad, and Y. W. Lee, 79–92. London: Kluwer Academic Publishers.

Mahoney, James, and Kathleen Thelen, eds. 2010. *Explaining Institutional Change: Ambiguity, Agency, and Power*. New York: Cambridge University Press.

Mahoney, Matt. 2011. Making Friends. *Technology Review Magazine* 114 (January–February): 20–21.

Mann, Catherine, Sue E. Eckert, and Sarah Cleveland Knight. 2000. *Global Electronic Commerce: A Policy Primer*. Washington, DC: Institute for International Economics.

March, James G., and Johan P. Olsen. 1984. The New Institutionalism: Organizational Factors in Political Life. *American Political Science Review* 78: 734–749.

March, James G., and Johan P. Olsen. 1999. The Institutional Dynamics of International Political Orders. In *Exploration and Contestation in the Study of World Politics*, ed. Peter J. Katzenstein, Robert O. Keohane, and Stephen D. Krasner, 303–329. Cambridge, MA: MIT Press.

March, James G., and Johan P. Olsen. 1989. *Rediscovering Institutions: The Organizational Basis of Politics*. New York: Free Press.

Maugis, Vincent, Nazli Choucri, Stuart Madnick, Michael Siegel, Sharon Gillett, Farnaz Haghseta, Hongwei Zhu, and Michael Best. 2005. Global e-Readiness— For What? Readiness for e-Banking. *Information Technology for Development* 11 (4): 313–342.

May, Robert. 2001. Risk and Uncertainty. *Nature* 411 (June): 891.

Mayer, Franz C. 2001. Review Essay: The Internet and Public International Law—Worlds Apart. *EJIL* 12 (3): 617–622.

Mayer-Schonberger, Viktor. 2009. *Delete: The Virtue of Forgetting in the Digital Age*. Princeton, NJ: Princeton University Press.

Mayer-Schonberger, Viktor, and Deborah Hurley. 2000. Information Policy and Governance. In *Governance in a Globalizing World*, ed. Joseph S. Nye and John D. Donahue, 330–346. Washington, DC: Brookings Institution Press.

Mayer-Schonberger, Viktor, and David Lazer, eds. 2007. *Governance and Information Technology: From Electronic Government to Information Government*. Cambridge, MA: MIT Press.

Mazarr, Michael, ed. 2002. *Information Technology and World Politics*. New York: Palgrave Macmillan.

McCann, Kevin Shear. 2000. The Diversity-Stability Debate. *Nature* 405 (May): 228–233.

McGee, John. 2003. Strategy as Orchestrating Knowledge. In *Images of Strategy*, ed. Stephen Cummings and David Wilson, 136–163. Malden, MA: Blackwell.

McKnight, Lee W., and Joseph P. Bailey. 1997. *Internet Economics*. Cambridge, MA: MIT Press.

McNeill, J. R. 2000. *Something New Under the Sun*. New York: W. W. Norton.

McNeal, Ramona, Kathleen Hale, and Lisa Dotterweich. 2008. Citizen-Government Interaction and the Internet: Expectations and Accomplishments in Contact, Quality, and Trust. *Journal of Information Technology & Politics* 5 (2): 213 –229.

Merali, Yasmin. 2006. Complexity and Information Systems: The Emergent Domain. *Journal of Information Technology* 21:216–228.

Michael, David C., and Greg Sutherland. 2002. *Asia's Digital Dividends: How Asia-Pacific's Corporations Can Create Value from e-Business*. New York: John Wiley & Sons.

Midlarsky, Manus I., ed. 1989. *Handbook of War Studies*. Boston: Unwin Hyman.

Miller, David, and Sohail H. Hashmi, eds. 2001. *Boundaries and Justice*. Princeton, NJ: Princeton University Press.

Mingst, Karen. 1999. *Essentials of International Relations*. New York: W. W. Norton.

Mitchell, Ronald B. 1993. Intentional Oil Pollution of the Oceans. In *Institutions for the Earth: Sources of International Environmental Protection*, ed. Peter M. Haas, Robert O. Keohane, and M. A. Levy, 183–247. Cambridge, MA: MIT Press.

Mitchell, Ronald B. 1994. *International Oil Pollution at Sea: Environmental Policy and Treaty Compliance*. Cambridge, MA: MIT Press.

Modelski, George. 1996. Evolutionary Paradigm for Global Politics. *International Studies Quarterly* 40:321–342.

Morgenthau, Hans.1948. *Politics among Nations: The Struggle for Power and Peace*. New York: Alfred A. Knopf.

Morowitz, Harold J. 2002. *The Emergence of Everything: How the World Became Complex*. Oxford: Oxford University Press.

Moses, Lincoln E., Richard A. Brody, Ole R. Holsti, Joseph B. Kadane, and Jeffrey S. Milstein. 1967. Scaling Data on Inter-Nation Interaction. *Science* 26 (May): 1054–1059.

Mueller, Milton. 2002. *Ruling the Root: Internet Governance and the Taming of Cyberspace*. Cambridge, MA: MIT Press.

Mueller, Milton, and Mawaki Chango. 2008. Disrupting Global Governance: The Internet Whois Service, ICANN, and Privacy. *Journal of Information Technology & Politics* 5 (3): 303–325.

Murdoch, Steven J., and Ross Anderson. 2008. Tools and Technology of Internet Filtering. In *Access Denied: The Practice and Policy of Global Internet Filtering*, ed. Ronald J. Deibert, John G. Palfrey, Rafal Rohozinski, and Jonathan Zittrain, 57–72. Cambridge, MA: MIT Press.

Neef, Dale, ed. 1998. *The Knowledge Economy*. Boston: Butterworth-Heinemann.

Negroponte, Nicholas. 1995. *Being Digital*. New York: Knopf.

Newell, Allen and Herbert A. Simon. 1972. *Human Problem Solving*. Englewood Cliffs, NJ: Prentice Hall.

Newman, M. E. J. 2003. The Structure and Function of Complex Networks. *SIAM Review* 45 (2): 167–256.

Norris, Pipa. 2001. *Digital Divide: Civic Engagement, Information Poverty, and the Internet Worldwide*. Cambridge: Cambridge University Press.

North, Robert C. 1990. *War, Peace, Survival: Global Politics and Conceptual Synthesis*. Boulder, CO: Westview Press.

North, Robert C., and Nazli Choucri. 1996. New Perspectives on the Fourth Image: Report on a Global System. Presented at the International Studies Association annual convention, San Diego, CA, April 16–20.

Nye, Joseph S. 2011. *The Future of Power*. New York: PublicAffairs.

Nye, Joseph S., and John D. Donahueeds. 2000. *Governance in a Globalizing World*. Washington, DC: Brookings Institution Press.

O'Connell, Pamela Licalzi. 1999. Beyond Geography: Mapping Unknowns of Cyberspace. *New York Times,* September 30, E1.

Ohmae, K. 1999. *The Borderless World: Power and Strategy in the Interlinked Economy*. New York: Harper Business.

Organisation for Economic Co-operation and Development. 2003. *ICT and Economic Growth Evidence from OECD Countries, Industries and Firms*. Paris, France: OECD Publications Development.

Organisation for Economic Co-operation and Development. 2008a. Net Support: Critical Information Infrastructures. *OECD Observer* (268) (June): 8.

Organisation for Economic Co-operation and Development. 2008b. Security and the Internet: Fighting Malware. *OECD Observer* (268) (June): 10.

Organisation for Economic Co-operation and Development. 2008c. Widening Broadband's Reach. *OECD Observer* (268) (June): 14–15.

Organisation for Economic Co-operation and Development. 2008d. Space to Grow. *OECD Observer* (268) (June): 28.

Organski, A. F. K., and J. Kugler. 1980. *The War Ledger*. Chicago: University of Chicago Press.

Osgood, Charles, George Suci, and Percy Tannenbaum. 1957. *The Measurement of Meaning*. Urbana: University of Illinois Press.

Ostrom, Elinor. 1990. *Governing the Commons: The Evolution of Institutions for Collective Action*. New York: Cambridge University Press.

Ostrom, Elinor. 2005. *Understanding Institutional Diversity*. Princeton, NJ: Princeton University Press.

Ostrom, Elinor, and Susan J. Buck. 1998. *The Global Commons: An Introduction*. Washington, DC: Island Press.

Ostrom, Elinor, Joanna Burger, Christopher B. Field, B. Richard Norgaard, and David Policansky. 1999. Revisiting the Commons: Local Lessons, Global Challenges. *Science* 284 (April): 278–282.

Pielke, Roger, Jr. 2002. Better Safe Than Sorry. *Nature* 419 (October): 433–434.

Pimm, Stuart L., Márcio Ayres, Andrew Balmford, George Branch, Katrina Bustamante, et al. 2001. Can We Defy Nature's End? *Science* 293 (September): 2207–2208.

Pinker, Steven. 2011. *The Better Angels of our Nature: Why Violence has Declined*. London, England: Viking.

Pirages, Dennis. 1977. *The Sustainable Society: Implications for Limited Growth*. New York: Praeger.

Pirages, Dennis. 1978. *The New Context for International Relations: Global Ecopolitics*. Scituate, MA: Duxbury Press.

Pirages, Dennis, and Ken Cousins, eds. 2005. *From Resource Scarcity to Ecological Security: Exploring New Limits to Growth*. Cambridge, MA: MIT Press.

Pollins, Brian M., and Randall L. Schweller. 1999. Linking the Levels: The Long Wave and Shifts in U.S. Foreign Policy, 1790–1993. *American Journal of Political Science* 43 (2) (April): 431–464.

Population Council. 2006. *Global Reach, Global Impact, Annual Report, 2006*. http://www.popcouncil.org/pdfs/ar06/AR2006.pdf

Powell, M. J. 1993. Professional Innovation: Corporate Lawyers and Private Law-Making. *Law & Social Inquiry* 18:423–452.

Poznanski, K., and G. Modelski. 1996. Evolutionary Paradigms in the Social Science. *International Studies Quarterly* 40:315–319.

Price, Derek J. de Solla. 1965. Networks of Scientific Papers. *Science* 149: 510–515.

Price, Monroe E. 2002. *Media and Sovereignty: The Global Information Revolution and its Challenge to State Power*. Cambridge, MA: MIT Press.

Promises and Threats of the Knowledge-Based Economy. 1999. *Nature* 397 (January): 1.

Provos, Niels, Panayiotis Mavrommatis, Moheeb Abu Rajab, and Fabian Monrose. 2008. All Your iFrames Point to Us. *Google Technical Report provos-2008a.* February 4.

Rattray, Gregory J. 2001. *Strategic Warfare in Cyberspace.* Cambridge, MA: MIT Press.

Reddy, R. 1996. The Challenge of Artificial Intelligence. *Computer* 29:86–98.

Redner, Sidney. 2002. Networking Comes of Age. *Nature* 418 (January): 127–128.

Reidenberg, Joel R. 1997. Governing Networks and Rule-Making in Cyberspace. In *Borders in Cyberspace: Information Policy and the Global Information Infrastructure,* ed. Brian Kahin and Charles Nesson, 85–105. Cambridge, MA: MIT Press.

Renouvin, Pierre, and Jean-Baptiste Duroselle. 1967. *Introduction to the History of International Relations,* trans. Mary Ilford. New York: Praeger.

Richards, Deanna J., Braden R. Allenby, and Dale D. Compton, eds. 2001. *Information Systems and the Environment.* National Academy of Engineering. Washington, DC: National Academy Press.

Richardson, Lewis F. 1960. *Statistics of Deadly Quarrels.* Pittsburgh, PA: Boxwood Press.

Rodríguez, Francisco, and Ernest J. Wilson III. 2000. Are Poor Countries Losing the Information Revolution? World Bank infoDev Working Paper 26651. May. University of Maryland, College Park.

Rogers, Richard. 2004. *Information Politics on the Web.* Cambridge, MA: MIT Press.

Romer, Paul. 1986. Increasing Returns and Long-Run Growth. *Journal of Political Economy* 94(5): 1002–1037.

Rosecrance, Richard N. 1963. *Action and Reaction in World Politics: International Systems in Perspective.* Boston, MA: Little Brown and Company.

Rosecrance, Richard N. 1999. *The Rise of the Virtual State.* New York: Basic Books.

Rosenau, James. 1961. *Public Opinion and Foreign Policy: An Operational Formulation.* New York: Random House.

Rosenau, James. 1969. *International Politics and Foreign Policy: A Reader in Research and Theory.* New York: Free Press.

Rosenau, James N. 1990. *Turbulence in World Politics: A Theory of Change and Continuity.* Princeton, NJ: Princeton University Press.

Rosenau, James, and J. P. Singh. 2002. *Information Technologies and Global Politics: The Changing Scope of Power and Governance.* Albany: State University of New York Press.

Rothenberg, Jerome. 1993a. Economic Perspectives on Time Comparisons: An Evaluation of Time Discounting. In *Global Accord: Environmental Challenges and International Responses,* ed. Nazli Choucri, 307–332. Cambridge, MA: MIT Press.

Rothenberg, Jerome. 1993b. Economic Perspectives on Time Comparisons: Alternative Approaches to Time Comparisons. In *Global Accord: Environmental Challenges and International Responses*, ed. Nazli Choucri, 355–398. Cambridge, MA: MIT Press.

Rourke, John T. 2001. *International Politics on the World Stage*, 8th ed. New York: McGraw-Hill/Dushkin.

Rourke, John T. 2003. *International Politics on the World Stage*, 9th ed. New York: McGraw-Hill/Dushkin.

Rourke, John T. 2008. *International Politics on the World Stage*, 12th ed. New York: McGraw-Hill/Dushkin.

Rudolph, Christopher. 2003. Security and the Political Economy of International Migration. *American Political Science Review* 97 (4): 603–620.

Ruggie, John G. 1982. Multilateralism: The Anatomy of an Institution. *International Organization* 46 (3): 561–598.

Ruggie, John Gerard. 1986. Continuity and Transformation in the World Polity: Toward a Neorealist Synthesis. In *Neorealism and Its Critics*, ed. Robert O. Keohane, 131–157. New York: Columbia University Press.

Ruggie, John Gerard. 1998. *Constructing the World Polity: Essays on International Institutionalization*. London: Routledge.

Ruggie, John Gerard. 1999. "What Makes the World Hang Together? Neo-utilitarianism and the Social Constructivist Challenge." In Peter J. Katzenstein, Robert O. Keohane, and Stephen D. Krasner, eds., Exploration and Contestation in the Study of World Politics, 215–245. Cambridge, Mass: MIT Press.

Russett, Bruce M., ed. 1972. *Peace, War, and Numbers*. Beverly Hills, CA: Sage.

Sala, Osvaldo E., Stuart F. Chapin III, Juan J. Armesto, Eric Berlow, et al. 2000. Global Biodiversity Scenarios for the Year 2100. *Science* 287 (March): 1770–1774.

Sassen, Saskia. 1991. *The Global City: New York, London, Tokyo*. Princeton, NJ: Princeton University Press.

Sassen, Saskia. 1998. *Globalization and Its Discontents: Essays on the New Mobility of People and Money*. New York: New Press.

Saurin, J. 1993. Global Environmental Degradation, Modernity and Environmental Knowledge. *Environmental Politics* 2 (4): 46–64.

Sawyer, Steve, Rolf T. Wigand, and Kevin Crowston. 2005. Redefining Access: Uses and Roles of Information and Communication Technologies in the US Residential Real Estate Industry from 1995 to 2005. *Journal of Information Technology* 20:213–223.

Scheer, Herman. 2002. *The Solar Economy: Renewable Energy for a Sustainable Global Future*. London: Earthscan.

Schiermeier, Quirin. 2002. How Many More Fish in the Sea? *Nature* 419 (October): 662–665.

Schmidt, Eric, and Jared Cohen. 2010. The Digital Disruption: Connectivity and the Diffusion of Power. *Foreign Affairs* 89 (6): 75–85.

Shabecoff, Philip. 1993. The Enemy Is Us. *Nature* 366 (November): 385.

Sengupta, Somini. 2006. India blocks blogs in wake of Mumbai bombings. *The New York Times,* July 18. http://www.nytimes.com/2006/07/18/world/asia/18cnd -india.html.

Shepsle, Kenneth A. 1989. Studying Institutions: Some Lessons from the Rational Choice Approach. *Journal of Theoretical Politics* 1 (2): 131–147.

Simon, Herbert A. 1955. A Behavioral Model of Rational Choice. *Quarterly Journal of Economics* 69 (1): 99–118.

Simon, Herbert A. 1972.Theories of Bounded Rationality. In *Decision and Organization.* ed. C.B. Marschak, and Roy Radner, 161–176. Minneapolis, MN: University of Minnisota Press.

Simon, Herbert A. 1980. The Behavioral and Social Sciences. *Science* 209 (July): 72–78.

Simon, Herbert A. 1983. *Reason in Human Affairs.* Stanford, CA: Stanford University Press.

Simon, Herbert A. 1985. Human Nature in Politics. *American Political Science Review* 79 (2): 293–304.

Simon, Herbert A. 1994. *The Sciences of the Artificial.* Cambridge, MA: MIT Press.

Sindjoun, L. 2001. Transformation of International Relations: Between Change and Continuity. *International Political Science Review* 22 (3): 219–228.

Slaughter, Anne-Marie. 2004. *A New World Order.* Princeton, NJ: Princeton University Press.

Smelsner, Neil J., and Faith Mitchell, eds. 2002. *Terrorism: Perspectives from the Behavioral and Social Sciences.* Washington, DC: National Academies Press.

Solow, Robert M. 1993. The Economics of Resources or the Resources of Economics. In *Economics of the Environment: Selected Readings.* 3rd ed., ed. Robert Dorfman and Nancy S. Dorfman, 162–178. New York: W. W. Norton.

Solow, Robert M. 2005. Sustainability: An Economist's Perspective. In *Economics of the Environment: Selected Readings.* 5th ed., ed. Robert N.

Solum, Lawrence B., and Minn Chung. 2003. The Layers Principle: Internet Architecture and the Law. Public Law and Legal Theory Research Paper 55, University of San Diego School of Law, June.

Sorokin, Pitrim A. 1957. *Social Change and Cultural Dynamics.* Boston: Porter Sargent.

Souter, David. 2008. Louder Voices and the International Debate on Developing Country Participation in ICT Decision Making. In *Governing Global Electronic Networks: International Perspectives on Policy and Power,* ed. William J. Drake and Ernest J. Wilson III, 429–462. Cambridge, MA: MIT Press.

Spinello, Richard A. 2002. *Regulating Cyberspace.* London: Quorum Books.

Sprout, Harold, and Margaret Sprout. 1968. *An Ecological Paradigm for the Study of International Politics.* Princeton, NJ: Center of International Studies, Princeton University.

Sprout, Harold, and Margaret Sprout. 1971. *Toward a Politics of the Planet Earth*. New York: D. Van Nostrand Co.

Star, S. L., and K. Ruhleder. 1996. Steps toward an Ecology Infrastructure: Design and Access for Large Information Spaces. *Information Systems Research* 7 (1): 111–134.

Starr, Chauncey. 1997. Sustaining the Human Environment: The Next Two Hundred Years. In *Technological Trajectories and the Human Environment*, ed. Jesse H. Ausubel and H. Dale Langford, 185–198. Washington, DC: National Academy Press.

Stefik, Mark.1990. *The Internet Edge*. Cambridge, MA: MIT Press.

Sterman, John D. 2000. *Business Dynamics: Systems Thinking and Modeling for a Complex World*. New York: McGraw-Hill.

Stone, Richard. 1992. The Biodiversity Treaty: Pandora's Box or Fair Deal? *Science* 256 (June): 1624.

Tainter, Joseph A. 1988. *The Collapse of Complex Societies*. Cambridge: Cambridge University Press.

Talbot, David. 2010. Moore's Outlaws. *Technology Review* 113 (4): 43. http://www.technologyreview.com/computing/25564.

Talbot, John, and Dominic Welsh. 2006. *Complexity and Cryptography*. New York: Cambridge University Press.

The Economist. 1998. "A survey of world trade: Turtle wars: Greenery and globalisation do not mix." October 1, 1998.

The Economist. 1998. "World trade survey: Why trade is good for you." October 1, 1998.

The New York Times. 2005. Op-Ed, November 20, A31.

Thouez, Colleen. 2004. *Global Migration Perspectives: The Role of Civil Society in the Migration Policy Debate*. New York: UNITAR.

Towards a "Knowledge Nation." 2001. *Nature* 411 (June): 619.

Towards New Standards in University-Industry Collaboration. 2000. *Nature* 411 (June): 723.

United Nations Common Data Source, http://unstats.un.org/unsd/default.htm.

United Nations Commission on Sustainable Development. 1995. "Transfer of Environmentally Sound Technologies, Cooperation and Capacity-Building: Report of the Secretary General." UN Document E/CN.17/1995/17. 1995.

United Nations Conference on Environment and Development. 1992. *Agenda 21: Programme of Action for Sustainable Development*. Rio de Janeiro, Brazil: UN Document E.93.1. 11.

United Nations. 1994. Technology and Finance: New Opportunities & Innovative Strategies for Sustainable Development. United Nations Development Programme. Prepared for the Commission on Sustainable Development Intersessional Working Group on Technology Transfer, New York, February 22–25.

United Nations. 1999. *United Nations Human Development Report*. New York: Oxford University Press.

United Nations. 2001. *World Population Prospects: The 2000 Revision. Comprehensive Tables No. E.03.XIII.6.*.Vol. I. United Nations, Population Division. New York: United Nations.

United Nations. 2003a. *The Arab Human Development Report 2003: Building a Knowledge Society*. United Nations Development Programme and The Arab Fund for Social and Economic Development. New York: United Nations.

United Nations. 2003b. *World Youth Report 2003: The Global Situation of Young People*. New York: United Nations.

United Nations. 2004 . *World Population Prospects: Analytical Report. ST/ESA/SER.A/233. United Nations*. vol. 3. The 2002 Revision. United Nations, Population Division. New York: United Nations.

United Nations. 2005a. *World Population Prospects*: The 2004 Revision. Vol. 3, Analytical Report. United Nations, Population Division, Department of Economic and Social Affairs. New York: United Nations. http://www.un.org/esa/population/publications/WPP2004/WPP2004_Vol3_Final/WPP2004_Analytical_Report.pdf

United Nations. 2005b. *World Youth Report*. New York: United Nations.

United Nations. 2008a. *UN e-Government Survey 2008: Assessing E-Government Readiness: From e-Government to Connected Governance*. New York: United Nations.

United Nations. 2008b. UNPAN Data Center. New York: http://www2.unpan.org/egovkb.

United Nations Conference on Environment and Development. 1992a. *AGENDA 21: Programme of Action for Sustainable Development*. New York: United Nations.

United Nations Conference on Environment and Development. 1992b. *A Guide to AGENDA 21: A Global Partnership*. Geneva: United Nations.

United Nations Conference on Trade and Development. 2002. *World Investment Report 2002: Transnational Corporations and Export Competitiveness*. New York: United Nations.

United Nations Conference on Trade and Development. 2008. *World Investment Report 2008: Transnational Corporations, and the Infrastructure Challenge*. New York: United Nations.

Urstadt, Bryant. 2005–2006. A Tangle of Wires. *Technology Review*, December 2005/January 2006, 80.

Vicsek, Tamas. 2001. A Question of Scale. *Nature* 411 (May): 421.

Vincent, Jeffrey R. 1992. The Tropical Timber Trade and Sustainable Development. *Science* 256 (June): 1651–1655.

Vitousek, Peter M., Harold A. Mooney, Jane Lubchenco, and Jerry M. Melillo. 1977. Human Domination of Earth's Ecosystems. *Science* 277 (July): 494–499.

Waggoner, P. E., and J. H. Ausubel. 2002. A Framework for Sustainability Science: A Renovated IPAT Identity. *Proceedings of the National Academy of Sciences of the United States of America* 99 (12): 7860–7865.

Waltz, Kenneth. 1959. *Man, the State, and War: A Theoretical Analysis.* New York: Columbia University Press.

Waltz, Kenneth. 1979. *Theory of International Politics.* New York: McGraw-Hill.

Wareham, Jonathan, Jack G. Zheng, and Detmar Straub. 2005. Critical Themes in Electronic Commerce Research: A Meta-Analysis. *Journal of Information Technology* 20 (January): 1–19.

Warsh, David. 2006. *Knowledge and the Wealth of Nations: A Story of Economic Discovery.* New York: W. W. Norton.

Watts, Duncan J. 2003. *Six Degrees: The Science of a Connected Age.* New York: W. W. Norton.

Weiner, Myron, ed. 1993. *International Migration and Security.* Boulder, CO: Westview Press.

Weiner, Myron, and Sharon Stanton Russell, eds. 2001. *Demography and National Security.* New York: Berghahn Books.

Weiner, Norbert. 1948. *Cybernetics or Control and Communication in the Animal and the Machine.* Cambridge, MA: MIT Press.

Weiss, Edith Brown. 1992. *Environmental Change and International Law: New Challenges and Dimensions.* Tokyo: United Nations University Press.

Weiss, Edith Brown. 1989. *In Fairness to Future Generations: International Law, Common Patrimony, and Intergenerational Equity.* Dobbs Ferry, NY: Transnational Press and United Nations University.

Wellenius, Björn, Carlos Alberto Primo Braga, and Christine Zhen-Wei Qiang. 2000. Investment and Growth of the Information Infrastructure: Summary Results of a Global Survey. *Telecommunications Policy* 24 (September): 639–643.

Westland, J. Christopher, and Theodore H. K. Clark. 1999. *Global Electronic Commerce: Theory and Case Studies.* Cambridge, MA: MIT Press.

Wheeler, Quentin D., Peter H. Raven, and Edward O. Wilson. 2004. Taxonomy: Impediment or Expedient. *Science* 303 (January): 285.

Wilson, Ernest J. III. 2004. *The Information Revolution and Developing Countries.* Cambridge, MA: MIT Press.

Wilson, Ernest J. III, and Kelvin Wong, eds. 2006. *Negotiating the Net in Africa: The Politics of Internet Diffusion.* Boulder, CO: Lynne Rienner.

Wickboldt, Anne-Katrin. 2007. Growing Clean? In *Mapping Sustainability: Knowledge, e-Networking and the Value Chain*, ed. Nazli Choucri, Dinsha

Mistree, Farnaz Haghseta, Toufic Mezher, Wallace R. Baker, and Carlos I. Ortiz, 277–300. Cambridge: Springer.

Wickboldt, Anne-Katrin, and Nazli Choucri. 2006. Profiles of States as Fuzzy Sets: Refinement of Lateral Pressure Theory. *International Interactions* (32): 1–29.

Wils, Annababette, Matilde Kamiya, and Nazli Choucri. 1998. Threats to Sustainability: Simulating Conflict within and between Nations. *System Dynamics Review* 14 (2–3): 129–162.

Wilson, Edward. O. 1988. *Consilience: The Unity of Knowledge*. New York: Knopf.

World Bank. 1995. *Social Indicators of Development*. Washington, DC: Socio-Economic Data Division, International Economics Department, World Bank.

World Bank. 2002. *World Development Report 2003: Sustainable Development in a Dynamic World: Transforming Institutions, Growth, and Quality of Life*. New York: World Bank/Oxford University Press.

World Bank. 2010. *World Development Indicators*. Washington, DC: World Bank. http://data.worldbank.org/indicator

World Bank Institute. 2009. *Governance Matters 2009: Worldwide Governance Indicators 1996–2008*. http://info.worldbank.org/governance/wgi/index.asp

World Watch Institute. 2002. *State of the World 2002*. New York: W.W. Norton.

World Watch Institute. 2004. *State of the World 2004*. New York: W.W. Norton.

World Resources Institute. 1996. *World Resources 1996–1977: A Guide to the Global Environment*. New York: Basic Books.

World Summit on the Information Society. 2003; 2005. *World Summit on the Information Society*.

Wurster, Thomas S. 1999. *Blown to Bits: How the New Economics of Information Transforms Strategy*. Boston: Harvard Business Press.

Young, Oran. R. 1993. Negotiating an International Climate Regime: The Institutional Bargaining for Environmental Governance. In *Global Accord: Environmental Challenges and International Responses*, ed. Nazli Choucri, 431–452. Cambridge, MA: MIT Press, 1993.

Young, Oran R. 2002. *The Institutional Dimensions of Environmental Change Fit, Interplay, and Scale*. Cambridge, MA: MIT Press.

Zacher, Mark W. 2001. International Organizations. In *The Oxford Companion to Politics of the World*. 2nd ed., ed. Joel Krieger, 418–420. Oxford: Oxford University Press.

Zagare, Frank C., and D. Marc Kilgour. 2000. *Perfect Deterrence*. Cambridge: Cambridge University Press.

Zhao, HongXin. 2002. Rapid Internet Development in China: A Discussion of Opportunities and Constraints on Future Growth. *Thunderbird International Business Review* 44 (1): 119–138.

Zittrain, Jonathan L. 2005. *Technological Complements*. New York: Foundation Press.

Zittrain, Jonathan L. 2008. *The Future of the Internet—And How to Stop It.* New Haven, CT: Yale University Press.

Zolberg, Aristide, and Peter M. Brenda, eds. 2001. *Global Migrants, Global Refugees: Problems and Solutions*. New York: Berghahn Books.

Zook, Matthew. 2000. Internet Metrics: Using Host and Domain Counts to Map the Internet. *Telecommunications Policy* 24:613–620.

Index

Italicized numerals indicate pages with figures.

Hardin, Garrett, "tragedy of the commons," 83
HarperCollins Atlas of World History (Barraclough), 49
HB Gary, 166
Held, David, "Globalization," 45
Hess, Charlotte
"knowledge commons," 83, 84
Understanding Knowledge as a Commons (Hess and Ostrom), 84
High politics, 104, 126, 176
in Arab countries, 59–60
and cyberspace, 3
defined, 3
Homo cybericus, 30
Homo economicus, 29, 30
Homo individualis, 30–31, 228
Homo politicus, 29, 30
Homo sustainabilis, 228
Hong Kong, Facebook use in, 66
Huberman, Bernardo A., on cyber venues, 11–12
Human activities, 3, 258nn2
Human capital index, 110, 112, 113
and GDP, 116, 117
Human demands, volume and nature of, 27, 28, 30
Human interactions. *See* Politics
Human rights, 21, 204, 222, 253n13
in Arab countries, 59
consolidating global norms, 171–172
as global norm, 157–58
political filtering of content, 135
politicizing cyber rights, 170
threats to, 30
Human Rights Council, 171, 253n15
Human trafficking, 197

Identity theft, and cyber security, 39
Illegal trade in drugs and alcohol, 197
Illegal use of drugs and alcohol, control of, 135
Image, 17
Imperialism, 5

India
controlling content in, 138, 251n12
cyber access in, 53, 57
profile of, 34
Individual, 19, 22
in lateral pressure theory, 17, 27–31
multiplier effects of individual message, 139–140
power and influence of, 226–228
Indonesia
Facebook use in, 66
profile of, 34
Influence. *See* Power and influence
Information and communications technology. *See* Technology
Information commons, 83
Information content. *See* Content
Information revolution, 241n22
Information service providers, control of, 139
Infrastructure, 110, 112, 113, 248n11
cyber threats to, 21, 151–152
and GDP per capita, 120, 121
institutions for cyber management, 159
threats to, 225
Institutional bargaining, 82
Institutionalism, 15, 241n25
Institutionalization, 156–157
Intellectual property rights. *See* Property rights
Interest articulation and aggregation, 30
Intergovernmental institutions, 43–44
International civil society, 46
International collaboration. *See* Cooperation and collaboration
International Computer Security Association, 166
International conflicts. *See* Conflicts
International Meteorological Organization, 204
International migration. *See also* Refugees and displaced persons
and "diaspora," 255n17
multiplier effects of, 191
and national security, 255n15
patterns of, 190
and remittances, 189